D1368386

HOW YOU CAN
PROFIT
FROM THE
S & L
BAILOUT

HOW YOU CAN
PROFIT
FROM THE
S & L
BAILOUT

WHY THERE'S NEVER BEEN A BETTER TIME TO BUY REAL ESTATE

SONNY BLOCH
CAROLYN JANIK

BANTAM BOOKS
NEW YORK ▪ TORONTO ▪ LONDON ▪ SYDNEY ▪ AUCKLAND

The comments, observations, and recommendations in this book are the opinions of the authors and are based on Sonny Bloch's twenty-seven years and Carolyn Janik's twenty-two years in the real estate and development business. Because every real estate deal is unique, the marketplace is constantly changing, and the relevant laws and regulations will probably change after this book goes to press, readers should consult with their attorneys and tax consultants before making any financial decision or investment.

HOW YOU CAN PROFIT FROM THE S&L BAILOUT
A Bantam Book / April 1991

Library of Congress Cataloging-in-Publication Data

Bloch, H. I. Sonny.
  How to profit from the S&L bailout/Sonny Bloch and Carolyn Janik.
    p.   cm.
  Includes index.
  ISBN 0-553-07161-0
  1. Real estate investment—United States. 2. Savings and loan associations—United States. I. Janik, Carolyn. II. Title.
HD 1382.5.B65   1991
332.63'24—dc20   90-21073
                                                                          CIP

Published simultaneously in the United States and Canada

Bantam Books are published by Bantam Books, a division of Bantam Doubleday Dell Publishing Group, Inc. Its trademark, consisting of the words "Bantam Books" and the portrayal of a rooster, is Registered in U.S. Patent and Trademark Office and in other countries. Marca Registrada. Bantam Books, Inc., 666 Fifth Avenue, New York, New York 10103.

PRINTED IN THE UNITED STATES OF AMERICA

0 9 8 7 6 5 4 3 2 1

This book is dedicated to the memory and ongoing inspiration
of my father, A. Howard Bloch,
who passed away October 14, 1990.

—S.B.

"Yet in my lineaments they trace
Some features of my father's face."
—Lord Byron

For my father, Leon V. Lech, with love.

—C.J.

ACKNOWLEDGMENTS

Traveling 200,000 miles a year and being on the air twenty-four hours per week requires a tremendous backup team to put together a book as complete as this one. First, my coauthor Carolyn Janik is the person who made this book happen. I am an oral communicator, and her ability to blend my thoughts and hers into this book is an extraordinary one. Thank you, Carolyn. I would also like to thank my administrative assistant, Susan Passarelli in New York, and the members of the broadcast industry production teams and others who gave me the space to get my work done. The following people deserve special recignition: at WABC in New York, Duke Brodsky and Fred Weinhaus; in Washington, D.C., my co-host and producer of *Living With Animals,* our nationally televised PBS show, Gale Nemec; my brother, Stuart Marshall Bloch, an attorney in Washington, D.C., who helped us put together some of the information on the Resolution Trust Corporation; my brother Ivan Bloch and my sister Harriott Fuller. Special thanks to Larry Wyman, Chairman of the Sun Radio Network, who has given me tremendous support in that part of my professional life; my executive producer of *The Sonny Bloch Show,* Steven Weigner; our enthusiastic editor, Barbara Alpert and my mentor Dan Green, the person who published and promoted my first real estate book. Thanks also to Phillip Jones with the Resolution Trust Corporation,

Bill Seidman, the chairman of the Federal Deposit Insurance Corporation, and Danny Wall, former chairman of the Federal Home Loan Bank Board.

—S.B.

I want to thank Connie Sayre, who struck the match that lit the spark, and Ellen Levine, who put it all together.

—C.J.

CONTENTS

INTRODUCTION

Fifty years ago, Uncle Sam appeared on army recruiting posters, a tall man dressed in stars and stripes, pointing his finger and saying I WANT YOU! How do you think that poster artist would draw Uncle Sam today? Probably in a red blazer, white shirt, and star-studded blue tie, holding a ballpoint pen in one hand and a real estate contract in the other. Why? Because as of 1990, Uncle Sam is the world's biggest real estate seller!

What has he got to sell? Well, the last time we looked, he was selling garages and parking lots, uranium mines, time-share apartments, half-finished condominium developments, oil and gas fields, hotels, commercial warehouses, mobile homes, land, single-family houses, athletic clubs, ranches and pasturelands, nursing and retirement homes, multi-family houses, condominium apartments, co-op apartments, vacation cottages, marinas (including one that goes dry with every low tide), vacation resorts, gas stations, and one coal mine. Eighty-four percent of the 35,908 properties listed in his Spring of 1990 publication, however, were residential.

"Thirty thousand properties . . ." you say. "Gosh, that's not a lot for a whole country!"

Right! But that was only the first publication and Uncle Sam hadn't even scratched the surface at that time. There are another half million properties soon to come on to the market. And as a follow-up, there are about three million more hidden in the cracks, crevices, and dusty files of currently faltering lending institutions.

Does the world's biggest real estate seller have something for you? The odds are good, better than good. And he probably has something for your mother-in-law and your best friend too.

No, you won't see Uncle Sam standing at the gateway to a fairgrounds shouting "Something for everyone!" But it's almost like that. The world has only seen the beginning of the bailout volcano so far. In among the smoke and rumblings of the current eruption, and certainly among the shower of properties expected from future thrift and bank failures, there are a lot of potential investments for a lot of different people. You could almost sort the listings, and place them under headings that read: THE GOOD! THE BAD! THE BOGUS! THE BARGAINS! and THE STEALS!

There may not be something for everyone in the Savings and Loan Bailout, but there could be for anyone who has the desire, the skill, and the perseverance to make money in real estate. What you have to do is find the right property, then figure out how to buy it at a price that makes sense for you, and that will be profitable in the not-too-distant future.

This book will help you take that step, by explaining what the bailout is, how it may affect you and the rest of the country, and perhaps most important, how to analyze the properties available, choose the one that could be your best investment ever, and comfortably travel the often hazardous path to ownership by using this book as a resource guide. If you've never bought property before, or if you own a house but are considering buying real estate as an investment, HOW YOU CAN PROFIT FROM THE S&L BAILOUT provides clear-headed information on how to do it, and do it well.

Ready? Here goes.

CHAPTER 1

WHAT IS THE S&L BAILOUT—AND WHY DID IT HAPPEN?

Do you resent paying $60 for a visit to your doctor? Are you especially annoyed when all you're getting is a prescription for the antibiotic you already suspect you need to cure your bronchitis? Think about it. You'll probably spend half an hour in the waiting room, ten minutes in the examining room, and 45 seconds writing your check. Sixty dollars!

Now hold on to that feeling a minute and compare it with the feeling you'd probably get while writing a check made out to the United States Government for, let's say, $300. Think about writing a check for that amount, or maybe more, in each of the next ten years. Think about the fact that these checks will be your annual contribution to the patch-up of a national banking disaster of criminal proportions that took place in broad daylight and was permitted by Congress. At least your doctor's prescription will make you feel better.

To take this little exercise just one step further, think about the time and effort exerted to earn the money that your check-writing turns over to the payee. Your doctor had to attend endless hours of classes to earn the right to prescribe that antibiotic. He also has to maintain an office, employ a staff, pay insurance, and put in a full work week. Well, the people who lost or used the money that millions of Americans trusted to their friendly bankers may not have spent much time studying anything related to investment strategy, may have worked no more than one or two days a week, and had no legal responsibility to anyone for what they did with the money invested. Most of them are very, very rich right now. Meanwhile, your annual $300 check, combined with a similar check from every working American in the nation, will be used to repay guaranteed deposits and restructure the banking system that many of these guys essentially robbed and very nearly destroyed.

"Okay," you say. "It's going to cost me $300 a year to secure my life savings. Bad . . . but not horrible. At least I still have the savings."

Yes, but those $300 checks are also going to guarantee that the well-heeled ex-manipulators of your money and many other wealthy groups and individuals won't lose a penny of the money that *they* had on deposit in the same banks. (In many cases of thrift failures, various monied groups or individuals had numerous accounts in the same banking institution, each account just under the $100,000 guarantee limit.)

To add still more insult to injury, there's virtually no hope of getting all, or even most of the squandered money back and there will be little punishment for the thieves, con-artists, and manipulators. The government will be able to prosecute only a minute percentage of bank officers—only those who are considered the very worst offenders among the highfliers of the greedy 1980s. A few bankers and developers will also be sued by the groups of people whose money they are thought to have taken under false pretenses. The rest of the S&L crowd, however, are legally innocent of any wrongdoing. They made "mistakes" or they put the money in their charge wherever the interest rates were most inviting, knowing that the deposits were guaranteed by the federal government and therefore caring nothing about how the savings institutions were being run or how the borrowers who agreed to pay high interest rates were using the money they borrowed.

Tighter regulations and new attitudes toward speculation have probably ended the "working" days of these gambling bank executives, but the money they personally have on deposit in federally insured financial institutions is still guaranteed. And your tax dollars are paying for that guarantee.

Is your blood pressure rising? Keep calm or you'll end up with another unnecessary $60 bill at the doctor's office. And keep reading. This banking mess is a reality that isn't going to go away, a financial rape of the American people that cannot be undone and will take many years to resolve. *But,* and this is the part that's really important to you as an individual and to your checkbook, the bailout of the nation's thrift institutions can be turned into a veritable volcano of financial opportunities for those investors with a little inside savvy. You'll still have to pay the $300 plus per year for the bailout, but at the same time you can be using bailout properties to bring in what may be many, many thousands of dollars each year.

In this chapter, we'll tell you briefly what happened to cause the current banking catastrophe, just so that you'll have some perspective on where the turmoil is coming from. Then we'll spend the remainder of this book telling you how to turn this enormous lemon into lemonade.

THE FERTILE SOIL OF DEREGULATION

Among the slogans of Ronald Reagan's first campaign for the presidency was a promise to get government off the backs of American business. Among his official acts in pursuit of this promise was the signing of the Garn-St. Germain Act of 1982, a sweeping liberalization of the regulations governing the savings and loan industry. With this deregulation, fertile ground for new investments was opened for cultivation. The S&Ls rushed to see what they could grow in these new fields, and the greatest banking crisis in United States history began.

The seeds for the current S&L crisis, however, preceded Reagan's presidency and the Garn-St. Germain Act. With 20/20 hindsight, we can pin the beginning of the crisis to decisions made at the beginning of the decade. In 1980, during the Carter administration, Fernand St. Germain, the chairman of the House Banking Committee, was instrumental in drafting a bill to raise the maximum amount of federal deposit insurance to $100,000. With this higher insurance limit, the government's guarantee was no longer restricted to the protection of savings deposited by the average, working American. The wealthy could now move their money into selected financial institutions with the same impunity. For example, by opening joint accounts and trust accounts in addition to individual accounts, an investor could deposit over a million dollars in one savings institution, and every penny would be insured by the United States government.

But even in 1980, St. Germain and other members of Congress knew that increasing the amount of deposit insurance alone would not stimulate enough business for the ailing thrifts. As long as the amount of interest that savings institutions could pay to depositors was regulated by law, the thrifts could not compete with other banking institutions who were offering more appealing investment vehicles such as money-market funds. So in addition to raising the limit on insured deposits, Congress agreed to lift the regulations on the amount of interest an S&L could pay its depositors. The theory was that savers and investors alike would then put their money wherever they could get the best return.

Thus the decade started off with support and deregulation that allowed thrifts to pay competitive interest rates on a great deal of fully insured money. But still the savings and loan industry was having a difficult time staying healthy. Because their investment options for the money they had on deposit were essentially limited to historically safe but relatively unprofitable home mortgages, they could not bring in enough income to pay out competitive interest rates and at the same time stay out of the red ink. This problem was "fixed" in 1982.

With the passage of the Garn-St. Germain Act, thrifts could invest in almost anything that might turn a profit. A weak S&L, therefore, could attract more deposits by offering higher interest rates. Then it could invest those deposits in high risk (and potentially high yield) ventures. If these investments proved successful, the thrift made money. If the projects failed and the investments went sour . . . Well, the depositors didn't really need to worry much about that, they were insured by Uncle Sam.

And finally, to add frosting to the cake, the Federal Home Loan Bank Board, which regulated the S&L industry, relaxed the capital requirement regulations for individual thrifts to a minimum. This meant that your friendly S&L needed to keep very little of its assets in real cash. Paper assets (mortgages and other loans) were acceptable building blocks in the eyes of the overseers. If its paper turned into real money, the S&L won big. If the paper crumpled and disintegrated, the S&L might go under. But only the Federal Savings & Loan Insurance Corporation (the FSLIC) would really lose any money.

Nice theory. Until S&Ls began to fall like a tapped row of standing dominoes and the FSLIC realized that it didn't have enough money to pay the bill. Then who was the loser? You guessed it: THE AMERICAN TAXPAYER. Estimates on how much the bailout is going to cost vary depending upon who is doing the estimating and they keep changing, but the figure being tossed about as of this writing is $500 billion.

WILD GROWTH

"Yikes! Looks like Congress blew it," you say. "But then again I can pretty much understand the motivation. Probably they were trying to stimulate free enterprise, probably they had good intentions . . . okay, they did go overboard. Their deregulation and insurance encouraged risky money-lending policies that were impossible to support when ventures failed. But *why* did it get so out of hand? This is a regulated industry! There are supposed to be bank inspectors on the job. Why is it going to cost $500 billion plus to mend the errors? Wasn't anybody watching?"

Yes, there were people watching. And there were very powerful people looking the other way. Understanding how we got into this mess is a lesson in human nature.

Let your imagination range free for a minute. Picture a beautiful mountain, add deep, powdery snow, install fine new chair lifts, include a luxurious resort with a roaring fire in the fireplace and a fine restaurant. Presto! Skiers appear. And no advertising was necessary.

That's just about what happened in the S&L industry during the 1980s. The government had set up a no-lose situation with the potential for some very smooth and rewarding "skiing." Aggressive, competent, risk-taking businessmen were attracted to the industry. So were some manipulative and unscrupulous opportunists. Unfortunately for this nation, the worst of these new-age bankers either already had or made extraordinary efforts to build political, social, and financial connections with people in key positions of power in our government.

In his book, *The Big Fix: Inside the S&L Scandal,* James Ring Adams names names and tells exactly who did what and when. The intricate web of government and business that he discloses is astounding and appalling. He demonstrates again and again that executive bankers discovered that "the best way to steal is to share a portion of the proceeds with those in a position to provide protection. The protectors may be in Congress or The White House or a governor's mansion. They may not understand just what they are doing, and their cut can be incredibly small. But they have stripped the defenses from the financial system, weakened banking and allowed the destruction of the savings and loan industry." [p. 32]

Probably the most publicized of the bank-failure scandals was that of Charles Keating and his Lincoln Savings & Loan Association in Irvine, California. When Federal Home Loan Bank Board examiners checked through its books in 1986, they found that Lincoln as a lender was almost completely out of the home mortgage business. Instead, the savings institution was putting its money into junk bonds and very speculative real estate ventures. Worse yet, loans were being made without credit checks on the borrowers and without appraisal of the properties that were being offered as collateral for the loans.

Besides the fact that depositors' money was being recklessly loaned, it was also being recklessly spent. Close relatives of Mr. Keating were found listed on the bank's payroll at salaries in the million-dollars-a-year range. At the same time, Lincoln was making huge donations to some of Mr. Keating's favorite charities and to selected political campaigns.

When the bank examiners cried STOP!, Keating shouted HARASS-MENT! He took his case to friends on Capitol Hill, an act that would later put his name and theirs on the front pages of the nation's newspapers. Five senators intervened on Keating's behalf: Dennis DeConcini (D., Arizona), Alan Cranston (D., California), John Glenn (D., Ohio), John McCain (R., Arizona), and Donald Riegle, Jr. (D., Michigan). The result was a delay in Bank Board action which allowed Keating to go on spending depositors' federally insured money. Later it was made public that the five had received a total of approximately $1.4 million in political contributions.

The Lincoln Savings & Loan story is just one case in the many bank failures at the close of the 1980s. No one knows exactly how much government/business collusion went on throughout the decade. It has been documented that some ethical and responsible men and women in the government's financial regulatory agencies did try to speak up. To a person, they were squelched and sequestered rather than rewarded. And this happened at *every* level in the bureaucracy, even to Edwin Gray, Chairman during the 1980s of the Federal Home Loan Bank Board.

On Sonny Bloch's national radio show, Ed Gray told the nation that he tried to warn President Reagan of the impending disaster but was not allowed access. According to Gray, Don Regan stood guard before the president and, as White House Chief of Staff, he told the man entrusted with safeguarding the nation's thrifts, not too politely, to be quiet.

The time came, however, when nothing could keep the lid down and the scandal erupted. As we move into the opening years of the decade of the nineties, no one yet knows the full magnitude of the banking fiascoes of the eighties. And the costs of setting the system right continue to mount.

Many, many thrifts failed as much of the paper they were built upon became just that: paper that was not producing income. The government forced bank closings, arranged mergers or acquisitions by other banks, or took over management. Because so many borrowers were in default at these failed or failing institutions, mortgaged houses, commercial buildings, land, and other collateral became the property of the government. In order to recoup some of the lost money, this property had to be unloaded. Thus it happened that Uncle Sam became the largest real estate seller in the world.

Among the pages and pages of property listings now on the government's books are many excellent investment opportunities and a few rotten eggs. The problem is that you can't always tell a rotten egg unless you crack it open. We'll tell you how to do that, but first let us introduce you to the machinery for property disposition that the government has set in place.

THE MACHINERY FOR REPAIRS

In August of 1989, President Bush signed into law the Financial Institutions Reform, Recovery and Enforcement Act. You'll hear it commonly called by its acronym, FIRREA. Among other things, this act created the Resolution Trust Corporation (the RTC) which was to be responsible for disposing of the assets of the failed thrift institutions. If you intend to profit from the S&L bailout, you'll have to work with the RTC, directly or indirectly.

The RTC has been establishing offices in critical locations across the nation and hiring people to staff those offices. We've included a list of agency VIPs in Chapter 5, but you can also call the Sonny Bloch Hotline for up-to-the-minute information and new names in your particular location. The toll-free number is (800) 878-8255.

The RTC is supervised by a five member oversight board which includes the cabinet-level Secretary of Housing and Urban Development (HUD). It appears that there will be slightly more than one thousand S&Ls under supervision by the RTC by the end of 1991, perhaps more. Besides supervising these S&Ls, the RTC will be responsible for managing many thousands of owned properties plus securities, mortgages, other loans, and other assorted assets totaling well over $180 billion.

The cost to the American taxpayer for this cleanup will be mind-boggling. The first numbers ventured were in the range of $50 billion; then $130 billion became the generally accepted estimate. As of early 1990, conservative estimates of the cost of the bailout exceeded $500 billion. Some analysts, however, are tossing around numbers with "trillion" after them.

Are you blurry-eyed and dizzy trying to picture those numbers in piles of paper dollars? It's just about impossible. Almost as bad as trying to visualize how many miles from the earth to Pluto. After all, the difference between fifty billion and five hundred billion is just a strategically placed zero. And no matter which of those estimates you choose to believe—even the smallest—its expenditure in real money will assure that the S&L bailout will be the most expensive domestic event in United States history to date.

Government officials are still hopeful that the sale of the real estate that the RTC has acquired by foreclosure and default will help to defray some of this cost. The National Association of Realtors and other local groups, however, have expressed fear that "dumping" such vast holdings on the open market would cause havoc, if not serious recession. Partly as a result of their energetic and persistent lobbies and partly because government is government, a beautifully bureaucratic collection of rules and procedures for the sale of RTC properties has been developed.

For example, at the insistence of a coalition of powerful people in the House of Representatives and some groups of nonprofit housing advocates, the RTC is required to give certain parties the first and exclusive opportunity to purchase eligible residential properties. "Eligible" includes single-family homes that are appraised at $67,500 or less, and multi-family properties with per unit values of $28,032 to $58,392 dependent upon bedroom size.

In Chapter 6, we'll tell you if you can qualify to become one of those "certain parties." It's important right now, however, that you realize that these rules of preference and their dollar guidelines are just examples of the requirements of an industry that is still growing. The RTC is a toddler as government agencies go and it's still working on its letters and numbers. We can promise you that many of its policies, rules, and guidelines will be subject to change in the course of the coming decade.

Right now, let us give you just a taste of how changeable "subject to change" really is. When the first listings of RTC property to be sold were published in January of 1990, 13,391 copies of the four-volume set were ordered by anxious would-be buyers on the first day of their availability. The 10¼ pound, 3,000 page best-seller titled *Real Estate Asset Inventory* could well have rivaled first day sales of a Stephen King thriller. But where was the thrill? The RTC had clearly announced that it would sell no property for less than 95 percent of its appraised value. Why were so many people interested in shelling out $50 to buy a list of properties that under no stretch of the imagination could be considered bargains?

Because most of these book buyers were savvy investors who knew that numbers change. They wanted the list so that they could watch, literally *watch,* the properties. Since appraised value represents an educated estimate, most of these would-be buyers suspected that the numbers might be revised or policy changed when the properties didn't sell within a few months. And sure enough, reappraisals were ordered with instructions to come up with a "more realistic" figure for those properties that were not moving. The RTC would still sell only at 95 percent of appraised value, but there was to be a new value assigned to the property. Watching investors could then reevaluate the worth of the investment in terms of their own appraisal of value in the area.

This approach was "policy" for about four and a half months. Then on May 8, 1990, the RTC announced that it would no longer hold to the 95 percent of appraised value bottom-price figure. The board of the RTC had voted unanimously to allow local managers and national directors to reduce the allowed selling prices on the properties it had for sale. Suddenly, purchase prices of up to 15 percent below appraised value would be allowed on all properties that had been on the market for at least four months. Managers would also be allowed to shave another 5 percent off the appraisal figure of these properties if they did not sell within three months of the first price reduction.

Approximately 20 percent off appraised value! Now that's almost always a good deal in the real estate marketplace. So the "watching" of specific properties by savvy investors will probably pay off handsomely in this round of sales. Why? Because they guessed that the numbers and rules would probably change and they were there to be first in line when it happened.

The moral of this tale is: *don't let the changeability of the RTC put you off.* Change can be a money-maker, especially if you can anticipate it and prepare for it. Two more examples, and then we'll go on.

At the outset of sales, the RTC also stated: (1) that properties would be sold only through conventional real estate channels with licensed real estate brokers representing the seller (your government), and (2) that there would be no seller financing available to the general public. Before the agency was a year old, both these rules were changed.

Seller financing is not only now available but the down payment minimum has been lowered. When the RTC first made the change that allowed seller financing, they required 25 percent of the purchase price as a down payment. As of this writing, they are requiring only 15 percent. There is also a plan for lower-than-prevalent rates of interest on financing for buyers who agree to provide low and moderate income housing in the properties they purchase.

And about the rule that all property would be sold only through conventional channels (read "channels" as real estate agents). Well, in the winter of 1990 when the first crocuses were just popping their heads out of the ground, the word "auction" could sometimes be heard (*sotto voce* to be sure) in some RTC offices in the nation. By May, the RTC had announced that it planned to sell $300 million in appraised inventory at its first major auction scheduled in July. And the Bush Administration had given its full backing to policy statements that would allow the RTC to accept purchase prices at this auction that were as much as 30 percent below the appraised values.

Is the focus in this snapshot of the bailout clear for you or are you rubbing your eyes and saying, "What focus?" Don't worry. Everyone else is seeing the same blurred image. It's obvious that the government is still feeling its way on this one. So remember as you work through and with the bailout that no numbers, no pronouncements, no rules are forever.

ABOUT THIS BOOK

This book was conceived in a moment when the air suddenly seemed so alive with electric snaps and pops that just breathing was exciting. Our literary agents had brought us together to explore the possibility of a series of books on general real estate topics. No one had planned to talk about the bailout that day. The topic just came up, probably inevitably.

Within minutes we knew everything else had to wait. *This* was our book! We both saw the bailout as a volcano, a volcano that would continue to erupt for at least a decade to come. In what seemed a white-hot current of recognition, each of us knew that *together* we had the magic to turn the smoke, fire, and ashes of the bailout volcano into a shower of riches for the real estate marketplace.

We honestly believe that every new savings and loan industry eruption, every new bank failure and its bailout, is going to result in a wealth of opportunities. We've joined forces to tell you how you can find those opportunities and how you can make them profitable.

As you read, do keep in mind that the specific numbers and policies we make reference to may be changed as the government bailout bureaucracy comes of age. Don't let that bother you. Bear in mind that the sale of S&L bailout properties is only a variation on one of the oldest and most reliable games in town: the real estate investment game. Procedures and success strategies have remained the same in the real estate marketplace for as long as we both can remember, and that's nudging up near a hundred person-years, much more if you add in the experience and recollections of both our fathers, and our grandfathers before them. Yes, both of us are from families where real estate was standard dinner table conversation!

When the two of us look at the changing S&L bailout rules, sometimes we laugh and sometimes we shrug. We know that dealing with the RTC is going to be like negotiating through a maze, and a fancy one at that with lots of doors to choose from. But we know which are the right doors and we know where to get the keys.

This is a book about how to profit from the federal government's rescue of your deposits in the savings and loan industry. More basically, however, this is a book about how to profit in the American real estate marketplace. It makes no difference whether your investment interest is a cottage in the woods or an apartment complex in a major city. It makes no difference who's heading the RTC or what set of numbers the RTC is using in the month you decide to buy. The numbers that matter for you are the numbers on your particular deal. By the time you finish reading this book, you'll know how to evaluate and use those numbers, you'll know how to use real estate facts, and you'll know how to use the RTC rules to your advantage.

Let's go look around this volcano.

CHAPTER 2

WHAT HAS THE GOVERNMENT GOT TO SELL?

Finding bailout properties to buy is not quite as easy as going to your favorite real estate broker for a day of house hunting. It requires some ingenuity, some action, and sometimes a little inside information.

Do the words "inside information" set off bells and whistles in your mind? Are you thinking, "Not me! I'm not going to get tangled up in any insider trading scam!"

Well, relax, get comfortable, and keep reading. The kind of inside information we mean is perfectly legal in the real estate marketplace. "Inside information" is your Aunt Mabel telling you that Mr. and Mrs. Throckmorton who live around the corner are planning to retire to Florida and will probably be selling their house soon. If you wanted to live around the corner from your aunt, it would be perfectly legal for you to knock on their door and make them an offer before the house was listed. It's also perfectly legal for you to buy that used car lot on Pleasantville Road right after you hear from a friend in a high place on the A&P staff that the supermarket chain is looking for a site in the Pleasantville Road area. (In fact, if you were really real estate savvy, you wouldn't even bother to buy the used car lot. You'd negotiate an option on the property. Then if A&P happened to like the land you selected for them, you could make a fortune. If they didn't, your loss would be the cost of the option. Little risk, big profit potential, and all legal.) The point is: *inside information in the real estate marketplace is legal.*

Okay, so you're now feeling comfortable with "inside information" (and we're going to give you quite a bit of it), but what about ingenuity and action? That sounds a lot like work, doesn't it? Well, it is. Investing in real estate is *not* play. But it could be the most rewarding work you ever do.

In Chapter 4, we're going to tell you how to separate the *good* deals from the *bad* and the *bogus,* and how to spot the *bargains* and the *steals.* In Chapter 5, we'll tell you where to look for and how to find bailout-related properties. Right now, however, hold the reins on your enthusiasm for a few minutes while we take you on a brief survey of the investment vehicles in the bailout inventory that are most likely to interest you. This section is full of facts that can mean the difference between success and failure, or, more bluntly, the difference between making money and losing money!

REO = REAL ESTATE OWNED

Fact one is that Uncle Sam is selling REOs. REO is the banking acronym for *real estate owned* and it refers to properties that the lending institution has foreclosed upon because of mortgage default.

Are you still with us? What we're talking about is sometimes referred to in conversation as "repossessed property." You've heard repossession stories: Joe didn't make the payments on his car so the car dealer came by and took it back. That's the automobile equivalent of *mortgage default:* not making the payments that are due. Now technically, "repossessed property" is not quite the same as "foreclosed property," since *repossessed* refers to goods and *foreclosed* to mortgaged real estate, but the effect is the same: the person who took out the loan no longer has the property.

Carrying foreclosed properties on their books costs banks and the RTC money and usually produces little or no income. As a result, lenders and the RTC want to sell their REO properties. In other words: THEY WANT OUT!

With new REOs coming into the bailout inventory almost every day and the old stuff generating more carrying costs every day, we have highly motivated sellers. In every real estate marketplace, highly motivated sellers set the stage for fabulous deals (for the buyers). To allow the sell/buy drama to unfold, all that's needed is a savvy buyer with money (or the ability to get money).

But we still haven't really told you about what all this REO really is. That's next on the itinerary. We're about to take you on an investment vehicle tour. As your guides, we'll be talking about generic profiles and we'll pepper those profiles with bits of advice specific to each particular vehicle. To start off, we've divided our tour into three main areas, arranged in order of riskiness and complexity: HOUSING (places where people live), COMMERCIAL INVESTMENTS (places where people work), and VENTURES (high risk real estate that costs a lot and /or screams for a creative owner).

HOUSING

Housing is usually the beginning investor's first step in real estate. Often, a first purchase is personal housing which later turns into an investment. With this experience behind them, neophytes usually go on to the purchase of housing to be rented for a time and then sold, or to housing to be fixed up and then rolled over for quick profit. Some of the following housing investment vehicles lend themselves to personal use, some to both personal use and rental, some to rental only. Some are long-term commitments, others cry out for rapid turnover. It's important to recognize your particular goals of the moment before you choose what to buy.

And—pardon us for being a little obvious—we'd like to remind both new and seasoned investors of a maxim that works in every buy/sell situation: *Never buy something just because it's cheap.* The word SALE can be the downfall of investors as well as shoppers. Before you put down money in the real estate marketplace, ask yourself: *Is this what I really want? Is it a good deal? Can I sell it tomorrow for more than I'm paying today? Will it bring in positive cash flow? When?*

SINGLE-FAMILY HOUSES

In the late 1970s/early 1980s, several best-sellers encouraged every person in the nation to make a fortune by buying, fixing up, and then selling old houses. Some of the authors of these books have since declared bankruptcy.

"So?" you ask. "That's behind us. What about *now*? Can a person make a fortune by buying fixer-uppers? And is the government selling them?"

Yes, to both questions. But you'd better know what you're doing! Fix-up and carrying costs are considerably higher now than they were at the end of the 1970s and appreciation is slower. A prospective turn-around investment has to be selected very carefully.

The RTC does have a considerable number of boarded-up properties on its lists, so there is opportunity here (at the right price). But according to RTC procedure guidelines as of this writing, these properties must be purchased in *as is* condition. Whenever the words *as is* appear in a listing, you absolutely *need* to use a professional property inspection firm to help you evaluate the condition of the building and estimate the probable cost of necessary repair work. You'll also need to do a careful and accurate estimate of what the expected market value would be once repairs are completed. We'll give you some formulas for success in Chapter 4.

"How about getting rich slowly?" you ask. "Have they got any houses that can be rented until the market heats up again?"

Again, yes. But if you are considering the purchase of a single-family house with the intention of renting it, be aware that these properties generate much less income per square foot of space than most apartments and condominiums. On the other hand, houses sell more quickly and usually for more profit than either individual condominium apartments or apartment buildings. The major key to success in this endeavor is a balancing act: buying at a price low enough and renting at a rate high enough to come out with positive cash flow.

A decade plus ago, positive cash flow wasn't nearly as important as it is today because housing appreciation was spiraling. It didn't matter if you lost a thousand or two a year while renting, you made it up ten- or twenty-fold plus a handsome profit when you sold the place. But you can't count on appreciation to pull you out of a bad judgment in this market. The 1990s are the decade of the *savvy* investor.

If you're not yet an "investor," if you just want to be a "homeowner," the bailout may also be *your* ticket. But it's not a free ride. If you think some helpful real estate agent is going to hand you a home wrapped in ribbon with a gift tag reading *Love from Uncle Sam,* think again. Bailout properties are being sold in a competitive marketplace. You must learn to compete and then you must get good at it.

To overcome the lack-of-experience handicap of the first-time buyer, we suggest that you do some reading in a basic how-to-buy-a-house book or two. (Forgive us for recommending our favorites: *Sonny Bloch's Inside Real Estate* and *All America's Real Estate Book* by Carolyn Janik and Ruth Rejnis.) To the universal savvy-and-skills of house buying that you'll read about, add the following two tactics that are specific to dealing with bailout properties.

1. *The countdown watch.* As of this writing, official government policy allows local supervisors to accept 20 percent less than the appraised value of a property after it has been on the market four months. We think the real sales figures will go even lower! In a countdown watch, you identify the property, estimate its market value, decide on the price you want to buy it at, get to know whoever is supervising the sale (a real estate agent can tell you when other offers are being made), prearrange approval for financing, and wait.

   Yes, wait. You must keep track of exactly how long the property has been on the market and make your first low offer just before a publicized price reduction. Now you're in on the bidding even if that price reduction is big enough to bring out buyers in a thunderstorm. The RTC wants to move properties, and if you raise your bid to a new lowered price with a contract all written and the financing looking good, your chances of getting the nod are excellent. Be aware also that you can keep a countdown watch on more than one property at a time. We'll tell you more about negotiating with the RTC in Chapter 8.

2. *The end run.* Sometimes the best way to deal with the RTC is to do an end run around them. With a little extra effort, you can deal directly with a lending institution in financial trouble that is trying desperately to sell its REO before the RTC shuts it down. Some of these foreclosed houses are real plums that have not been advertised

to the general public. We'll tell you how to get lists of unpublicized REO and deal directly with still-alive thrifts in Chapter 5.

MULTI-FAMILY HOUSES

Any building that contains at least two but no more than six separate housing units is usually considered a multi-family house. More than six units and you have a small apartment building.

Multi-family houses are often an excellent place for the small investor or first-time homebuyer to begin. In many cases, by choosing to occupy one of the units and to act as the super, the owner can cut down on his/her housing costs and on the maintenance/management costs of the building.

One of the good things about buying a multi-family as a first home is financing. The rental income from the units that you do not occupy is considered when you apply for a mortgage. Some buyers therefore will qualify for a mortgage on a multi-family house when they would be turned down for the same mortgage amount on a single-family house. There are also some tax advantages for homeowners of multi-family houses. For example, the owner can deduct on IRS returns the maintenance expenses for the portion of the house that is not owner-occupied. Prorated depreciation is also allowed. If this sounds appealing to you, do some research in tax advice books or talk with a good CPA before you sign on the bottom line, even before you start imagining where you'll place your furniture.

For the investor who does not plan to occupy a unit in the multi-family house, purchase decisions should be made according to all the customary investment guidelines: probable market value, condition, rental income, cash flow, and current and future demand for housing in the area. (More about each of these items in Chapter 4 and others.) Emotion *(do you like it?)* should not factor into the decision to buy or not to buy.

The disadvantages of multi-families? Well, they sell less quickly than single-family houses so you should consider them as a less liquid asset. If you choose to make one of the units your home, you will be sharing your yard and the common areas of the building with your tenants. Some landlords (both live-in and absentee) are also bothered by the seemingly constant demands of their tenants for repairs or improvements.

The RTC has a good number of multi-family houses for sale in several areas of the nation. Some of these are going to be offered on a priority basis to not-for-profit groups and low-income housing advocates. Becoming a not-for-profit low-income housing advocate can be very profitable indeed. More about this in Chapter 6.

VACATION HOMES

Among the REO properties of the nation, you can probably find a log cabin in Arkansas, or a fourteen room bungalow on the California coast, and a lot of other vacation home choices in between. Which means that someone looking for a second home where he/she can summer, winter, or just weekend in peace might well regard the bailout as an answer to some long-standing prayers.

If you're buying vacation property as an investment, however, you'll have to be very careful in your selection. In the first place, the IRS gets into the act with very complicated tax rules on how much personal time you can spend in the place in proportion to rental time. Then there are the considerations of seasonal occupancy and long distance maintenance and management. And most important of all, you've got to ask yourself why this particular property has become REO. Did the buyer overextend himself? Or are rental prospects in the area dismal because of a fall from popularity, overbuilding, or generally depressed economic conditions? If someone else couldn't keep a property rented enough days to show a positive cash flow, you might not be able to do it either.

Vacation areas have a way of coming into and going out of fashion. If you buy in an area that's on its way out, you may not see any discernible appreciation for years to come and renting may become a yearly ordeal. Conversely, when vacation areas get hot, their real estate usually appreciates well above the national average and brings rents in the premium range. A well-timed investment purchase in a desirable vacation area could be a virtual gold mine.

TIME-SHARES

For those of you who haven't had the opportunity to sit through a time-share sales presentation, let us tell you about this late twentieth century form of property ownership. Time-sharing is a kind of condominium ownership where, rather than buy full ownership of the unit, you buy one week (or one month, or some specified period of time) per year in a given unit. In other words you not only buy a particular space in a condominium community, you also buy a particular time or amount of time each year. Now this may seem rather intangible, but the ownership is real, fee simple, and can be sold or passed on to your heirs. (Be aware, however, that there is a kind of time-share sales program called right-to-use which is *not* real estate ownership.)

Fee simple ownership is the reason behind the appearance of time-share units in the RTC lists. You see, some lenders actually loaned people the money to buy these units and secured their loans with mortgages on the property. When buyers defaulted on their payments, the banks became time-share owners.

Then they had a problem because no bank wants to own a time-share. Why? Because maintenance cost per dollar value is very high, rental income is neither high nor dependable, and resale time-share units are notoriously hard to sell, seldom bringing in more than a fraction of their original selling price. It's not at all unusual for a week's ownership in a two bedroom unit that originally sold for $10,000 to change hands on the resale market for $4,000. You might use those figures as a guideline when evaluating what's a bargain in RTC time-share sales.

The price is *not* the only factor to consider in time-share purchases, however. You should also examine the health of the condominium community as a whole. Because of high-pressure sales programs and a handful of other reasons, there has been an unusually high percentage of defaults in some time-share resorts. When units are in default, they are not contributing the annual maintenance fee. This puts a greater load on the other unit owners, their maintenance fees going up slightly with each unit that goes into default. Bad, but the alternative is worse. If the Owners Association refuses to take on the added cost of units in default, the maintenance budget shrinks and eventually the condition of the resort deteriorates. In a worst case scenario, a condominium community could lose its land for nonpayment of back taxes.

Fortunately, the great time-share shakeout has already taken place and most resorts are now well managed and viable. Before buying, however, check the maintenance of the resort (preferably by spending a week there) and compare its maintenance fees with those of similar resorts in the area. Also ask how many unsold apartments there are. (One hundred percent ownership is best!)

And finally, never buy a time-share as an investment property. With the vacation exchange clubs that are available, owning a time-share week or two can be a wonderful way to see the country or the world inexpensively, but the units almost never show a profit. If you find a bailout time-share in an area you know and love and the price is right, you may just want to snatch it up. But don't do so under the fantasy that you're adding substance to your investment portfolio.

MOBILE HOMES

The manufacturers of mobile homes now call their products "manufactured homes" and the homes no longer look like aluminum shoe boxes. In fact, many cannot be distinguished from traditional "stick built" houses and all must meet stringent federal construction standards.

Having established these standards in the 1970s, the government stood behind its "seal of approval" and arranged that manufactured homes set upon a foundation could be mortgaged exactly like stick built homes and the mortgages could be insured by the FHA or guaranteed by the VA. Which is why some S&Ls are now the owners of "manufactured homes." (The mortgages were foreclosed.)

Mobile homes *not* set on a permanent foundation are financed exactly like cars. And, yes, some S&Ls made this kind of loan also and then repossessed the "trailers" when payments weren't made as scheduled. So you might find something closer to an oversized shoe box than a traditional house among the RTC inventory after all.

But are they good investments? That depends. Price is a factor, but more important is location and appearance. Statistics show that manufactured homes set on permanent foundations in neighborhoods of similar housing are appreciating at the same rate as nearby properties. Manufactured homes without foundations and standing upon rented sites, however, depreciate. How fast? That depends upon the surrounding area. (Some appraisers regard them as not very different from automobiles.)

CONDOMINIUM APARTMENTS

Condomania came into full flower in the eighties and no other housing species has ever been so overbuilt. In most parts of the country today, there are simply more condos than there are condo buyers. Knowing that, you don't need an MBA from Harvard to come to the conclusion that prices are probably not going up very fast, if at all, and that the pace of sales is probably a little less than swift.

That doesn't mean, however, that there aren't some good money-making opportunities in among the lists of REO condos. You just have to get the purchase price down low enough and check out all the other factors that contribute to the quality quotient of the condominium community.

"The quality *what?*" you ask.

What we mean is the answer you get after you examine, consider, and calculate all the aspects of a community that contribute to the valuation of its individual units. When you own a condo, you yourself own a particular space, nothing else, no bricks and mortar, no driveway space, no land. You share in the ownership of all those things, however, with all the other unit owners. Why? It's what owning a condo means. With your condo apartment purchase you get an undivided interest in all the common elements of the condominium community. You also get an obligation to help support and maintain those common elements.

What are "common elements"? What's an "undivided interest"? If those are your questions and you're feeling overwhelmed, don't worry. That's normal. Condominium ownership is more complex than most offering plans would like you to believe.

Common elements are everything except the spaces (apartments) that are individually owned. The roof, the walls, the foundation, the stair-cases, the balconies, the roads, the shrubbery, the swimming pool, the tennis courts . . . you get the idea. An undivided interest is a share that cannot be split off from the whole. As a unit owner, for example, you own an undivided interest in the swimming pool, but you cannot remove one single tile from that pool because everyone owns an undivided interest in each and every tile.

When you buy or sell a condo apartment, then, you are buying or selling a community as well as a home. House rules and by-laws and the quality of the maintenance as well as the amount of the monthly main-tenance fees all count toward the potential appreciation of your pur-chase.

As an investor, you will want to consider the vacancy rate in your area as well as the ratio of maintenance fees to rent. Remember, your rental income must cover not only the financing costs but also the maintenance fees and still show positive cash flow. The good news is that rented condos require minimal time commitments, since maintenance complaints go directly to the staff hired by the Unit Owners Association.

CO-OP APARTMENTS

Owners of co-op apartments do not own real estate. They own shares in the corporation that owns the building and they have a proprietary lease on the apartments they call their own. Co-op apartments therefore are not mortgaged. Financing is arranged by holding the stock certificates as collateral. Because co-op loans are considered more risky than mortgages, most lenders have required larger down payments and have been more careful about qualification guidelines when lending in this market. As a result, there are not a great many co-ops among the bailout properties that are now for sale or are likely to be offered in the near future.

Individual co-op apartments and entire co-operative buildings are more likely to appear on bailout lists in the areas where this kind of ownership is most common. So if you've got your heart set on a co-op, watch lists for New York City, Buffalo, northeastern New Jersey, the Baltimore/Washington area, Chicago with scattered occurrences in the rest of Illinois, San Francisco, the greater Miami area with scattered occurrences in the rest of Florida, Connecticut, Massachusetts, Michigan, and South Dakota. In other parts of the nation, many people won't know what you're talking about if you ask where the nearest co-op is, or they'll think you're referring to a food-buying plan.

If you find a bailout co-op (individual apartment or whole building) being offered for a good price in a good area, evaluate it just as you would a condo, except for one thing. Be much more careful in reading the financial statements. In fact, it's a good idea to hire an accountant or a real estate attorney to examine the financial statements of the co-op for you.

"Why spend that extra money?" you ask, thinking that you're pretty good at numbers.

Because some professional help here could save your neck. If the co-op community (the building) goes under, you have *nothing* to call your own. This is different from the guy next door in a condominium losing his unit to foreclosure. In that case you still own your unit. The effect of the foreclosure might be a bit of a strain on the condo community's maintenance budget but each unit owner still owns his/her unit with no other ill effects from the foreclosure. In a co-op building, everyone sinks or swims together.

In some areas of the country (notably New York City) failure of sponsors and/or developers to make underlying mortgage payments on the building has made some co-ops financially shaky. There have also been some reports of quasi-authorized re-mortgaging of buildings which (unknown to or not understood by individual apartment holders) puts the co-operative as an operating entity in jeopardy.

Does that make you nervous? With good reason, but a pleasant co-op apartment in a well-run building can be a good investment with potential appreciation and all the tax advantages of homeownership. Just choose carefully and investigate the numbers thoroughly!

APARTMENT BUILDINGS

Many, if not most, pension funds and insurance companies avoid investing in apartment buildings.

Does that surprise you? After all, there *is* a shortage of rental housing in many areas of the nation. Why are these powerful and well-financed investors shying away from this vehicle? Because supply and demand is not the primary factor in their decisions. When asked, pension fund managers will tell you that apartment buildings are "too management-intensive" for their portfolios.

Translated into English, "too management-intensive" means that the success (read as *positive cash flow*) of the building depends too heavily on how well it is managed. Now if you think you're a good manager, or that you can hire and oversee good management, don't let the prejudices of the big investors influence you. Just take the information and use it in your decision making.

Apartment buildings come in all sizes, shapes, and price ranges. Some are bought by individuals and some are bought by investor groups. Besides price, condition, maintenance requirements, the time demands of ownership, management costs, and cash flow, *probable holding time* should be a factor in the decision to buy. If you intend to buy for a long-term investment, the building must not only carry itself, it must produce real cash income annually. If you think you can buy cheaply enough to do a fix-up and resell quickly for a profit, you can assign less weight to the positive cash flow aspect of your considerations, figuring that you might show a loss in one year that will be made up by a large profit when the building is sold. This is not a bad investment strategy, just a slightly more risky one. Remember, apartment buildings take a lot more time to sell than your typical suburban cottage with a white picket fence (if there are any of those left).

COMMERCIAL INVESTMENTS

One of the reasons commercial property is not usually recommended for beginners is turnover time. Commercial space often stands empty between tenants much longer than residential space. Also, once a tenant is found, the lease is invariably more complex than a housing lease.

Let's look at an example. If you buy the building where a shoemaker has his business and the shoemaker decides to move across the street, you must pay mortgage principal, interest, taxes, and maintenance costs on that building until you find another tenant. Which could be many months, long enough to wipe out any hope of positive cash flow for several years to come! And when you do find a prospective tenant, you'll almost certainly be asked to do some extensive interior remodeling, since this new person is unlikely to be a shoemaker whose burning desire is to compete with the shoemaker across the street.

Okay, so let's say your new tenant is going to be a dry cleaners. You're willing to repaint, put in new floor tile, even a new counter, but are you willing to foot the bill for one of those monster carousels that the cleaned clothes ride around on until they are picked up?

You won't pay for the carousel, you say. Okay, but you need a tenant and the dry cleaner is pressing you to pay for at least the installation costs. You agree and congratulate yourself that you have the place rented at last. When you get the lease back from your new tenant's lawyer, however, you discover that, if the dry cleaner moves at the end of his lease, you're the one who's stuck with the repair costs that result from the dismantling and removal of the giant go-round in question.

Spots in the shape of dollar signs begin to appear before your eyes. You want to tear the lease up and tell the dry cleaner where to go, but you *need* a tenant! Okay, you'll eat the repair costs. And besides, this guy might stay for twenty years. So what's the worry?

You're just beginning to feel better about the deal when the word *electricity* catches your eye. No! Not the electricity. That's too much! You were willing to include electricity in the shoemaker's rent, but not a dry cleaner! All that ironing!

Are you beginning to get the idea about a more complex lease? Besides tenant problems, commercial property often demands more maintenance and management time, is more sensitive to the economy, and costs more than comparable residential property. It can also be more profitable.

If you have some past experience in housing investment, some spare money to invest, and a desire to expand your circle of influence in the real estate marketplace, don't cross out the possibility of a commercial investment. The bailout and its bargains may just be the perfect opportunity for you to step into a new investment vehicle. Let's look at some of the possibilities.

MIXED-USE BUILDINGS

A mixed-use building isn't going to let you escape the complexity of commercial leasing. In fact, leasing is going to be your learning experience in this investment vehicle, with the pain cushioned by cash. While you're learning about commercial leasing, the residential portion of your building should carry you financially.

But we're jumping ahead of ourselves here. We haven't even defined mixed-use property yet. You've certainly seen it though, even if you didn't recognize it by name. Mixed-use property is the building that houses a hairdresser, or pharmacy, or candy store, or doctors' offices, or any other business on the first floor (or in any part of the structure) and residential apartments in the remainder of the space.

There is a considerable amount of mixed-use property for sale in the bailout. If this investment vehicle interests you, buy only at a price that will allow you to structure the financing so that the residential income will cover the expenses of the building. This guideline will guarantee you healthy positive cash flow when the commercial portion of the building is leased. It will also guarantee that your investment will not cause sleepless nights if the commercial portion stands empty for six or nine months.

Taking this advice into consideration, remember also that all other criteria of getting a good deal apply to mixed-use property. Don't let numbers or emotions carry you into an investment that you won't be able to sell for a profit, or perhaps sell at all.

LAND

Back in the good old days (when federal regulation was still a genuine reality), financial institutions just didn't make loans with raw land as collateral. What is called "raw land" is land without "improvements," that is, land without buildings. Most land deals therefore were cash transactions or land purchase contracts in which the seller effectively held a mortgage on the land for the buyer.

But everyone knows that financial institutions, including the thrifts, got into holding mortgages on raw land because there is a lot of land for sale in the bailout. Is it worth buying? Each piece must be judged individually, but "worth" is usually a combination of price tag and your plans and experience.

Raw land is considered among the less liquid assets in the real estate marketplace, which overall is considered nonliquid. You can see where that puts land. To express it on a more personal level: don't put a penny of your money into raw land if you think you'll need that penny in the next five years. Yes, five years is usually considered the minimal turn-around time for land investments. There are some exceptions, however, and we'll go into those in Chapter 4.

"All right, it's hard to sell if you need fast cash," you say. "But on the other hand, it doesn't demand any time or attention while it's appreciating. Besides being illiquid, is there anything else wrong with investing in land?"

First of all, appreciation is *not* guaranteed, in land or in any other real estate investment. Second, and maybe more important, raw land does not usually generate any income but it does require the payment of property taxes. With a few exceptions therefore, land is a negative cash flow investment.

"So you're saying that most investors should stay away from land," you surmise.

No, we didn't say that. Land can be an excellent investment vehicle. But you've got to be aware of its negative aspects before you buy. If you are willing and financially able to make the long-term commitment, go right ahead. Purchase of the right land at the right time and price can bring a return of 500 percent or more in five to ten years. The most important factor in collecting this kind of windfall is foresight. You must anticipate, either through your own intuition and research or through some accurate insider information, where the need and demand for land will be *before that demand is there.*

How does one do that? Well, "intuition and research" might be your observation that a huge and elegant shopping mall is being built in the middle of a vacant field near a small town. Now you know those builders paid a lot of money for a lot of professional market research before committing millions to mall-building. You can guess pretty accurately that either a large company is moving into the area or demographic studies show that an upscale population is moving toward the area. In either case, the land within easy driving of that shopping mall is likely to appreciate faster than normal.

"Accurate insider information" might be that your brother-in-law's mother is hired as an appraiser for IBM. She passes on the word that they were favorably impressed with a parcel suited to a new production plant far from any major city. (As we said earlier, this kind of insider information is perfectly legal.) You watch public records of land purchase. As soon as that deal goes through, start shopping for land in the area! There *will* be a demand for housing and if you buy good land it will appreciate. Fast!

But what's good land? That question is why we put land in the experience-required section. "Good" depends upon the suitability of the terrain and the location to the goals of the developer and upon the regulations governing land use in the local community. Land for housing must have adequate drainage and a source of water (either wells or the ability to tap into a city water supply). It must be accessible by road and it must be safely removed from environmental hazards. Commercial development has these same requirements but also raises questions about the potential effects of the new businesses on the environment.

Zoning regulations can actually prohibit any kind of development except that chosen by the city fathers. If you plan to invest in land, therefore, you'd best become acquainted with the workings of your local planning board. It's also a good idea to get to know its members personally if you have the opportunity. Extra attention to the community, its needs and concerns, and its governing groups can make a tremendous difference in the profits from your land investment. If you want a zoning change, you've got to take your plans before the local planning board and you've got to change the mind-set of the community. Take it from us, community minds don't change easily.

If you are considering buying land from the bailout inventory, ask yourself why it's for sale. What was proposed for the land when the S&L took a mortgage on it that just didn't happen? Why didn't it happen? Can the proposal be reconsidered by whatever board or whoever blocked the original development? Can the environmental problem encountered by the former owner be remedied? Is there another feasible use for the land that might make it more valuable in the near future?

If you have money to invest, but little experience in land investment, this may be a time to investigate a partnership deal with a reputable builder. Your money and his knowledge might just make a profitable marriage.

STRIP MALLS

No, we're not talking about a place where caged dancers dodge strobe lights! Strip malls are to be found all across the nation and the finest families shop at them. They are your typical suburban shopping centers. Not Main Street, but a group of small stores, one or two large stores, and a large paved parking area. The usual small businesses include a pharmacy, bakery, pizza parlor, hairdresser, bank, barber, etc. When a strip mall has only one large store, it is almost invariably a grocery store. When there are two, they are usually at either end of the strip and the second store is usually a clothing store or a household goods store like Woolworth's or Kmart.

The developers of strip malls often keep title to the property and lease the spaces in their malls. If income from leased space cannot cover the mortgage payments on the property, the mortgage might be foreclosed. And thus there are strip malls available in the bailout.

Before you rush out to buy one, you've got to find out why the developers couldn't make those mortgage payments. Can you buy the mall at a price low enough (we're still talking seven figures) to reduce rents, attract 100 percent occupancy, and still have positive cash flow? This may be a good deal, but bear in mind that you may well need a good deal of down payment money. Strip malls are often the investment vehicle of choice in newly formed investor groups. More about that in Chapter 9.

OFFICE BUILDINGS

About the mid-1980s, word got around that office buildings were overbuilt. The press quoted statistics showing that much space was standing empty, and in many parts of the nation, this was true. So what do you think happened? Builders stopped building office buildings. Which gave the demand for office space a beautiful chance to catch up to the supply.

In the usual pattern of things, the next phase of the real estate cycle is for the demand to exceed the supply. Then, in the space of time between the realization that there is a shortage of office space and the completion of a new phase of overbuilding by money-motivated developers, those people who own office buildings will make a lot of money. (This is a cycle of at least ten years.) These office building owners will make an especially handsome profit if they buy the buildings cheaply and then discover that they can charge higher rents because there's a shortage of space. From there it's a short road to office condominium conversion or the sale of the building.

Buy low, rent high, sell higher could be a bailout scenario for office buildings in many parts of the country during this decade. Foreclosed office buildings available in the bailout might come partially filled, however, with leases that run many years at stated rents. Your number-working will have to determine the chances of filling the unfilled spaces with tenants paying high enough rents to make the cash flow for the building positive.

Besides the cash flow, condition, and lease situation of a building, you should also know its geographic area well enough to anticipate growth or stagnation. Finally, you should know who's building what in the town and in nearby towns and you should know what new proposals are before the local planning boards.

Office buildings are another of those lots-of-zeros investments and you might need a group effort to get together 15 percent of the purchase price as a down payment. If you can do that, however, Uncle Sam might hold the mortgage for the balance. Just be absolutely certain that income will cover costs because this is not a liquid investment vehicle.

HOTELS

There may be more hotels for sale in the bailout inventory than you would expect. Unless, that is, you consider the fact that the 1980s were a decade when the already rich got richer and when a lot of otherwise ordinary people got rich quite suddenly.

Most people with money to spare want to have more fun, and leisure-time industries expanded rapidly in the eighties. But the rainbow and its pot-of-gold attracted too many hopefuls, and leisure-use construction is yet another story of overbuilding. Some luxury hotels and resorts never brought in their expected return; others were never completed. You can find failures and incompletions and a few other situations among the stories behind the bailout hotel properties.

Many of the bailout's hotels and resorts will be sold at auction. If you're thinking of participating be aware that "auction" doesn't mean plaid shirts and jeans. We're talking the equivalent of white-tie affairs here with opening bids in the multimillions likely and competition named Hilton, Sheraton, Marriott, and maybe even Trump. Oh, and you probably won't *go* to the auction site, you'll just tune in on the special television channel and place your bids by phone.

In discussing the pros and cons of hotel ownership, we're talking about profit margins that are so "management-intensive" they could make owning an apartment building look like a sure thing at the races. Add that characteristic to a business that's sensitive not only to the economy but also to the whims of fashion, and you'll know why we don't recommend that you spend a lot of time dreaming about buying a resort hotel.

Unless, of course, you know the hotel business, you have considerable financial resources, and you're looking for a new career or perhaps a retirement income. If that's your story, do check out the addresses on the bailout lists. There may just be a small hotel that the big names have overlooked. It could be your passport to an interesting and profitable occupation, if not riches.

WAREHOUSES AND MANUFACTURING SPACE

There aren't a lot of warehouses or factories for sale, but the right one in the right hands could be a gold mine. The floor space that once was the warehouse or factory of a large company might be divided up in any number of ways and leased to any number of small and/or new companies. Some commercial warehouses might be converted into storage facilities for the general public, some factories into telemarketing centers or factory outlet centers or day-care centers. The possibilities are almost endless, except for one thing: the zoning restrictions of the town.

There's a lot of research required on this investment vehicle but it can pay off handsomely. Before you buy, check all the usual factors and then triple-check the zoning ordinances that apply. Look at the building creatively, asking yourself: What exactly can be done with this property? How much would that cost? How much income would the changes bring in? What are the possibilities of profitable resale if the restructuring is successful?

Check also on facilities. Is there enough parking space for the use you foresee? Is there adequate electrical supply? Waste disposal? Air conditioning? What's the access like? If what you convert the space to draws crowds, can the current roads carry the load?

The converted warehouse can be the birthplace of many small businesses, but remember, as those businesses grow they will want more space or they will move out. And others will surely fail. You must be prepared for a high turnover rate if you decide to house a start-up manufacturing center. The warehouse business is more stable, but less lucrative. The other ideas? You'll have to make your own judgments or hire professionals to render opinions.

VENTURES

We've labeled this final group of the bailout investment vehicles as *ventures* because they require a certain amount of expertise in order to be transformed into money-makers. They also require the graceful presence of Lady Luck, who, we might add, is not exactly known for her reliability and fidelity. But if you have the expertise and you can risk the money, there might be something here for you.

CONDO OR CO-OP CONVERSIONS

Once a sponsor or developer gets his conversion plan approved by the state, he is responsible both for selling the units and for carrying the maintenance share for all unsold units. If condo or co-op units do not sell fast enough, the sponsor can find himself in trouble. The building in a co-op and all the unsold units in a condominium community can revert to the mortgagee (the lending institution) when the sponsor is in default. And some did. Some of these in turn are now in the hands of the RTC.

Even if you have the cash in hand to buy an incompletely sold conversion, think twice, or three times, before you do it. There are problems aplenty, not the least of which are the people living in the building. The owners have complaints, the tenants have complaints, and neither group particularly likes the other. Or that's the way it often goes. The owners get together and form a Unit Owners Association, the tenants form a Tenants Association, and then it may feel like you're dealing with the Teamsters Union.

If that's not challenging enough for you, there are the outside people to add interest to your life. Housing inspectors, health inspectors, fire inspectors, rent control boards, eviction procedures, housing courts . . . Should we go on?

So why would anyone want to do this? Because there really is big money in conversion. When the building or complex, or what portion of it remains unsold, can be bought for a low enough price, the sale of the units can bring in huge profits, even if those units are sold at prices that are discounted enough to induce prospective buyers to line up at the door at 6 A.M. The problems don't always end with the sale, however, since you may be required to move out the renters, or at least to stick around long enough to get the Unit Owners Association operational. This sometimes means a significant contribution to the Condominium's Contingency Fund or a generous go-round of repairs and refurbishing.

If the condo conversion you take over is a time-share, there is still another added expense: sales. Time-share developers spend a huge portion of their development budget on sales. And until all the units are sold, you will still have to bear some responsibility in the maintenance and management of the resort.

INCOMPLETE CONSTRUCTION

Like the guest who eats and runs, some developers are inconsiderate enough to declare bankruptcy right in the middle of construction. When the mortgage lender takes over the property, everything stops because lending institutions are not builders. So every person who made a deposit on one of those incomplete units or houses begins screaming for someone to get the building going again or for their money back, neither of which will happen unless someone buys the incomplete construction.

Lending institutions are usually very anxious to get rid of incomplete construction because it is a source of annoyance and because it's expensive. These properties can often be bought for a fraction of their worth, but with the purchase you buy the headaches.

There are invariably workman's and materialman's liens on the property. You should negotiate with the lender until you are assured that all of these liens are to be paid off before you take title. If they aren't, you will not get clear title and your money may be tied up in a stalemate.

Then there are all those people with unfinished living quarters. Part of your negotiations with the lender will be a definition of the terms under which you take over those contracts. And if you negotiate cash and terms to your satisfaction and then go on to make all the homeowners-to-be happy, your public relations problems still won't be over. Besides the construction-contract owners, you must also convince the general public that you are a reputable builder, one who will finish the work promised by the guy who just vanished. The report of a bankruptcy sale often destroys the bankrupt builder and injures the credibility of everyone else involved.

If you take on someone else's construction project, you may also have to take over responsibility for agreements made with the local municipality for roads, sewers, curbing, and sidewalks. Agreements with public utilities for electrical supply, water, and gas will also survive the change of ownership.

Construction bankruptcies, even at a dirt-cheap price, are risky ventures. Expenditures for unforeseen problems and legal entanglements can wipe out a potential profit almost in the blink of an eye. On the other hand, we both know some very wealthy people in construction.

FARMS

Sad to say, there are some foreclosed farms among the bailout properties and there probably will be more. Some of these are going to be offered at prices far, far below market value for a comparable working farm in the area. Should you snatch them up? Not so fast.

Farms are usually a bargain only to the farmer next door or to the nearby wealthy farmer trying to get his new son-in-law established in a situation that will allow the wealthy farmer's daughter to live in the manner to which she became accustomed in his house. Farms only rarely appeal to the prospecting investor.

But what if you *want* a farm? If you are a farmer from another state or another area and you find an attractive farm listed in the bailout inventory, you had better find out why that farm was foreclosed before you buy it. The former owner's problem might be your problem too!

Then again, if you can buy the farm cheap, cheaply enough so that your mortgage is relatively small, and you really do know something about farming . . . Well, maybe you can get some of the equipment thrown in with the purchase. And maybe the bailout will turn out to be your bonanza.

If you're thinking about "stealing" a farm in the bailout and then turning it into suburban homesteads, think again. If the farmland were close enough to the spreading suburbs to be of value for housing development, don't you think the farmer would have tried to sell it to land developers rather than letting the bank foreclose? If he were so naive in the world of real estate that he did overlook the possibility of a sale, don't you think that the professional developers will be in there bidding against you? And if they aren't, what's wrong?

Usually, farmland is just too far from suburban sprawl to attract developers. But yes, if you want to invest in a farm now as you propose a toast to your newborn baby in the hopes that the sale of the farm will pay that child's college tuition, you may be all right. If you pay cash, that is, and if you can afford the annual taxes, although some farmland can be rented to cover expenses.

GAS STATIONS, MARINAS, AND OTHER SERVICE FACILITIES

A small airport anyone? How about a restaurant in an old sidewheel paddleboat? Well, maybe the RTC doesn't exactly have those . . . yet. But they have some lovely gas stations, marinas, convenience stores, and other businesses.

At the right price, these can be good investments if you know the business that was established in the place. If you know little or nothing about the business, however, you are very likely to make some fatal errors. That doesn't deter you from the bargain? Okay, then pay as little as possible and get as much professional advice as you can possibly afford.

Some successful start-up business people buy into a franchise and thus get the guidance, training, and buying power they need. Or you might consider converting a bargain property to a business that you are familiar with. In either case, find out why the previous owner failed before you buy. If you are planning to change the nature of the business, do a community study to see if the community can support the business you want and if there is enough parking and access.

WHITE ELEPHANTS

Deserted churches, abandoned barns, nonconforming city lots sandwiched between skyscrapers, houses illegally converted to four units in a one-family residential zone, closed school buildings, dead restaurants . . . What else can you think of? We're talking about properties that are for sale cheap because they are no longer being used for what they were built to be.

These are risky ventures because they require both creativity and lots of luck to become money-makers. Some of them do, however. *If* you can come up with a grand idea (like a defunct restaurant reborn as a day-care center), *if* you can sell your idea to the town fathers, *if* you can get the necessary approvals, and *if* you have the money to do the work, you might make some profit. *If* you can find a buyer for your finished project (ideally you should have one lined up before you do the conversion). If you plan to run the converted facility yourself, this bailout white elephant might just become your life's work.

THE CHANGING INVENTORY

Only two things can be said with absolute certainty about the bailout: (1) the inventory of properties to be sold is immense, and (2) that inventory will keep changing for several years to come, probably many years.

It's very possible then that you could be a participant in the bailout bonanza many times, choosing several different kinds of investment vehicles along your way and experimenting, learning, and growing in marketplace savvy all the while. The key to this success scenario is to make your first purchases very profitable. This means choosing investments that fit your pocketbook and your time demands, getting them at bargain prices, financing for your best interests, and selling for a profit. If you do all this, you'll be able to go back to the bailout bonanza again and again.

CHAPTER 3

WHAT ARE YOU LOOKING FOR?

If Macy's or Neiman Marcus were going out of business and had slashed the prices on everything in their stores nationwide, you'd have to compete with hordes of bargain hunters to snatch up the best merchandise. Such a sales event would not be a good time to wander about the stores "shopping" for something that might catch your fancy. At any big inventory-liquidation sale, the customers most likely to come away with the best bargains are those who go in knowing exactly what they want to buy and what competitive market value is for those items.

To buy bailout properties profitably, you should take a lesson from the smart going-out-of-business shopper. The United States Government is running the sale of the century and you can't possibly browse all the departments. So before you go shopping, decide what it is that you're shopping for. What do you want? Take a good look first at your goals and then at yourself. Why do you want to buy real estate anyway? What do you want to own? What do you expect to get out of that ownership? How much do you have to spend?

Keep in mind whenever you enter the real estate marketplace that a "good deal" is only a good deal if it's right for *you*. The golden goose that your neighbor or your spouse's cousin brags about could be a honking annoyance in *your* backyard.

WHY BUY?

Why invest in real estate? If you need an answer to that question, you probably shouldn't be reading this book. But then again, you won't be the first person to stumble into something and then go back five steps to find out why it's so good. If you really want an extensive, theoretical answer to the *why real estate?* question, you might stop by at your local library and read in either of our two previous investment books: *Sonny Bloch's 171 Ways to Make Money in Real Estate* or Carolyn Janik's *Money-Making Real Estate*.

For the purposes of this book, let's transpose *why buy?* into *what do you want to get out of buying a bailout property?* There are three common answers: quick profit, good income, and a roof over your head.

QUICK PROFIT

Buy low, sell high. And do it as soon as possible. Isn't that everyone's idea of a bargain in the real estate marketplace? If rapid turnover for profit is your motivation, be sure that you do some serious investigating before you sign anything. When a property has been on the market long enough for several price reductions and you think that you can negotiate the purchase price even lower, you should always make an effort to define for yourself exactly what is impeding the sale. Bluntly, ask yourself, "What's wrong with it?" Then find out if the situation can be remedied and how much the fix-up will cost before you make any kind of an offer. Purchase price, the estimated cost of refurbishing or improvement, and resale potential are the key factors in evaluating quick-profit real estate. We'll tell you how to use them in the next chapter.

GOOD INCOME

One of the more pleasurable experiences in life is getting up from the hammock, going out to the mailbox, and picking up a handful of checks for $600 or $700 each. Just think, all that money coming in while you're listening to the grass grow. Well, it's never quite that easy, but checks-in-the-mailbox is a very good reason for investing in real estate. If that's your motivator, you'll need to be particularly aware of cost-to-income ratios, cash flow, maintenance and carrying costs, time commitments demanded by ownership, and probable future appreciation or depreciation. Income property ownership is not a money-making opportunity that is without risk, work, or responsibility. Before jumping in, ask yourself if you have what it takes to be a landlord.

A ROOF OVER YOUR HEAD

If you're just starting out in the real estate marketplace and you want a place to live as well as a means of increasing your net worth, you should ask yourself one question in addition to investigating all the standard criteria for judging a good deal: *Do I love it?*

When buying investment real estate, emotions and personal taste should not enter into purchase decisions, but if you're going to put yourself and your family as well as your money into a property, you'd better love it, at least a little. If no stretch of your imagination will allow you to see HOME SWEET HOME above a doorway in the prospective building, you may be buying emotional stress that will affect both your life at that address and the property's future resale potential. Unloved, owner-occupied properties are often maintained less carefully and sold sooner (usually without optimum appreciation) than those in which the owner feels comfortable.

WHAT TO BUY?

Once you know why you're buying, you must decide what you want to buy. This is not always as easy as it may sound because many different kinds of property can be a means to accomplishing the goals we just mentioned. You've got to decide what among the types available will be best for you. Even the most careful evaluation of the numbers in a deal, however, won't guarantee you a right decision. You must also look at yourself as you relate to your investment. Consider the following five factors.

TIME

Most of us are not full-time real estate investors and even those who are don't want to spend eighteen hours a day at it. Before you dive into a real estate purchase, consider how much time it will demand and how much you have to give. For example, if you plan to refurbish a run-down single-family house, doing most of the fix-up work yourself, and then resell it, you'd better have a lot of time and a few friends you can count on. Every day between the day you buy and the day you sell costs you money! On the other hand, managing a small apartment building is usually regarded as a time-consuming investment, but if your cash flow is positive enough to allow you to hire an excellent super, you'll probably have minimal time demands from the investment.

When evaluating property purchases in terms of their impact upon your life-style, be sure to differentiate between customary and usual time demands for a particular type of property and the demands of any special plans you may have for it. Land, for example, is usually considered an undemanding investment. All you have to do is wait for it to go up in value, right? Right. Unless you should want to speed that appreciation up by getting subdivision approval or a zoning change. Then you'll have to spend many hours at planning board meetings, not to mention a good many dollars on engineering and legal costs. Likewise, managing an apartment building with a good super may not take much of your time, but think again about time commitments if you are considering a condominium conversion.

KNOWLEDGE

The adage goes: *It's not what you know, it's who you know.* In the real estate marketplace, however, what you know can pay off just as well as who you know. For example, to make what you know powerful insider information when making purchase decisions, just property-hunt in those places where you don't need a street map to get around. And for even more market advantage, hunt where you recognize particular buildings or where you know the names of property owners. In the real estate investment game, it's almost always best to buy property in places that are familiar to you because your intuition grows out of your knowledge of the area. That knowledge also guides you in getting crucial facts, quickly and accurately.

When hunting for that investment vehicle with an inside track on the road to riches, consider first those properties that are close to your current home. Then consider areas where you once lived and areas that you visit frequently. Only if everything comes up zeros should you consider the hot turnaround area three hundred miles away that the guy in the next cubicle at work has been bragging about. And then only very cautiously.

Before you choose a property, give some thought also to the value of knowledge you have accumulated through your past experience. Have you owned this kind of property before? Is this a common investment vehicle in your family? Are you employed in a field that requires some dealing with people who own this type of property?

Familiarity with the problems and procedures inherent in a type of investment vehicle can increase your odds of making profitable decisions about that kind of property. It can also expedite the completion of any work that has to be done in the process of buying, selling, or maintaining the property. If you are purchasing with partners, tap the knowledge of all the members of the team—their relatives too.

SKILLS

When you saw the word *skills*, you probably thought: carpentry, plumbing, electrical work, roofing, painting, wallpapering, tile installation, and so on. And yes, those are all skills that help in certain kinds of real estate purchases. But also consider negotiating skill, organizational ability, tact, patience, perseverance, and persuasive powers, to name but a few special talents. Ask yourself if the talents and personality traits that you bring to an investment will help to achieve its maximum potential profitability. Usually, it's best to choose those investment vehicles where your particular skills will make a difference.

MONEY

What you can buy will be affected by how much money you have to invest. But don't slam the book closed saying, "That does it! I'm broke!

I'll never get in on this bonanza!" There are creative ways to get purchase money and we'll tell you about them. At this time, however, you should be concerned with evaluating the ongoing money demands of an investment vehicle. Generally, it's a bad move to invest in any kind of property that will put undue financial stress on your day-to-day life-style. The question to evaluate in terms of money therefore is not how much can you buy, but how much will this investment cost per month until you sell it?

INTEREST

No, we don't mean the interest rate you'll be paying on your mortgage. We're referring here to interest in owning the kind of property under consideration. Does the idea of refurbishing a house or turning around a floundering apartment complex light up your eyes? Do you want to talk about it to anyone who'll listen? Would you rather sit at the kitchen table planning the addition of a backyard deck or some tasteful landscaping than watch a prime-time movie on television? Do you talk about real estate deals at cocktail parties?

Despite the opportunity to choose among an incredible variety of real estate investment vehicles, there are some people who simply are not interested in the real estate marketplace. There are also many who would do well in some investment vehicles but be impatient, anxious, or uncomfortable in others.

If you really are not interested in investing in real estate but are going into a project because someone told you that this is the hot spot of the 1990s, think through the risk/opportunity ratio before you put down your investment dollars. Remember that land and buildings are relatively non-liquid investment vehicles. Weigh the money-making potential of the real estate purchase you are considering against other opportunities such as coins, oriental rugs, or even the stock market.

If you *are* interested in real estate but you aren't sure about your skills or preferences, spend some extra time thinking about various kinds of property ownership from a conceptual perspective. What does each demand of its owner? Examine your attitudes toward devoting your free time to a money-making endeavor that may seem like all work and no play.

But then perhaps *Monopoly* was your favorite board game as a child and your attitude is that dealing in the real estate marketplace *is* play. You just want to learn to do it better (and for real money). Keep reading!

This book will give you a lot of information and advice, but *you* must decide why you're in the marketplace and what you want, and there are no right or wrong answers. Except one. *Don't invest in real estate or in a particular kind of real estate just because someone tells you it's a quick way to get rich.* It may be, but be warned that you won't get rich without some risks, work, time demands, setbacks, and disappointments. If you're interested in what you're doing, the obstacles become challenges. If you're doing what someone tells you to do just because that someone told you that this was the road to riches, the obstacles can become colossal headaches.

Investing your money and then dedicating a good deal of your time to doing something that you find genuinely distasteful can make you sick, literally. So spend a little extra time and find something you'll enjoy doing. There are probably more varied choices in the real estate marketplace than in any other investment field. If you choose your vehicle wisely and to your liking, your investment career will probably be longer and more profitable for it.

HOW MUCH?

As we've said, there are many ways to finance and buy real estate. The Resolution Trust Corporation can attest to that and to the fact that some of the available methods don't always turn out as expected. That's why we got to write this book, and why you have a chance to profit from the bailout. The question is: how much risk are you and your lender willing to take?

The first consideration in good financing is always an evaluation of the economic trends of the day. Let's look at the 1970s as an example of how the national economic mood can influence real estate investment. Throughout most of that decade, prices were spiraling and financing was available at relatively low interest rates. *No money down* (or as little as possible) was considered the best real estate investment strategy. Nationally recognized gurus proclaimed that maximum leveraging was the secret to creating wealth. And very often, it worked!

In today's marketplace, we have slower appreciation and higher interest rates. This requires a change of investment strategy in order to keep real estate up there among the world's best opportunities for becoming a millionaire.

A major part of that change is in arranging appropriate financing. Today, minimal down payments can mean *negative* leveraging. In this situation, the annual cost of carrying the property is greater than its annual appreciation, which means you lose money each year! In the 1990s, positive cash flow is usually much more important than minimal down payment.

Part of your job as an investor will always be to keep abreast of what's going on in the economy. In learning how to deal with the S&L bailout, you'll also be learning how to judge the factors that will affect your future deals in the marketplace.

Balanced with economic awareness in the financing aspect of real estate investment is an evaluation of your personal abilities and capabilities. So don't buy on impulse. Before you even walk into the marketplace to look around, think about how much money you have, how much money you owe, and how much money you'd like to have. Then think about how much or how little anguish, anxiety, and just plain discomfort you're willing to go through to get what you want. Think about how stressful money questions in general are to you and your family. The goal here is to arrive at an estimate of your own tolerance factor before you learn exactly what that factor is by having to live through the intolerable.

Some people can borrow from Peter to pay Paul for years on end, always juggling their checks, often seeming to stay afloat by lucky break after lucky break, yet they seem not to be bothered by it all. Some people can buy property with absolutely no idea how they're going to pay for it, and still sleep at night. Some people can eat spaghetti and beans and hover around the television as their only entertainment for years on end without complaint because they sincerely hope and believe that "when it's all over" they'll be able to name the streets in *their* development after family members and eat Beluga caviar for breakfast whenever they want.

Other people are into sugar binges, alcohol, and nail biting if a bad month forces them to be ten days late with a mortgage payment. Some landlords will start putting the word out that they might just have an apartment to let if a tenant is nine days late with the rent. Some investors wake in the middle of the night trying to remember if the last check they wrote was really covered by their bank balance. These people are not necessarily less likely to make money in real estate. (Actually, they're probably less likely to *lose* money than the investors who can't be bothered to worry.) They simply need to structure their deals in ways that put less stress on their budgets . . . and their psyches.

You probably fit in somewhere between those two examples, but only you can evaluate where. That evaluation is essential to good investing. Recognize that dealing in the real estate marketplace means dealing with money, often large sums of money. Then judge your position and your attitudes toward that special commodity. If you have much more than you need and you don't ever need to worry about how you're going to pay the bills, then you can buy pretty much whatever strikes your fancy as a good deal and arrange the financing in any way that's convenient. If you're like the rest of us, however, if your supply is somewhat limited and if handling money matters sometimes makes you nervous, factor financing arrangements and cash flow demands into your decision on what to

DETERMINING YOUR INVESTMENT COMFORT ZONE

Check the boxes that indicate your investment goals:

- ☐ Personal shelter (you plan to live in the investment property)
- ☐ Quick and profitable resale possibility
- ☐ Probable future appreciation
    - ☐ Profit goal reached in three years
    - ☐ Profit goal reached in five years
    - ☐ Profit goal reached in ten years
- ☐ Positive cash flow
- ☐ Hands-on personal involvement
    - ☐ In planning
    - ☐ In management
    - ☐ In rehabilitation
- ☐ Interpersonal contact
    - ☐ As a landlord
    - ☐ As a developer
    - ☐ Minimal time demands
- ☐ Tax advantages

buy. Think about how the money aspect of your prospective purchase will affect your life and then decide if the potential profit is worth the risk and its associated stresses. Sometimes it definitely is and sometimes it isn't. It's your call.

FROM DELIBERATION
TO DECISION

This introspective evaluation should bring you to some decisions on what kind or kinds of property you want to buy, how much time you are willing to put into your investment venture, how much profit you hope to achieve from the venture and how soon, and how much of your money you're willing to put at risk. But all these decisions are just warm-ups to the big decision: actually buying something. To do that successfully, you've got to have the second attribute of the successful going-out-of-business-sale shopper that we mentioned at the outset of this chapter. You've got to know the competitive market value of whatever you're shopping for.

Since you're shopping in the bailout marketplace, you've got to know the value of similar pieces of real estate in the local area. Until you develop this market savvy, you cannot be certain that you're getting a good deal.

"Why not?" you ask. "This isn't a jungle. A person can get professional evaluations. Or you can get advice from friends or relatives."

Yes, you can. But the person who is likely to look after your money better than anyone else is *you*. In the real estate investment marketplace, you must learn to rely first upon your own judgment. Think about that. Everyone knows you can't rely on the government's appraisal figures. Those properties are being repriced every four months or so. You certainly don't want to take a broker's word for value. That's taking someone else's assurance that your money will make more money for you in the future while your purchase is making money for that person in the present. And goodness knows Uncle Archie doesn't always have the right answers. Sometimes, just sometimes, his evaluations are colored by feelings more than facts.

So it all comes back to you. To put the matter in its simplest terms:

before you decide to buy, you've got to know what makes a good deal good and you've got to be able to find the good deals. Turn the page, and we'll help you learn how.

CHAPTER 4

HOW TO SPOT A GOOD DEAL

Everyone knows there's no such thing as a real estate marketplace. After all, a real estate buying ground isn't exactly a flea market where you can wander from display table to booth to tailgate, rummaging for good deals. The real estate marketplace is everywhere and nowhere and forever moving, it exists wherever a piece of property is for sale, wherever a deal is being made.

But if there were *real* real estate marketplaces across the nation, places where you could pass through a gate and wander among prospective properties, then we'd have a sign to hang over every one of those gates. It's the translation of a French saying that dates back to the middle of the ninteenth century: *Plus ça change, plus ç'est la même chose.* Those words may be over a hundred years old but they speak loud and clear to end-of-the-millennium Americans. Our sign would read: THE MORE THINGS CHANGE, THE MORE THEY STAY THE SAME.

Talk about change! We have the nation's banking industry trying desperately to keep its nose above water, and not certain of succeeding. We have the United States Government selling everything from tract houses to hotels. We have auctions advertised weekly in the Sunday papers and foreclosures and tax sales becoming an everyday happening.

For a little spice, we have the exciting, the puzzling, and the paradoxical: little things like drug-related property seizures and sales, overbuilding and housing shortages in the same area and at the same time, condominium failures, and deserted co-op conversions. If you stand back to review the past two decades, you'll also see falling home prices and escalating home prices moving across the nation like huge tidal waves. To help blend all this together, the lending industry seems to have created some new variation on home mortgaging practically every month.

Does all that make you nervous? Maybe you're beginning to think "This is no place for me! Or my money!" But don't make that judgment so quickly. Behind virtually every headline announcing the latest development in this national real estate circus is a story that demonstrates anew the timeless and universal principles of real estate investment. The U.S. real estate market still offers a great majority of the most accessible and potentially profitable investment vehicles available to the American public.

But to succeed in this changing industry, you must understand and work by its tried, tested, and enduring principles. Just about all of those principles revolve around two words: *market value.*

In the real estate marketplace, most appraisers, mortgage lenders, and salespeople will tell you that market value is the highest price a ready, willing, and able buyer will pay and the lowest price a ready, willing, and able seller will accept. But market value for the success-oriented investor must be more than an industry-accepted term designating the amount of money that changed hands at the closing table. Market value must mean price as a factor related to supply and demand, location, condition, and cash flow. As such, an evaluation of a property's market value will include its potential for profit.

If you want to learn how to make money in real estate, you must study in two areas, both concerned with market value and both essential and inseparable in the making of every deal. (1) You must learn how to recognize a good investment property. (2) You must learn how to make it yours at the least possible cost, with the best possible terms, and with clear title. The mastery of these two must-learns will be an ongoing experience throughout your days as an investor. You can't possibly learn everything about real estate by reading one book, even this one. We can, however, give you a damn good basic course, with special skills in bailout properties.

The recognizing-a-good-investment-property part of a Ph.D. in real estate dealing is the same no matter who or what the seller happens to be (including the federal government). In this chapter, we'll provide you with property evaluation information that will enable you to spot a good deal when you see one. It'll take us the rest of the book, however, to complete the basic course in how property can be bought effectively, efficiently, and safely under current distress-sale conditions.

Is that a contradiction? you may wonder. We said that nothing changes, that it's all timeless and universal, but added that it will take us the better part of this book to explain how to "beat" the new system!

Actually, it's not a contradiction at all. Most of the negotiating techniques, self-protecting legal procedures, and financing options involved in buying real estate *are* timeless and universal—and they're as appropriate to prime ocean-side estates as they are to distressed property. Even in an era when real estate is making front-page headlines, the same rules still apply to practically every deal. It's just that these tried-and-tested principles have been embellished with some intricate scrollwork for purposes of the S&L bailout.

These rules and procedures, these bits of specialized information, are essential to success in this specialized market. But you can learn to use the system—and how to keep current with its changes. Knowing what to do and what's happening or about to happen can make the difference between augmenting your workaday salary with a few property investments and quitting your job to sail the Caribbean in your own yacht.

But before you can begin setting speed records for getting through the bailout's maze, you've got to know how to recognize a good deal when you see one. Let's begin with that.

CRYSTAL BALLS

If you could look into a crystal ball that accurately reveals the future, you'd be rich. So goes the old folk tale anyway. And isn't it true? After all, we already told you in the previous chapter that the key to success in land investment is knowing where the demand will be before it gets there. So if a little future knowledge is good in land investment, it's probably good in any booth at the real estate fairgrounds. Right?

Yes, but with qualifications. Real estate, like most industries, is driven by the oldest sales principle of all: supply and demand. So knowing *where* the demand will be has got to be helpful. But there's another factor. You also have to know *what* will be in demand. Land transcends the *what* question because, under favorable zoning regulations, it is available for whatever it is that is needed. When buying buildings, however, you buy into a function. If no one wants what you have, you can be sitting in the middle of the highest demand area in the nation and still not have a successful investment property.

Try to sell a New England connected farm (house, barn, chicken coop, and other outbuildings contiguous and stretching out into something that looks vaguely like the letter Z) in San Diego. San Diego is a healthy market, with lots of growth and good demand for real estate, but how much interest do you think you'd get in your farm?

"Not much," you answer. "But this is a ridiculous example. You're not going to *find* a New England connected farm in San Diego. Unless you built it—and who in their right mind would do that!"

Exactly! The structure must meet demand. But let's take a less imaginative example. In the late 1970s/early 1980s, a highly recommended investment plan involved buying yet-to-be-built condominiums at preconstruction prices. The idea was to choose a unit scheduled for completion near the end of construction time (usually scheduled about eighteen months to two years away), sign a contract, put down a deposit, and wait.

Let's say you put down $10,000 earnest money at the signing of the contract to buy. In many parts of the country, by the time the builder finished building enough of the condo community to get to your unit and ask you to close and take possession, prices had gone up as much as $6,000 to $10,000 or more on that size unit. Some investors assigned their contracts for a cash fee of $5,000 plus the $10,000 escrow money. (A cash return of 50 percent in perhaps eighteen months!) Other investors closed on the deal and flipped the property, selling for maybe $9,000 more than they bought it, and pocketing approximately $7,000. And some investors decided to rent the condo unit for a while, anticipating even greater returns in another year or two when all the landscaping and the tennis courts were in.

It worked then, but it wouldn't work now. Condos are so overbuilt in most areas of the nation that prices are stagnant or falling. There is less demand than supply and many of the people who *are* buying condos are doing so because they can't afford anything else. Surveys show that what most first-time homebuyers really want is a moderately priced house on a little patch of grass. Now that was the rage in the late 1940s! But it's here again.

Using good old real estate horse sense including the supply/demand instinct, a smart investor observing the condomania of the 1980s could have anticipated the state of today's market without the help of a crystal ball. He or she could have bought run-down Cape Cods built in the late 1940s and early 1950s, done some minor fix-up, rented the properties for enough to cover carrying costs, and then, in the early 1990s, put in a new bathroom or two and some cosmetic updates. Assuming the neighborhood was attractive, that investor would now own properties in greater demand than their competition (the overbuilt condo units). Properties in demand always bring better prices.

"Okay, we get the idea," you say. "But how do we know what will be in demand? How do we know what will be overbuilt? A crystal ball would help."

True. But since good ones are hard to find, let's look at some supply/demand facts.

DEMAND

The demand for various types of real estate is directly related to population growth and character. Anticipating future demand requires watching current happenings, which is just one of the many reasons we recommend that you invest locally. The majority of the happenings that affect real estate values are local happenings! The following are five things to watch for.

1. *Demographic changes.* Is the population in the area increasing or decreasing? Is the median age of the population going up or down? Is the median income going up or down? Are more people commuting to work outside the area? You can get most of these answers from

the local Chamber of Commerce. If they can't help you, material is available from the Census Bureau in Washington. For statistics call (301) 763-4040.

2. *Transportation.* You probably learned in grade school that transportation is very important to a society. Now that you're grown-up, you can just transpose that lesson into "Transportation is *very* important to real estate values, both residential and commercial." As an indicator of future growth and real estate demand, watch for new highways, especially proposed interchanges which have a positive effect on nearby commercial property. Check out airports in the state. New airports or increased activity at already functioning airports is usually another indicator of growth. Then check out rail lines. If yours is an area where commuting to work is common, proximity to a rail line usually improves resale value.

3. *Desirability.* You might say that some communities "come into fashion." The catalyst that stimulates people to rank Pleasant Village above its neighboring communities might be publication of a study ranking the schools among the ten best in the state, or growing recognition of special recreational facilities, or low taxes for extensive municipal services, or improved commuter connections, or beautiful upscale housing being built at several different sites within the town. Whatever it is, however, it's valuable to the real estate investor. Be aware of the talk in your community. Get into what's going to be hot while it's just warming up.

4. *A Draw.* If someone were to write a best-seller titled *The History of Disney World,* it would be the prototype tale for how one enterprise can affect an entire area. But the factor that draws people and businesses to your area doesn't have to be of Disneyesque proportions. It might be the designation of a stretch of river as a national recreational area. It might be the building of a convention center or new sports complex. Or maybe the ghost of Elvis Presley has begun to appear regularly in your local library. (You never know.) Be sure that the draw you identify is real and likely to be long lasting. From there, it's a matter of choosing your investments well, because whenever people are attracted to an area, property values go up.

5. *Corporate Development.* When a major corporation locates office facilities or a production plant in an area, the demand for housing and services is going to go up. Be aware, however, that the reverse is also true. Corporate pullout equals sliding real estate values.

SUPPLY

Once you've determined that demand for real estate is likely to increase, you must do some careful research on supply. Ask yourself: *What's in short supply now? What will be in short supply here two, three, or five years from now?*

Part of the answer to these questions goes back to demographics. You want to find out about the people in the area and about the people likely to come to the area. What will they want? Luxury houses? Low-maintenance houses? Recreation facilities? Day-care facilities? Shopping?

To determine what will be in short supply in the near future, do some detective work. Find out what is being built in the area now. You can do this by attending meetings of the planning board, reading local newspapers, and talking with real estate agents. Be aware that what's most popular right now, whatever is being built most frantically, is not likely to be a good investment in two to five years. Why? Overbuilding *means* oversupply. Too much of anything means lower prices.

The northeast corridor in the late 1980s is a good example. Luxury houses were in! Huge bathrooms with whirlpool tubs, skylights, European kitchens. Price tags were consistently over half-a-million dollars. The problem is that there are only so many people in the world who can afford half-a-million-dollar houses.

If you build more houses than there are people who can afford them, they stand empty. And then? You guessed it! Prices come down.

At the very same time that the northeast was being peppered with mini-estates, there was nowhere near enough rental housing being built in this same area. Now if there are not enough apartments for people who want to rent, guess what goes up. Right, the rents. So what would be the better investment, an old apartment building that needed some remodeling but was located in a desirable area near public transportation or an unfinished luxury home development in foreclosure?

You probably think that we expect you to say, "The apartment building, of course!" But don't jump to an answer so quickly. The investment quality quotient still depends on the price. It should be obvious, however, that supply and demand must be factored into the decision.

Having said all this about the importance of supply and demand, we'd like you to suspend it in a particular *what if* situation. What if you can buy something so cheaply that if you were to resell it immediately at 15 percent below the current going rate for that kind of property, you would still have made a handsome profit? In that case it doesn't matter much if your type of investment property is overbuilt or if the market for real estate is sluggish with little or no growth. Remember, almost all real estate investments are liquid assets *at a price*. There will be a buyer for a genuine bargain. You, as an investor, just have to be sure that you can buy the property so cheaply that you can offer it for resale well within the bargain category. This is a real possibility in the bailout but it does require careful attention to facts and numbers.

WHAT'S A BARGAIN?

Methods of determining value in real estate vary according to the kind of real estate you're buying. What we can give you here are guidelines that have stood the test of time and trial. In the end, you are the one who must determine whether a piece of property is a bargain in its unique circumstances.

SINGLE-FAMILY RESIDENTIAL PROPERTIES

If you can buy bailout single-family houses, condo apartments, or co-op apartments at 15 percent below the current going rate for similar real estate, that's usually a bargain. If the property is in run-down condition, requiring considerable expenditure of time and/or money to be made salable, however, you should estimate the costs of the repairs and then calculate your bargain so that your top-dollar purchase price plus your estimated cost of repairs is still 25 percent below the going rate for similar real estate.

"Why so much lower?" you ask.

Because repairs to a fixer-upper virtually always take longer and cost more than you estimate. Fixing up run-down houses is not a hobby! You want to make money at this and you want your purchase price to give you some assurance that making money is pretty certain.

Here's how it works. Two houses, both three bedrooms, one and a half baths, and each with a one-car garage, located next door to each other. One, in move-in condition, sold last month for $200,000. The other, the one being sold by the RTC, has water in the basement, needs a new roof, and has an interior painful to the eyes of the vast majority of conventional buyers. Besides paint inside and out and floor covering everywhere, it also needs cosmetic surgery on its shrubs and lawn.

You estimate $22,000 for fix-up costs, doing a good deal of the work yourself. Using our guideline, you'll want the purchase price plus fix-up to be 25 percent less than market value. Since virtually the same house in good condition sold next door recently, let's take that figure as probable market value. With that guideline, 25 percent less than market value is $150,000. Subtract your $22,000 from the $150,000, and make your offer. (Your initial offer should not be $128,000, however. That's the top dollar you want to pay for this gem.)

But what if there is no house or condo next door that recently sold? If determining a bargain in single-family residential real estate is predicated upon market value, how do you determine market value?

Comparables are the key. Professional appraisers go through the motions of using several other determinants like replacement cost and tax assessments, but most of them will admit freely that it's comparables that determine their appraisal figure. So what are comparables? And how do you get them?

In a real estate office, the term *comparables* refers both to the listing sheets describing properties that have been recently sold and to the properties themselves. A real estate agent might say to you, "There's a house around the corner that is a comparable." Or she might say, "I have a comparable right here," as she pulls out a sheet of paper from her briefcase.

The printed comparables sheets contain all the pertinent information about the property that has recently been sold: a property description, usually including room dimensions and extras included in the sale, the original asking price, all the price reductions, and the actual selling price. They also contain information as to length of time on the market and the date of the actual closing.

Comparables are kept on file in virtually every real estate office in the nation. If you have a working relationship with a real estate agent, simply ask to see them. That agent should help you to choose those properties that are most like the one you are interested in and will therefore be most helpful in determining market value for the property you are considering.

If you have not yet established a working relationship with a single real estate professional, now is a good time to start. Most RTC properties are listed with local brokers and most brokers are Realtors, sharing their listing information through a Realtor Board. Working with an agent of your choice therefore will give you access to comparables for the entire local area.

Many novice real estate investors see real estate agents as "the enemy." Don't. Real estate professionals can be immensely helpful in your investing career. Make friends with them, use their knowledge and skills, and then be guided by your own decision-making capabilities.

For investors planning to hold single-family residence property longer than the time it takes to do a remodeling job, another factor, probable appreciation, is just as important as the initial purchase price. Now any economist will tell you that there's no certain way to predict what the economy will do, and likewise there's no certain way to predict property appreciation. But the past is often a clue to the future. Working with your favorite real estate professional or with the local Chamber of Commerce, get figures on home appreciation in the area for the past two to three years. The Chamber will probably give you median figures for the area. Your Realtor will be able to help you calculate the appreciation in the exact neighborhood where your prospective property is located.

And finally there's the question of cash flow. With today's tax laws, you should look for bargains that will allow you to structure your purchase so that the income from renting the property covers its expenses, including mortgage and tax payments. If you think a particular single-family house is an especially good investment that will appreciate rapidly in the next two years, you can sometimes take a little additional risk and carry a slight negative cash flow. But be sure the drain on your checkbook won't be too painful or anxiety-provoking.

MULTI-FAMILY RESIDENTIAL PROPERTIES

Comparables are a good source of market value information in the multi-family market as well, but here there is yet another important factor to consider: income. The income-to-cost ratio is always a factor in estimating the value of a rent-producing property. A three-family building that brings in $700 per unit is obviously a better buy than one bringing in $650 per unit if both can be purchased at the same price and both are in relatively good condition and in comparably good locations.

Use the same bargain-defining guidelines for helping to choose a multi-family house as in choosing single-family housing but factor in the rents. If you plan to occupy one of the units, the rental income from the space that you do not occupy should cover or almost cover mortgage principal, interest, and taxes.

APARTMENT BUILDINGS

Theoretically, comparables should work also with apartment buildings, but they don't because there aren't usually enough, if any, apartment buildings just like yours sold within the past year. Estimating market value for apartment buildings therefore relies more heavily on numbers. What is the income? What is the debt service? What are the taxes? What are the management and maintenance costs? When you answer these questions, you should have a positive number that is your cash flow. The market value of an apartment building is often determined, at least in part, by the amount of positive cash flow it generates each year.

Even before working out cash flow, however, some investors use a rule-of-thumb guideline of an eight to one cost-to-income ratio before they will even consider other factors in an apartment building investment decision. This means that if a building has a price tag of $800,000 it must show gross rent receipts of $100,000 per year before it is even considered.

The worksheets on pages 62–64 will help you to evaluate your prob-

WORKSHEET FOR EQUITY POSITION—APARTMENT BUILDINGS

1. Purchase price of building .... $_____

   ADDRESS _____

2. Total cash investment .... $_____

   a. down payment .... $_____

   b. estimated fix-up costs .... $_____

   c. legal fees .... $_____

   d. title insurance .... $_____

   e. points paid for mortgage .... $_____

   f. other mortgage costs .... $_____

   g. inspection fees .... $_____

   Enter total on line 2 .... $_____

3. Estimated market value with fix-up .... $_____

4. New mortgages needed for purchase .... $_____

5. Equity after closing (line 3 minus line 4) .... $_____

If you got a good deal, your equity after closing should be more than your total cash investment (line 2).

YEARLY ESTIMATE OF CASH RETURN ON CASH INVESTED

A. Total cash invested .... $_____
   (Line 2 from Equity Position Worksheet)

   1. Monthly rental income × 11 .... $_____
   (1 month vacancy cushion for each apartment)

   2. Annual management fees .... $_____

   3. Annual maintenance costs .... $_____

   4. Annual utility fees .... $_____

   5. Insurance .... $_____

   6. Municipal property taxes .... $_____

   7. Mortgage interest .... $_____

   8. Total expenses .... $_____

B. Positive cash flow .... $_____
   (line 1 minus line 8)

To calculate your rate of cash return on the cash you invested divide line B by line 1.

DOLLAR SIGN GAZING

To estimate the probable appreciation return on the cash you invested, each year do the following exercise.

A. Total cash invested .... $_____

B. Estimated current market value of the property .... $_____

Year 1 use your original market value estimate (Equity Position Worksheet line 3). Calculate the appreciation using the percentage guideline for the local area. Add this figure to the original estimated market value and enter on line B. In each succeeding year, begin with the figure on line B for the previous year.

C. Subtract existing mortgage principal balance ....– $_____

D. Your estimated current equity .... $_____

To calculate your rate of estimated appreciation return on the cash you invested divide line A by line D.

---

able equity position (how much cash you have invested in a building) and the yearly return on your cash investment.

In an ideal situation of a bailout apartment building, you will purchase at least 15 percent below what you estimate as market value, your income from rents will cover all debt service, maintenance, and management costs, and perhaps add some pocket money to your life each month, and you will project appreciation that will add *at least* 5 percent per year to the value of the property.

Keep in mind all the factors we mentioned under SUPPLY AND DEMAND and do a little extra detective work before you buy. What has been the vacancy rate in this building? What is the vacancy rate in the area? (Anything under 4 percent is good.) How does the vacancy rate in your prospective building compare with the rate in the area? Can you explain the relationship? (Why is the building doing better? Or worse?) Can anything you do change this relationship? Is there anything you might do that would increase the potential appreciation of the property? Is a condominium conversion possible? Would it be profitable? (Is there a demand for condominiums in the area?)

COMMERCIAL PROPERTY

Cash return on your investment (the rental income minus expenses and carrying costs) is the most important criterion for judging value in commercial properties. Another important factor, however, is the quality and term of the leases. If you have a five-star tenant like A&P or Kmart that will probably be there for twenty years and has agreed to a net, net, net lease (in a triple net lease, the tenant pays all expenses, including property taxes and insurance), the investment is more secure than one in which there is possible frequent turnover of tenants.

If you are considering the purchase of commercial bailout property, don't try to do it alone. There are some great deals out there, but each must be evaluated on its own terms and there are no hard and fast guidelines that are dependable in all situations. Work with a commercial broker, an experienced business accountant, and a lawyer familiar with commercial real estate.

LAND

What's a bargain in land? That question is hard to answer because there are no comparables, there is usually no income, the land is considered indestructible so there is no replacement cost evaluation, and the future appreciation depends not only upon demand but also upon the use to which the land can be put. This is why land is a risky investment.

There is one bargain indicator that works most of the time, however: road frontage. If a large piece of land can be subdivided and it has considerable frontage on an established road, lots can usually be divided off and sold to cover costs or to fund the development of the remainder of the parcel.

Before you scoop up bailout land parcels, ask yourself how anything built on the land would get water, electricity, and waste disposal facilities.

What would it cost to bring in these necessities? Many novice investors forget to factor the cost of development into their land purchase bargains. When they do, they often discover they don't have bargains at all.

WHERE IT'S AT

Here we are playing the old real estate tapes again: Location, location, location, location. . . . But like it or not, location is the *sine qua non* of the real estate game. Without that unique space, there is no ownership. And the space can never be moved. All of which you should read as: CHOOSE CAREFULLY.

TOWN, NEIGHBORHOOD, AND LOT

In all residential real estate, location translates into town, neighborhood, and lot. The space you choose, your address, the buildings around you, and the lay of the land is as important in choosing vacation property as it is in choosing your primary residence, it's as important in evaluating price and market value for a single condominium apartment unit as it is in evaluating price and market value for a multimillion dollar garden apartment complex.

When you find yourself wondering "How good is this good deal?" take a walk. Walk around the property and walk through the neighborhood. Then, if you don't know the town intimately, head for the local library and do some local research. The following are questions to ask yourself and/or others about town, neighborhood, and lot.

About the town:

1. What is the character of the community? Towns are like people, with personalities and bank accounts. There's no hard and fast guideline for good or bad investment opportunity here except: Does the property fit in with the town? A million dollar mansion that you can *steal* for $700,000 in a primarily blue-collar town is probably not as good an investment as a well-maintained two-family house that you can buy for 15 percent off market value.

2. What is the accessibility of this town to workplaces? When you are investing in residential real estate you must remember that what you have to market as a result of your purchase is a home. Most people who have a home also have a job. How close your property is to transportation to common workplaces or to the work sites themselves will have an effect on its future value.

3. How are the schools? This is the second-most-often-asked question that real estate agents hear from buyers and renters. Even home hunters without children to educate ask the question because the reputation of the school system is tied to resale value in the community.

4. What services and recreation facilities are available? Think about things that make places into good places to live. Does the town have: firehouses, police stations, hospitals, shopping malls, movie theaters, restaurants, community swimming pools, golf and country clubs, places of worship, and maybe an old-fashioned bandshell in the park?

5. What are the taxes? This is the *most* often asked question that real estate agents get to answer. Maximum services and minimum taxes will help a sale along every time. For investment purposes, be absolutely certain that the local taxes are pretty much in line with neighboring communities. If they're higher, find out why.

About the neighborhood:

1. What is the median price for homes in this neighborhood? Even if you think you're getting the bargain of the century, be wary if its price tag is more than 10 percent above the median price in the area. The biggest house in the neighborhood is often hard to sell.

2. What's the zoning here? You might be buying what you think is a two-family house only to find out that it's in a single-family zone and has been converted illegally. You could lose that two-family income. Check that the property you're buying fits into the neighborhood.

3. What's two blocks over? It's not just what's on your street that counts. It's also what's nearby. You can check the zoning for contiguous area

in the municipal planning board office or you can drive or walk around. If the character of the streets changes radically (from residential to commercial, for example) it's usually detrimental to investment growth potential.

4. What are the plans for that open land? Open land behind the property you're planning to buy may seem like a plus. It gives the house a sense of privacy, which is fine if it's dedicated parkland. But what if it's zoned industrial and a perfume factory is planning to start building its plant there next year. Always check out the zoning for undeveloped land near any property you plan to buy.

5. Who lives here? People want to feel secure and comfortable in their neighborhoods. They want friends for their children and people they can borrow a cup of sugar (or Johnnie Walker) from. Look for signs of community caring. Neighborhood helping hand signs in the windows for children. Neighborhood watch signs. People talking over a hedge on a sunny spring day. Children playing together. Good maintenance of lawns and exteriors.

About the lot:

1. What is the size and shape of the lot? You really want to see a survey drawing which will give you exact dimensions and boundaries. You also want to favor regular (rectangular) over strange angles and pie-shaped pieces. If you are purchasing a condominium unit, you want to see a survey map of the condominium-owned land to see where your unit is in the community and to get an overview of the community as a whole.

2. What is the terrain? Usually relatively flat is best in residential real estate. It's hard to sell buildings that are hanging on the edges of cliffs or hidden at the bottom of gullies.

3. How good is the drainage? You may not care about drainage on a sunny day, but you'll be wishing you had while you bail your basement during a thunderstorm. Does the land slope toward the property? Sloping terrain could be an even greater problem if your lot is collecting the runoff water from an entire development.

If you are buying in an area where septic tanks are used for waste disposal, drainage becomes a major issue. You may want to pay to have a percolation test done if you are suspicious of problems.

4. What's beneath the grass? Especially when buying relatively new construction, you will want to know what the land was like before housing was built upon it. Was the area once a farm? A landfill? A forest? A swamp? The answer could affect the livability of your building, not to mention resale value.

5. What do you see from the windows? Views have value in the real estate marketplace. Trees, the ocean, even city lights across the river can add value. Flashing neon signs will certainly detract.

ACCESS

In commercial real estate the most important word is access. If you are an experienced investor or part of an investor group and you are considering commercial property, ask yourself questions about how people and things will get to and from, into and out of your building or buildings. The answers will make a difference in the success of your investments.

Check roads, trains, and planes. Does your piece of commercial real estate need these? Why? How often? Is what currently functions adequate? In other words, are the roads wide enough? The trains frequent enough? The planes close enough? If the answer is no, can you do anything to improve the situation? Anything cost-effective, that is.

What about parking? It's the bane of the commercial developers' existence. All that land devoted to empty cars! But you'd better have adequate parking if you want your commercial venture to bring in a positive cash return.

WHAT YOU SEE AND WHAT YOU DON'T

Too bad that nineteenth century barns don't usually make good investment vehicles. When you buy an old barn, you can see exactly what you're getting. Hewn beams, mortise and tenon structure, well-fitted bracing, sills, eaves, it's all there for the eye or the hand to examine. In just about every other kind of real estate, we cover over the structural elements with nice smooth surfaces. Which means that you're buying more than you can see. It also means that those structural elements and working systems that you can't see can make a tremendous difference in the profit margin of your investment.

Chapter 8 tells you what you need to know about professional property inspections, and includes how to do it yourself if you insist, so we won't get into what to look for here. Suffice it to say that you must take the *condition* of a piece of property, the *cost* of repairs, and the *time* it takes to do them into consideration before you buy. Also, think ten times ten again before you buy something that is structurally unsound.

IT'S A GOOD DEAL WHEN . . .

1. The type of investment vehicle is right for you.

2. The property can be bought well below market value.

3. Necessary repairs are minimal and/or have been factored into your purchase price.

4. Cash flow is positive or the property carries itself.

5. Your estimate of supply and demand in the area indicates the strong probability of resale profit.

TIPS ON FINANCIAL SUPPLY AND DEMAND

Who's borrowing how much affects the cost of borrowing. If there is a large demand for borrowed money, interest rates will be higher. If the demand is down or if the supply of money is increased (a factor controlled by the Federal Reserve Board), interest rates will decline. This supply/demand balance in the financial marketplace can affect your real estate investment decisions. A low interest rate on a mortgage could change a property profile from tentatively break-even to positive cash flow, and conversely, a mortgage with a high interest rate could push a property profile into negative cash flow.

By watching certain indicators, you might be able to time your real estate purchases to catch a somewhat lower interest rate. The following are the indicators we watch.

THE FEDERAL RESERVE BOARD'S REPORT ON THE MONEY SUPPLY

The Fed keeps track of several categories of money. In terms of housing, the most reliable is M1—the amount of cash, traveler's checks, checking account funds, and similar deposits held by the American public. When announcements are made that M1 supply is expanding, you can usually expect lower mortgage interest rates within a few months.

Another Federal Reserve Board indicator is the national *discount rate.* The discount rate is the interest rate at which banks and other lending institutions borrow money from the Fed. A reduction in the discount rate has a trickle-down effect on the real estate consumer. In a competitive marketplace, when local banks begin to believe that the reduction is real (that it will last for a while), they are stimulated to reduce their *prime rate,* that is, the rate they charge their best customers. A reduction in the prime usually results in a reduction in mortgage rates within thirty to forty days.

You can watch both of these Federal Reserve Board indicators in your local newspapers or in specialized financial newspapers.

GOVERNMENT SPENDING ON MONEY

You've certainly heard about the deficit. Like the rest of us, the government borrows money to cover its expenses, and like the rest of us, it pays interest. The most common government securities are Treasury Bills (called T-bills) and bonds. When rates on T-bills go up, it means that the government is paying more for the money it borrows, which usually means that money is more in demand (and less available). Less money available will result in higher interest rates.

CHAPTER 5

HOW TO FIND BAILOUT PROPERTIES

"Don't show them the pictures!"

That was the broker talking. Actually, it was two different brokers in two very different parts of the country saying exactly the same words at about the same time (twenty plus years ago). And who were those two brokers admonishing? You guessed it! Two neophyte sales agents who would later become real estate writers.

Both of us got the same message drilled into our heads when we were each spending seven days a week showing houses. And you know what? Both of us broke that rule. (It's a lot easier to sit in the office and look at pictures on the listing sheets than it is to drive buyers all over town.) We broke it, that is, until we found out why our bosses kept repeating it. Then our annual earnings started to go up.

What we learned in those real estate offices so long ago is that *pictures don't sell property.* Each of us could tell you a few stories about customers who said, "No, we don't want to see that one," while looking at the pictures on listing sheets of properties chosen for the day's tour. Then we'd call them a week or two later as a follow-up and they'd tell us they had just bought a place through another agent. And the place would turn out to be the one they said they didn't want to see in our offices. The other agent had taken them there, just "happening" to stop between other showings.

Why is this relevant to looking for good investments? Pictures don't sell property because real estate is not only three-dimensional but also bigger than people. To evaluate it, you have to stand in it, walk around it, see it, touch it, sometimes even smell it. No four-volume edition of RTC listings, no computer disks, no on-line property descriptions, no videotapes, and no televised auctions are going to allow you to find good investment properties without getting out of your favorite chair.

Investing in real estate is an *active* business; it doesn't happen to you, you make it happen. In the bailout decade, if you want to invest in real estate successfully, you must be prepared to put forth aggressive action, along with more than usual perseverance and a good deal of creativity. You must learn not to take "No" or "That's not possible" for an answer. You must learn to ask endless questions and not to believe everything you read in the press. You must get to know who's in charge of what and talk directly to those people, calling them by name and helping them to remember *your* name. You must see things that other investors don't see. Not ghosts—*possibilities!* And you must become a detective, following leads that other people give up on. If you can do all this, you can pick up a lot of profitable pieces from the bailout volcano.

WHO'S THE SELLER?

Perhaps some of you remember the first four-volume set of printed property listings that the RTC published in January of 1990. Perhaps some of you even bought it! Well, that publishing phenomenon was out of date and incomplete before it hit the market. The listings were peppered with inaccurate prices and statistics and, even in four volumes, only a small fraction of the bailout properties available at the time were identified. By the day that you're reading these words, the highest and best use for any one of those four original volumes might well be as a doorstop on a windy day, or perhaps a booster seat for your toddler.

That may sound pretty bad, but your government was not out to deceive you. Many of the errors and inaccuracies were simply the result of the normal bureaucratic blundering that occurs whenever administrators are assigned to work in a field that is totally unfamiliar to them. Mistakes are inevitable!

Some of the omissions in the first publication were also due to bureaucratic error. More often, however, many bailout-related properties were omitted from the list because the two-stage process by which the government "rescues" the deposits of failed or failing thrifts locked them out. Understanding this process can lead you to an inside track on some excellent real estate opportunities. The two stages of the deposit-rescue process are *receivership* and *conservatorship*. Only the REO of thrifts in receivership is listed in RTC publications.

Receivership. When a failed S&L is closed by the Office of Thrift Supervision and placed in receivership, all of its assets are taken over by the RTC. Meanwhile the Federal Deposit Insurance Corporation (the FDIC) pays back the depositors.

The real estate owned (REO) by these failed institutions had usually been acquired through foreclosure on non-performing loans. Some of it has been hidden away in file drawers for more time than anyone associated with the thrift in question or with the Office of Thrift Supervision would like to admit. It is this foreclosed property that makes up much of the RTC inventory—and the RTC is its sole owner/seller. Each prospective buyer for closed thrift REO, therefore, must work through the RTC prescribed sales procedures in order to purchase listed property. (More about that in Chapter 10.)

Conservatorship. Some troubled S&Ls have not been closed, however. Instead, the Office of Thrift Supervision has placed them in conservatorship. A dictionary definition of *conservator* reads: *A person, official, or institution designated, as by a court, to take over and protect the interests of an incompetent*. In a very real way, thrifts in conservatorship are alive and functioning but designated incompetent by Uncle Sam. The Office of Thrift Supervision, therefore, places a conservator in each institution to oversee operations and to dispose of (that means *sell*) REO.

The "dispose of REO" part is where you get an inside chance to make some money. Most of the property being offered for sale by these sick thrifts is low profile, and we don't mean one or two stories high! It simply is not listed or advertised anywhere. This is especially true when the institution first goes into conservatorship and the federal overseers are still sorting their way through the dusty files.

As a prospective buyer for real estate owned by thrifts in conservatorship, you do not work through the bureaucracy of the RTC. For example, what if Sick Thrift Savings & Loan Association owns the property that you want to buy on Nadir Drive? You can buy it directly from that institution. To do this, you work with the conservator who is assigned to handling Sick Thrift's REO. Despite the fact that this conservator is government appointed, you are still dealing with Sick Thrift, not with the RTC or any other branch of the federal government.

"So you avoid all that government red tape . . ." you're thinking. "That sounds pretty good. But how do you find out about these properties if they're not listed or advertised anywhere?"

Stay with us. We'll tell you how to do it under END RUNS in this chapter. First, however, let's answer the question, "Can an individual buyer from a small town in America really get accurate information about what the biggest real estate seller in the world has to sell?"

RTC SALES INFORMATION

The administrators in the Resolution Trust Corporation know that they're in for a long haul, probably ten years or more. And they're actively trying to make information on properties more accessible to the American public. Agency headquarters has been established in Washington, D.C., and the nation has been divided into four regions, each with a director and several area consolidated offices.

As of this writing (1990), there are several service telephone numbers available to the nation in the Washington office. The main operator at the RTC can be reached at: (202) 416-6900. If you know specifically what you're calling about, however, you might do better with one of the designated lines. They are:

> *Inquiries about assets for sale:* (800) 431-0600;
> *Information on rules and policies:* (202) 416-7115;
> *Freedom of Information Act inquiries:* (202) 416-7450;
> *Announcements on scheduled meetings:* (202) 416-6985;
> *Inquiries about becoming a contractor or broker for the agency:*
>   (800) 782-4033;
> *Public Affairs Office:* (202) 416-7557;
> *Other general information:* (202) 416-6940.

When you call one of these numbers, you will sometimes be given names and telephone numbers for one of the regional offices. It is in these consolidated regional offices that you'll find most of the information necessary to get the real work of finding and buying your particular pieces of property done. When calling any regional office, try to get the name of the person handling the particular property that interests you. If you have no specific property in mind, get the names of people overseeing the REO in the city or cities where you hope to invest.

The following is a list of the addresses and telephone numbers for Consolidated Offices in the four national regions. We have omitted the names of directors at the individual office level, however, because they are frequently subject to change. If you want or need the name of a particular director, you can get that information from the "Other general information" operator in Washington at (202) 416-6940.

EAST REGION

William M. Dudley
Director

Bayou Consolidated Office
10725 Perkins Road
Baton Rouge, LA 70810
(504) 769-8860

Northeast Consolidated Office
East 6th Street
Red Hill, PA 18076
(215) 679-9515

Southeast Consolidated Office
220 East Madison Street
Suite 302
Tampa, FL 33602
(813) 870-5000

Mid-Atlantic Consolidated Office
Colony Square
Building 400
Suite 900

Atlanta, GA 30361
(404) 881-4840
(800) 628-4362

CENTRAL REGION

Michael J. Martinelli
Director

Mid-Central Consolidated Office
Board of Trade Building II
4900 Main Street
Kansas City, MO 64112
(816) 531-2212
(800) 365-3342

Lake Central Consolidated Office
2100 East Golf Road
West Building
Suite 300
Rolling Meadows, IL 60008
(708) 806-7750
(800) 526-7521

North Central Consolidated Office
3400 Yankee Drive
Eagan, MN 55122
(612) 683-0036

SOUTHWEST REGION

Carmen J. Sullivan
Director

Metroplex Consolidated Office
300 North Ervay
22nd Floor

Dallas, TX 75201
(214) 953-2300

Gulf Coast Consolidated Office
1000 Memorial Drive
Houston, TX 77024
(713) 683-3476

Southern Consolidated Office
1777 NE Loop 410
San Antonio, TX 78217
(512) 820-8164

Northern Consolidated Office
4606 South Garnett
Tulsa, OK 74146
(918) 627-9000

WEST REGION

Anthony Scaizi
Director

Central Western Consolidated Office
2910 North 44th Street
Phoenix, AZ 85018
(602) 224-1100

Coastal Consolidated Office
1901 Newport Boulevard
3rd Floor
East Wing
Costa Mesa, CA 92627
(714) 631-8380 ext. 4239

Intermountain Consolidated Office
1515 Arapahoe Street

Tower 3
Suite 800
Denver, CO 80202
(303) 556-6500

Since the RTC wants to sell the real estate it owns as soon as possible, they are setting up programs to make getting information about specific properties quick and easy. As part of this effort, a computer program has been developed to dispatch notices of properties likely to be of interest to registered investors. All you have to do to get your name and address into this computer is call the property inquiry line at (800) 431-0600 and tell the operator that you want a property profile preference recorded for your name. You'll be asked questions about the type or types of property you're looking for, the price range, and the geographic location. Within a week or so, you'll begin to get notices of appropriate properties in your mailbox.

If you don't want to register with the RTC computer, there are several other ways to get listings of RTC properties for sale. None of these, however, can entirely supplant the benefits of establishing contact with a living, talking, thinking person in a Consolidated Office and calling from time to time to ask "What's new?"

What *are* those "other ways to get listings"? There is the published list at $50, currently coming out at six month intervals. This is outdated before you can possibly get it but it's sometimes handy for making market comparisons regarding what's being offered, at what price, and where. For $100, you can buy the property list on a CD storage disk that can be used with personal computers. This is also outdated, but not as quickly as the published account. For $375, you can get the same information on floppy disks. Ditto the CD disk on outdating. For a $39.95 hook-up fee, a $16 monthly fee, and 25 cents a minute, you can get telephone access to the RTC's internal computer, which is the most current listing of properties for sale, including the name of the real estate agent handling the sale.

"Well, this finding property business shouldn't be so hard," you say. "These guys do want to sell this stuff!"

Right. But remember the story about the brokers who said, "Don't show them the pictures!" When you're sitting at your kitchen table with all this RTC listing information in hand, *all* you have is the equivalent of *pictures*. To invest in real estate, you've got to leave your home, go out into the marketplace, and find these properties. You've got to inspect them, compare them, think about them. To repeat: *nothing will happen unless you make it happen.*

Getting to walk through, on, or in RTC properties is incredibly easy. They are listed with local real estate brokers. For an appointment, you can either call the listing broker or call any local broker who cooperates with the listing broker and you will be shown the property.

Keep in mind while you work with these brokers and their sales agents, however, that they are required by contractual agreement to represent the *seller*. If you want to work with a broker or agent who will represent *you* throughout the transaction, you can sign a buyer broker agreement. (More about that in Chapter 7.)

END RUNS

Some of the best deals in the bailout never get published. They are the REO of thrifts in conservatorship. If you want to do an end run around the forward line of the RTC and get to property *before* a thrift is closed and the RTC takes over, if you want to avoid a lot of politics and red tape, get to know the individuals acting as conservators in the sick thrifts near you.

"How do you do that?" you ask. "I've never been good at politicking."

You don't have to do any political maneuvering here. You simply have to get the names of the people in charge, make contact, and then phone regularly. Express interest, be pleasant, let them know what you're looking for, and with subtlety (through your talk and actions), show them that you are a serious and knowledgeable investor. Remember, these people want to sell the properties in their charge. They will work with you.

You can get the names of financial institutions that are in conservatorship by calling the Consolidated Office nearest you or by calling the RTC office in Washington. When you call, ask not only for the names of the institutions in conservatorship in your area but also for the name of the person in charge of REO disposal in each institution.

If for some reason you can't get the names of the actual people handling your type of real estate from the Consolidated Office, call the main office of the thrift and ask for the name of the person handling real estate owned in that institution. If you get an operator who isn't sure to whom you should be connected, try suggesting: *the officer in charge of non-performing assets*. And if you still can't get a hands-on person, ask for the thrift's public relations representative. You *will* get a name at that level and you should ask that person for the name of the officer in charge of REO. If you don't get satisfaction, you can use the name of the public relations person in your phone call or letter of complaint to the regional director. Even the hint of going to the regional director usually gets results without any more effort. But do make that call or write that letter if you must. This can be a test of your perseverance. There are real people out there handling this REO and you *can* get their names. Do not give up!

Usually, getting names is not difficult. But whether yours was a one-step process or a ten-step process, move on from your point of contact. When you finally get to talk with someone who uses the acronym REO as though it were an everyday word, find out exactly who's in charge of what. Nothing is more important in doing end runs than getting the right names and keeping in contact. Once your own name begins to be recognized when you call, you'll be on your way to some great investment opportunities.

You may already have spotted a little problem here. How does a prospective buyer get to go inside and look around a property when there's no broker involved? Somehow you can't quite picture a bank officer showing run-down two-family houses! And he or she probably won't. But someone from the thrift will. Or a broker will be hired for the purpose. Just be sure that you know who's paying the broker!

You can streamline the process of checking out the REO of thrifts in conservatorship by doing as much preliminary inspection work as possible on your own. Get the list of addresses and property specifications and drive to them. Do as much looking around the property as you can without violating trespassing laws. If you like what you see and are willing to consider purchase, then, and only then, should you ask for a guided inspection of the interior space. And don't forget, if you're buying income-producing property, you should also ask to see records of rents and expenses for the past two years.

BAILOUT BONUS PROPERTIES

Besides the REO of thrifts in receivership or conservatorship, there is another kind of bailout volcano gold being scattered across the nation. Because of a pendulum swing in response to the S&L disaster, bank examiners are beginning to use fine-tooth combs. Combine this with the fact that regulations regarding capitalization and the disposal of non-performing assets have been tightened both for surviving S&Ls and for federally insured banks and you get a banking industry that's operating under the gun.

So what's happening? REO that "no one" knew about is suddenly up for sale. Handling REO is a bit like sex in Victorian times. No one talked about it but everyone did it. Non-performing assets were hidden away in virtually every lending institution in the nation. And now they're on the market, just begging for buyers.

Across the nation, there's also a lot of real estate not owned by lending institutions or the federal government that's up for sale and being directly affected by the bailout. You can't dump billions of dollars worth of property on the market all at once and not expect it to affect the marketplace. In areas where bailout properties are being sold for bargain prices, there are also private sellers who must sell or want to sell their properties. These people may have to offer bargain-basement deals to entice buyers to compete with the area's bailout properties.

There are no source lists for contacts among the healthy S&Ls and banks, nor are there national lists of sellers in trouble. Not yet anyway! You've got to do your own detective work. If you persevere and get good at it, you'll be rewarded. Meanwhile, let us give you a primer on how to go about finding these bailout bonus properties.

ABOUT BANKS AND HEALTHY THRIFTS

It's a fact of life. The most conservative and healthy lending institutions sometimes make loans that go bad. Like warts, they happen in the best of families. But until recently, no one in a bank or healthy thrift wanted to talk much about the REO that had resulted from its non-performing loans. (Most ordinary people would call them "bad loans" but lending institutions prefer non-performing loans, or better yet non-performing *assets*.)

Until mid-1990 it was often very tough to get anyone to give you five minutes, never mind straight answers, when you approached a bank or functioning thrift about its REO. Sonny Bloch frequently had secrecy-and-access problems reported to him from across the nation on his radio talk shows and in his on-site seminars. In response, he came up with a plan to force attention from the recalcitrant bank officers. *Buy a share of stock!*

That's right. Sonny suggested that investors in search of good deals on REO buy a share of stock in the bank. Waving the stock certificate, the investor could demand a few minutes of time and the right to look at the corporation's books, particularly information on non-performing assets. The lending institution's REO appears in the lists of non-performing assets.

Did the plan work? Yes, but not as you might have thought. Usually any papers that may have been reluctantly dragged out in response to the waving of the stock certificate remained unopened at the interview. Once the bank official realized that the investor was serious, he or she became more cooperative and provided well-organized, neatly printed descriptions of property available for sale.

Listeners began reporting on national radio how Sonny's strategy was working in their particular deals. And then, suddenly, Sonny had to take back his suggestion. You see, between Mother's Day and Father's Day of 1990, a number of non-regular callers punched in Sonny's hot-line number. Who were they? Bank and thrift officers telling the nation that Sonny was wrong. They would be *happy* to talk with investors about their REO. Just stop by and ask for . . . (Many callers actually supplied names!)

Was Sonny wrong? Not at all. Things just changed. Until the tightening of capitalization rules and inspection procedures, many lending institutions were quite successful at keeping their REO hidden. Many top bank management personnel believed that it would be better to hide the REO than actively market it. They feared that aggressive marketing of foreclosed property would hurt their institution's image in the eyes of the public. And beside that, they didn't want the inspectors getting worried about silly things like insolvency. Once these lending institutions realized that there was no longer any benefit to keeping these properties secret, they suddenly wanted to get rid of them as soon as possible.

So be agressive. Shop around at the banks and thrifts in your area, find out what REO they have for sale. You'll almost surely get a much warmer welcome than an inquisitive investor got in the 1980s. And you may be surprised. These lending institutions are not only motivated sellers, they may also be motivated lenders. You could end up with a bargain and have that bargain financed at a better-than-market rate by the owner/seller/lending institution.

ABOUT SELLERS IN DISTRESS

Most investors feel somewhat uncomfortable at the thought of profiting from someone else's misfortune. "I couldn't buy a house in foreclosure," they say. "I couldn't put people out of their homes." But think of the situation from another point of view. By buying a house in the midst of foreclosure proceedings but *not yet* foreclosed, you might actually save the homeowner a great deal of his or her equity. By buying the property at, let's say, 15 percent below market value, you get a deal that will usually allow the former owners to move out with some cash in their pockets. Without your offer, they might lose their entire equity. Many homeowners facing foreclosure are very happy at the appearance of a prospective buyer.

You can get information about properties in the foreclosure process from the people in the banking industry that you have gotten to know through your activities as an aggressive investor. You might consider this "inside information," but it's *legal* inside information. Information on properties in foreclosure proceedings is public. You can get it at the local courthouse. Remember that a little effort might help *you* to find a bargain and might help *someone else* out of a tough financial situation.

And there's still more! Not every distressed seller is facing foreclosure. Some are carrying two mortgages because they bought a new house before selling their old one. Some need to sell for personal reasons like divorce or a death in the family. Some are caught up against the competition with the low prices on bailout REO.

You've got to work to find these bargain properties in the private sector, but they are out there. Follow ads in the local newspapers, watching for price reductions or for dead giveaways like "Seller will consider all offers." Watch for properties that have been on the market for many months and then suddenly have the FOR SALE sign disappear from the front lawn.

If you have not been shown through a property with a real estate agent or inspected it with the owner while it was under a listing contract, you can approach a homeowner the day after a real estate listing contract expires, make an offer, negotiate, and purchase the property without incurring the seller's obligation to pay a real estate commission. This automatically reduces the price by thousands. Then you can talk price knowing that "long time on the market" and "not sold" are trump cards in *your* hand.

You can also cold canvass. Yes, just like the real estate agents do. If you find an area where you would like to invest, you can actually go door-to-door on a weekend, telling whoever answers that you'd like to buy in the neighborhood and asking if they know anyone who is planning to sell. Often you'll get a lead and sometimes you'll get a deal. There have been numerous accounts of sale prices that were considered "great" by both the buyer and the seller because the buyer made the offer unsolicited and the seller was aware of the market conditions and was relieved at the thought of not enduring the home-marketing process.

Finally, if you see a vacant property that interests you, you can get the name of the owner from the local tax assessor's office. This, too, is public information. Many deals are made when a ready, willing, and able buyer approaches a seller who's given up hope of selling, at least temporarily.

GOLF COURSES AND PTA MEETINGS

Some of the best properties never get listed anywhere. Real estate deals are made because something came up in conversation at the most amazing places, like golf courses, the hairdresser's salon, PTA meetings, Little League games, and cocktail parties. If you plan to make your fortune in the real estate marketplace, you must learn to listen. Market information is everywhere. And when you get a lead, you must do the legwork to follow up on it as soon as possible.

Waiting or doing nothing is a decision, a decision not to act in an action-driven marketplace. But don't misinterpret that sentence! We're not saying "Run out and buy!" The decision not to act is sometimes the best decision. You should decide not to act, however, only after running down the facts and making a careful evaluation. On the other hand, you should be ready to act if a property meets the criteria of a good deal that we talked about in Chapter 4.

We'll say it again: *nothing will happen in this business unless you make it happen!*

CHAPTER 6

AFFORDABLE HOUSING

Out of the smoke and rubble of the S&L disaster, there are slowly emerging the first flickering lights of what we think will be a bright hope for America's working citizens. After a decade of manic spending by the rich in an effort to get richer while the government did a hatchet job on virtually every housing program for the not-at-all-rich, our legislators realized that it wasn't working. In the Financial Institutions Reform, Recovery and Enforcement Act of 1989 (FIRREA) there is the promise of help.

The act mandates that preferential opportunity will be given to low and moderate income families to purchase affordable housing. It also mandates that monied groups will be given preferential opportunity to buy apartment buildings and other shelters for the poor or elderly if they make a commitment to provide low income tenancy in those buildings.

The RTC are having bureaucratic problems in getting this affordable housing program established, however. The structure and the working team are being built, somewhat slowly to be sure, and it's still under-staffed. But the affordable housing issue is being addressed and home buying programs will be available soon for Americans who never bought a share on Wall Street and who've never had enough spare cash to invest in a tax-free bond, much less a high-flying junk bond.

Does that have meaning for you? Are you hopeful that maybe there's a chance for you in the real estate marketplace? Well, you should be. But don't think for a minute that someone will come to your door and offer you a nice Cape Cod house that you can afford or perhaps a small apartment building in need of only minor repairs at 20 percent off market value just because you left your name on a list in an office somewhere. If you want to get in on RTC affordable housing offerings, you'll have to make a commitment to pursue your goals aggressively.

Your purchase program will probably be very much like the process every consumer-advocate writer encounters with virtually every assignment. You start with a few leads, something like: *This government office handles that* or *I think there's a place somewhere in East Hilltown with a whole block of townhouses to sell.* Then you pick up the phone.

Expect to reach receptionists who have no idea what you're talking about. Don't let them hang up. Ask for names of people who might be handling what you want. If you still get an "I don't know" answer, ask for the person who handles public relations (there's always someone). Then explain your story, tell the PR person what you want, and ask for the name of the person in charge of that particular kind of housing.

Expect blind alleys, but don't give up. If your telephone efforts aren't bringing you the information you need, go to the areas where you think the housing might be. Stop and ask questions, everywhere. Stop at gas stations, police stations, the town hall, real estate offices, CHRBs (Community Housing Resource Boards, called cherubs).

Don't be bashful. "Do you know where the government has some houses for sale in this area?" is not a dumb question. It's a question that could lead you to a house you can buy or an investment that will make you money. From the answers you get, zero in on the area, try to get street names, and most important of all, try to get the names of the people in charge of selling these properties.

"Why not just call the Consolidated Office of the RTC?" you ask.

A good idea. But the answers you get from the person who answers the phone may not be the answers you need. There has been an Affordable Housing Disposition Specialist assigned to each of the nation's four regional offices of the RTC. Affordable Housing Disposition Specialists at the Consolidated Office level are still being named as of this writing. Not every office has someone in charge and even those that do are still grossly understaffed and sometimes not completely organized. Also, the RTC right now is very busy running public information seminars around the nation. In other words, the people who could give you answers may be out of the office.

And if you do get to an affordable housing person at an RTC office, you may get lists of REO from the lending institutions in receivership but you may not get information on affordable housing units that are not yet owned by the RTC because they are still being marketed by lending institutions in conservatorship. These may be the best bargains of all.

So, if you want to get in on the affordable housing bonanza, get out there and *start hunting*. Unless you're incredibly lucky, you're not going to make the deal of your dreams on your first day in the marketplace. But keep going back. Each day you'll know a little more. Each day you'll move a little closer to your goal. Push a little if you must. Be courteous, but be persistent.

Let's look at the rules of this hunt for affordable housing as set out by FIRREA. By knowing the rules and the opportunities for preferential financing for low and moderate income buyers and for tax credits for apartment building buyers, you'll know what to ask for and you'll get the maximum benefits available through current programs.

BUYING A HOME

You may find this hard to believe (or maybe you won't, if you're familiar with government publications), but in the sale of bailout properties, a single-family home is not necessarily a single-family home. *The RTC considers any residence built to house one to four families as a single-family home.*

Now this is great news for you, because if you choose to purchase what we've been referring to as a multi-family house, you'll be able to include rental income in your qualification for the mortgage! The top prices designated by the RTC to qualify for consideration as affordable housing also go up with the number of units. Multi-unit "single-family homes" therefore add to the number of qualifying properties available for your consideration.

WHAT CAN WE BUY?

As of this writing, a building is considered single-family affordable housing if its price does not exceed the following guidelines: one-unit residence—$67,500; duplex—$76,000; triplex—$92,000; and four-plex—$107,000. Currently, these price caps apply nationwide; however, both public agencies and the private sector have noted that the guidelines do not take into account regional differences and therefore are not equitable. You will almost certainly see the maximum amounts change over the course of time; you may also see the maximums set by region rather than nationally, just as the FHA guidelines for mortgages are now written.

To become a qualified buyer for these affordable "single-family" houses and apartments, you must meet certain household income standards. But the government has been generous here. If you plan to occupy the property as your principal residence, you are eligible for affordable housing preferential treatment if your household income is no more than 115 percent of the median income for your area.

What is this preferential treatment? When FIRREA was enacted in 1989, the Affordable Housing Disposition Program was authorized. The objective of this program is to create home ownership and rental housing opportunities for low and moderate income households through the disposition of residential properties by the RTC. Part of that objective is to be achieved by giving qualified individuals and groups an exclusive ninety-day marketing period for properties designated as affordable housing. That means no outside investors can step in and buy these properties until they have been offered to qualified affordable housing buyers for ninety days.

Eligible single-family properties that have been for sale for at least four months by a lending institution in *conservatorship* can be reduced to 15 percent below appraised value as soon as the RTC takes them over (no additional waiting period)! Which means that some properties are real bargains the very day they come into the RTC marketing program.

The RTC has also been given some discretionary powers as to actual acceptable sale price in affordable housing deals, especially in areas where there are many properties for sale and there is a risk to the vacant buildings. The amount of negotiating space against the asking price on these properties may differ therefore from one Consolidated Office to another. Do try to negotiate the best deal you can!

In fact, if you are a low-income household that can't quite qualify for an asking price, negotiate even harder and then stop at the best bid that will allow you to qualify for the mortgage you need. Even if it seems much too low, just get your best bid in! Oversight Board rules and regulations for the RTC state in the Federal Register that "Among substantially similar offers for an eligible single-family property, the RTC will give preference to an offer from a family which is in a lower income group."

BUT HOW DO WE GET THE MONEY?

Because of the mandate in FIRREA, the Oversight Board is putting pressure on the RTC to offer special financing considerations for affordable housing. On March 8, 1990, the Oversight Board authorized the acceptance of down payments as low as 5 percent for single-family residential property (remember, that means up to four-family buildings) in specified circumstances. Among the circumstances are properties located in distressed areas (distressed means the real estate market is very slow and the RTC has a lot of properties to sell); properties that have large operating deficits; and properties where the buyer will commit work and money to improving the property's value. (Be sure you read about 203 K loans in Chapter 12. These could help you to buy an affordable property in need of repair with no money down and with the lender actually providing the cash to do the fix-up work.)

Besides providing seller financing when necessary, the RTC has received a mandate to make use of state and local housing agency bond financing programs to facilitate the sale of affordable housing properties. The Oversight Board "encouraged" the RTC to enter into negotiations with state and local housing agencies to secure commitments of low-interest bond money to be used to provide financing to low and moderate income buyers.

To add frosting to this cake, these below-market loans are *not* to be restricted to REO acquired by the RTC from lending institutions in receivership. The mandate for special financing extends to conservatorship properties expected by the RTC to become subject to the affordable housing requirements of receivership REO. Which means that if you can find a lending institution in conservatorship (one that the RTC plans to take over but hasn't yet done so), you can make a deal for one of their affordable housing REOs and apply for the special financing rates being used by the RTC, but without dealing with the bureaucracy of the Consolidated Offices.

If it sounds too good to be true, be aware that there is a little problem. These below-market-rate mortgage funds generated by state and local bond issues are notoriously ephemeral—here today, gone tomorrow—

and we don't yet know how successful the RTC will be in obtaining their commitment. So you quite justifiably may be wondering if there's any-place else where you can go to get the mortgage money to buy an RTC affordable home. The answer is YES. There are still some healthy S&Ls in the nation and they have money to lend.

Another by-product of the S&L volcano was the Community Rein-vestment Act, which authorizes the Office of Thrift Supervision to oversee S&L compliance. According to the OTS's *Regulatory Handbook,* Community Reinvestment Act examiners will review an institution's housing-related activities to determine in part whether that institution is meeting the credit needs of its community.

What a wonder! S&Ls will no longer be buying junk bonds from Wall Street and financing condominium developments in deserts two thou-sand miles from the bank's offices! The S&Ls will be required to operate in certain prescribed ways. The operations that will help a lending institution to comply with the Community Reinvestment Act are:

- Origination of mortgages, housing rehabilitation loans, and home improvement loans within the community;

- Participation in government-insured, guaranteed or subsidized loan programs for housing, such as those available through FHA, VA, or state or local agencies;

- Investment in or assistance to community development projects of programs, such as those operated by Neighborhood Housing Services;

- Participation in federal community and economic development programs, such as HUD's Development Block Grant program;

- Financing for community development corporations or local develop-ment corporations;

- Purchase of securities of state and local housing agencies.

All Community Reinvestment Act lending is to be made "consistent with safe and sound lending practices," which means that you will have to qualify by standard guidelines for the loan you apply for. BUT, the loans will be available. Out-of-state highfliers will no longer take precedence over the needs of the immediate community. And affordable housing activity will count heavily toward an institution's compliance evaluation.

What's more, how well your community lending institutions are doing is going to be public knowledge. As of July 1, 1990, savings institutions must make public the evaluation of their Community Reinvestment Act performance for all CRA examinations. The Office of Thrift Supervision is also "encouraging" lending institutions to make public documents describing the steps the institution has taken to determine, communicate with the community about, and meet the credit needs of its market area. And all of this is a direct result of mandates in FIRREA.

Banks are already being deluged with affordable housing applications from community lending institutions. All signs indicate that this trend is likely to increase. New York is a good example. To encourage even more savings-institution/community-group partnerships for affordable housing, some of the New York banks have developed computerized databases to keep in touch with community-based housing providers in the market area. This use of computer match-up practices is likely to expand across the nation.

The price of the bailout is huge and the pain real, but from it is going to come a safer, saner lending policy in this nation. Which may, if we're lucky and if we work at it, provide much-needed housing for America's working households.

HOW DO WE FIND THE AFFORDABLE HOUSING THAT'S AVAILABLE?

The FIRREA legislation requires that the RTC market its affordable single-family and multi-family (apartment houses) property through clearinghouses during the ninety-day exclusive period. Currently, eligibility to serve as a clearinghouse is limited to the Federal Housing Finance Board, to State housing finance agencies, and to national non-profit organizations. These clearinghouses, however, are "encouraged" by law to disseminate information on a regular basis to state and local public agencies, nonprofit organizations, for-profit entities, and organizations representing special population groups, such as the homeless, the disabled, the handicapped, and the elderly. They must also publicize the availability of these properties through the various media.

"So how come we haven't heard about these properties?" you may ask.

Because the program is really just getting started. As of the summer of 1990 the RTC had signed memorandums of understanding with only six clearinghouses. (In Arizona, Florida, Georgia, North Carolina, Tennessee, and West Virginia.) They are working on the rest of the nation. This does not mean, however, that you can't buy affordable housing through bailout programs in the other forty-four states. You just have to work a little harder. Call the RTC Consolidated Office nearest you and ask what groups are handling property in your area. If you can't find an Affordable Housing Specialist at the Consolidated Office level, call the Regional Office. Or work through your state housing finance office. Remember, don't give up. Ask for names and keep gathering information. This is a paper trail, but it does lead to opportunity.

Meanwhile, the RTC will supplement the efforts of clearinghouses in disseminating information about eligible residential properties through publication of property lists, a computer bulletin board, a toll-free telephone number (800) 431-0600, and other marketing activities. If you want more information on current rules and regulations governing affordable housing sales, you can call the office of Stephen S. Allen, Director, Affordable Housing Disposition Program, in Washington at (202) 416-7348 or Muriel Watkins, Program Coordinator, Affordable Housing Disposition Program, at (202) 416-7137.

Once the RTC's clearinghouse program becomes well established, there will be still more help for qualified households in search of affordable housing. The RTC is working to train TAAs (Technical Assistance Advisors) across the nation. These people will work in and with the clearinghouses to qualify single-family property purchasers, assist qualified households in identifying suitable properties, and help them to secure appropriate financing.

The TAA idea is an excellent ideal, but if you want to get in on the ground floor of this bailout bonanza, don't wait until someone is appointed to help you. Go out and help yourself. Be persevering, creative, aggressive, dauntless, relentless, and anything else it takes to move through the telephone answering systems, fax machines, computer programs, reams of paper, and multitudes of departments that already characterize the bailout. You *can* do it. Think of each NO you hear as a MAYBE, and each MAYBE SOON as a step toward YES.

BUYING INVESTMENT PROPERTY

Not every low and moderate income person *wants* to own a home, and FIRREA has also provided for purchase incentives that should increase the number of affordable rental apartments in the American marketplace. For investors, the RTC's multi-family buildings sold under the Affordable Housing Program might just turn out to be some of the best deals available in the entire bailout inventory.

AFFORDABLE MULTI-FAMILY HOUSING

The RTC and Oversight Board regulations currently define eligible multi-family properties as consisting of more than four units with a value not exceeding $29,500 for each efficiency, $33,816 for each one-bedroom unit, $41,120 for each two-bedroom unit, $52,195 for a three-bedroom unit, and $58,392 for a four or more bedroom unit. These value guidelines are currently nationwide, although that factor may be redefined in the future and the numbers themselves will certainly change from year to year.

Qualified buyers are public agencies, nonprofit organizations, and for-profit entities that make a commitment to meeting the statutory lower-income occupancy requirements. Public agencies and nonprofit organizations are eligible for low interest and more favorable financing available through the RTC. For-profit organizations may purchase during the ninety-day privilege period but are not eligible for special financing options.

To qualify for affordable housing privileged buying, the purchaser must agree that not less than 35 percent of all dwelling units in an eligible multi-family property will be available for occupancy and maintained as affordable for lower-income families during the remaining useful life of the building. This restriction will be written into the deed of the property.

Qualification guidelines for low-income households change from time to time and you will have to maintain contact with HUD in order to comply with housing and rental amount rules. Most of the very low income apartments will be subsidized with state and federal rental assistance programs.

The program for purchasing multi-family affordable housing involves the use of an RTC letter of intent and then a formal contract after the

RTC notifies you that the property is ready for sale. We strongly recommend that you work closely with the RTC Affordable Housing Representative in your area and that you have your own attorney.

Besides rent restrictions, there are a number of other restrictions and entanglements in buying affordable multi-family housing from the RTC. For example, rules include non-eviction clauses for those households already occupying apartments and family size adjustments to income guidelines.

"Is it all worth it?" you may wonder.

Usually, yes. The properties are likely to be sold at prices below market value. The growing need for low-income housing in the nation practically guarantees against high vacancy rates. Cash flow is aided by government rent subsidies. And finally, there are tax benefits to providers of low-income housing.

TAX BENEFITS

Among the few real tax breaks left to real estate investors after the 1986 Tax Reform Act are the tax credits available for buyers, builders, and renovators of low-income housing. This is a two-tier incentive system that is potentially very valuable. But like most government programs, it is full of ifs and maybes. So read on through the good parts, but see your tax advisor before you buy a low-income property solely for its tax benefits. They may not all be available, or you may have to go to great lengths to get them. Proceed with caution.

Tier one: For new construction or rehabilitation expenditures, a tax credit is available at 9 percent for ten years. In other words, a $100,000 expenditure could bring about a tax credit of $9,000 a year for ten years. (A total of $90,000!) Does that mean you're buying the building for $10,000? Not quite. You must factor in the time value of money. And you must remember that we said to see your tax advisor. You are almost sure to find that not all of your expenditures qualify for the credit.

Tier two: For expenditures to acquire an existing building or new or existing construction financed with federal subsidies, the tax credit is 4 percent per year for ten years. Both this and the 9 percent figure are subject to change on a monthly basis by the IRS to reflect changes in the current going interest rates.

To qualify for this tax credit, you must meet one of two criteria, both having to do with the minimum portion of the building that must be set aside for low income families. Once the building owner chooses which of the ratios he will use, the decision is unchangeable.

The first arrangement requires that 20 percent or more of the residential units in the building or complex be occupied by households with incomes no larger than one-half the median income for the area. These are considered very low income families and their rent is almost always subsidized.

The second arrangement requires that 40 percent or more of the rental units be occupied by households with an income no higher than 60 percent of the median income for the area. Many of these apartment rents will also be subsidized.

The units designated for low-income housing must also be permanent housing—no transients and no hotel-type rentals are permitted.

The gross rents paid by the low-income families must not be more than 30 percent of the qualifying income level of the household. There is no policy limitation on the rents charged for the remainder of the units in a building, however. These unregulated rents often support the low-income amounts to produce positive cash flow and a viable investment property.

There are also somewhat complicated reporting programs to the IRS that certify how the project has met and complied with various requirements. If the building does not meet the requirements for a period of fifteen years, some of the tax credits will have to be returned to the IRS. Sale of the property can also set off IRS recapture of the credits unless certain steps are taken.

The tax credit is calculated on an eligible basis formula which establishes a ratio between the number of low-income units and the total number of the other residential units or between the floor space of low-income units and the total floor space of the other residential units. The IRS always uses the lower of these two figures.

If you've read through all of this, we don't need to tell you that low-income housing tax credits is no game for the amateur. Be certain you are using a competent tax advisor and attorney.

Remember also that you can't include the cost of land in your calculations for tax credit expenditures on low-income housing, only the buildings themselves. But you *can* include the cost of certain amenities like parking areas, swimming pools, tennis courts, or a day-care center.

SOME SOURCES

When the FHA first began insuring mortgages in the 1930s, there were a lot of people who didn't think it would work. Well, it *has* worked and millions of Americans owe their homeownership status to FHA programs. Like the work of the early FHA, the affordable housing efforts of the RTC are not yet solidified and they are sometimes the target of criticism. The criticism is being accepted and considered. The potential for success is definitely there, however.

As we've said, one of your biggest problems in this beginning stage is certainly going to be getting information. To help you, this chapter ends with a few places to call or write for help. HUD offices and Government bookstores which carry an immense variety of helpful publications are listed at the back of this book. Or you might try contacting one of the following three groups.

National Council of State Housing Agencies
444 North Capitol Street, NW
Suite 118
Washington, DC 20001
(202) 624-7710

Housing Opportunities Foundation
An Affiliate of the U.S. League of Savings Institutions
1709 New York Avenue, NW
Washington, DC 20006
(202) 637-8900

ULI—The Urban Land Institute
1090 Vermont Avenue, NW
Washington, DC 20005
(202) 289-8500

The addresses and phone numbers of State Housing Agencies are available at this National Council.

CHAPTER 7

PAID HELP

We'd like you to do something you've probably never done before. *Think about populations.* No, we don't mean world populations, we're talking about very, very local populations. Specialized populations. We want you to imagine yourself in places where most of the people around you are in that location not only *temporarily* but also *necessarily.*

What *are* we talking about? Prisons?

Not at all. We'd like you to think about groups of professional people. Focus your imagination on how the training, skills, and motivations of a working population might affect the atmosphere in the workplace. In a university, for example, you'll live and breathe among teachers; in a hospital, nurses, doctors, and technicians; in the United States Congress, Senators and Representatives; and in the real estate marketplace, real estate agents.

You knew we'd bring this fantasy back to *real* estate, didn't you? Well, everyone knows real estate agents exist—and that they can affect the atmosphere of the real estate marketplace. You might duck them in a deal or two, but if you're reading this book because you want to make money by buying and selling property, you're going to rub elbows with them. To make money in real estate you must learn to work with real estate agents. They're an essential part of the population.

So don't waste your energy fighting the inevitable. Instead, focus on how to get maximum benefit from the knowledge, skills, training, access, inside knowledge, and money-making motivation of your local real estate professionals. Because these people spend their working days in the marketplace, they have a running start on every deal. They are already marketing the current crop of RTC properties and they can be of immense help in finding and evaluating other bailout-related real estate.

As in every service industry, the key to maximizing the effectiveness of real estate professionals is finding good people. Finding implies a search, and "good" requires individual evaluations. You will need to create in your mind (or on paper) a continuum between terrible and excellent where you might place the agents you encounter.

But you shouldn't do this on gut feelings. To evaluate agents effectively, you must know something about professional designations and quite a bit about the usual working procedures of the profession. You must also have at your command a set of standards for judging the quality of performance. This chapter will tell you what you need to know about real estate professionals in their workplace. At the end of the chapter, we'll give you a sample checklist to help you rate the real estate agents who become a part of your investment activity.

LICENSED PROFESSIONALS

Overheard standing on the checkout line at a grocery store:

"But aren't you going to get a professional inspection?"

"What for? The property is listed with the biggest agency in the state and the Realtor we saw it with is great. Why waste money on a home inspection firm when there's the disclosure law?"

"What disclosure law?"

"Well, my cousin, Edith, is married to a lawyer and she says that her husband says that sellers have to disclose major faults in the house or they can be sued. And the real estate agents, the ones that list the house and the ones that show the house, they have to disclose major faults or threats to future property value too, or *they* can be sued. *And* they can lose their licenses! We've got nothing to worry about."

That home buyer should have stopped at the flower department for a bunch of four-leaf clovers, because she's going to need all the luck she can get! She's not entirely wrong, however. Some states do have disclosure laws that require home sellers and real estate agents to inform prospective buyers about faults in the property, when they have prior knowledge of those faults. But it's difficult to prove *prior knowledge* in court if nothing is written down!

It's an old story: *what's true in theory is not always true in fact.* Agents in the marketplace make a living by using their best efforts to help sellers and buyers in the transfer of property. The law says that's what they do. But a written law doesn't mean that you should turn over your brain power and your money to your helper. You've got to watch out for yourself in the real estate marketplace, and actually in all the world's marketplaces.

The fact that real estate agents are licensed and regulated is not an assurance of quality performance. Regulation of the real estate industry is done by each state independently, and although some states *do* have real estate disclosure laws, many states do not. There are no federally mandated rules. Each state sets up its own licensing standards and procedures, each state polices its own turf, and each state handles its own problems. The fact that a sticker reading "Licensed Real Estate Broker" appears on the front window of an office only means that someone in that office has fulfilled the state requirements for broker licensing and that the license has not been revoked. Usually, it takes flagrant misrepresentation, fraud, or outright stealing to get a license revoked.

What do we mean? It can be summed up in five points.

1. Most real estate agents are good people.

2. Their motivator for working with you in the real estate marketplace is making money.

3. They are quite naturally more concerned with the money they make for themselves than with the money they might make for you.

4. You should make use of their knowledge and skills, and the professional services they offer.

5. You should do your own watching-out-for-your-money.

WORDS IN THE MARKETPLACE

If you know only English, you can still travel pretty well through Germany, France, or Spain. But it's much easier (and more fun) if you know the local language well enough to read street signs and restaurant menus. In the business world, every industry also has a language, some of it composed of professional terms and some of it jargon and acronyms. If you're going to do business in an industry's marketplace, learning its language will often speed your progress and sometimes prevent you from making costly mistakes.

You may already have noticed that lessons in the language of the real estate marketplace make up a good part of this book, and there's more to come, right to the very last page. At this point, let's focus on the words that pertain to the business of real estate brokerage. They must become as familiar to you as the special words of your own profession.

BROKER

Each state defines what a broker can and cannot do in its licensing laws. Throughout the nation, however, it is generally accepted that a real estate broker is one who, for a fee, carries on activities related to the transfer or rental of real property for another person. The relationship between the person who hires the broker and the broker is called a fiduciary relationship. Fiduciary means trust, and the broker acts as an agent who has the trust of the party who hired him or her. It is generally accepted that in an agency relationship the person who hires the broker can expect to get reasonable skill and competence, loyalty, confidentiality, full disclosure, obedience (except if asked to break the law), and full accountability. Failure to meet these expectations is usually sufficient grounds for breaking a contract with a broker.

Only a broker can act as the agent of a seller or buyer in the transfer of real estate. The majority of professional people whom you'll meet in the marketplace, however, are *not* brokers. They are licensed salespersons.

"Whoa!" you cry. "Are you telling us that all those professional people in the real estate marketplace are not the same? They all look alike to me. How can you tell the difference between the brokers and the salespersons? I don't want to waste my time working with someone who can't really *act* on my behalf or on behalf of the seller. How do I get to a broker so I can get something done?"

Don't worry. You can do all you need to do very efficiently through a licensed salesperson. Many buyers never actually meet the broker whose

name is on the sign over the door to the office. The real estate
marketplace functions on a two-tier system: broker over salesperson.
Most of the work in the marketplace itself is done by the salespersons.

LICENSED SALESPERSON

By law in every state, a licensed salesperson must work under the direct
supervision of a licensed broker. The broker is responsible for the
salesperson's actions and the salesperson takes on the agency rela-
tionships of the broker. In other words, if a seller hires a broker to sell
his home and thus establishes an agency relationship with that broker,
the seller also automatically has a fiduciary relationship with all the
salespersons working in that broker's firm. These salespersons work as
agents of the seller because their broker is the agent of the seller.

When dealing with legal papers, however, it's a different story. All
contracts which hire a real estate broker *must* be signed by the broker.
The signature of a salesperson on a contract to employ the services of a
real estate professional is not sufficient to create an agency relationship.
You must get the signature of a broker of record in the firm. With that
signature on paper, however, you can proceed to work the day-to-day
problems and possibilities of your property hunt with the salesperson
whom you choose.

REALTOR

Despite a widely held popular opinion that has been fueled by flagrant
misuse of the word in the press, a Realtor is not any and every person who
works at the trade of marketing real estate. *Realtor* is a registered trade
name and the capital letter R is a registered trademark indicating a
member of the National Association of Realtors. Established in 1908, the
NAR is the nation's largest real estate trade organization with close to a
million members.

In the United States, the vast majority of licensed brokers and their
salespersons belong to the NAR, work according to its Code of Ethics,
and are therefore *Realtors*. There do exist, however, independent
brokers who belong to no trade group and brokers who are members of
other trade groups such as the Realtists. Realtists are members of the
National Association of Real Estate Brokers (NAREB), a trade group
founded in 1947 with the stated purpose of promoting the rights and

opportunities of minorities in real estate. Some Realtists are also Realtors. Some brokers who are Realtors also belong to the Real Estate Buyers' Agents Council (REBAC), a trade group formed in the 1980s for brokers who represent buyers. More about buyer brokers in just a bit.

REALTOR BOARD

Realtor Boards are geographically organized groups of Realtors who agree to cooperate with each other by making their listings available to all Board members. The Board has elected officers and an office apart from the sales offices of its members. It acts as the local overseer for ethics questions and generally keeps members informed of new trends. If you have a complaint on the local level, the Board of Realtors in your area is your first step toward resolution and satisfaction.

MLS

In the real estate marketplace, the initials MLS stand for Multiple Listing Service. As the name implies, this business group is a service, not a policy-making organization, functioning for and under the direction of the local Realtor Board. Members of the local Board submit all the pertinent information regarding their property listings to the MLS within a day or two of the signing of each listing contract. The MLS sends out a photographer to take a picture of the exterior of each property and then prints that picture plus all the listing information. This MLS listing is then distributed to all member brokers and salespersons either on a separate, loose-leaf sheet for each property or as an entry in a weekly or bi-weekly published book of property listings.

The MLS also disperses to its members notices of price changes or other new information as the listing broker makes it available. Finally, many MLS offices publish a comparables book at stated times during each year.

COOPERATING BROKER

When one broker lists a property for sale, another broker or salesperson brings the buyer to the property, and the two brokers agree to split the commission, they are said to be cooperating brokers. Members of a Realtor Board agree to cooperate with each other at a commission split that is agreed upon in advance. It is also possible for two independent real estate brokers to enter into a cooperating agreement. And cooperating agreements can be created between Realtors who are members of different Realtor Boards and between Realtors and independent brokers.

LISTING CONTRACT

A listing contract is the document that hires the broker to represent the seller. The seller then becomes the *client*. The buyer is the *customer*.

"What's the difference?" you ask.

Read on.

WHO'S WORKING FOR WHOM?

Here's a puzzle for you. Tom and Jerri have been working with Felix the broker for two months. They have been loyal customers and Felix likes them very much. On the advice of a salesman from another agency, Felix shows them a ranch style house in an area he doesn't usually work. He estimates, however, that similar properties in the area are probably worth between $175,000 and $185,000.

Tom really likes the place but he's doubtful about the asking price of $210,000. Jerri just wants it. Tom turns to Felix in confidence and says, "Look, let's make an offer of $180,000. I know it's low, but we don't want to stretch too far. If they don't like it, we'll go to $190,000."

How does Felix present the offer to the sellers or to the sellers' listing agent? What would you do?

Felix tells the sellers and the sellers' listing agent that his customers are offering $180,000 but that they are willing to pay $190,000.

Does that make you want to throw rotten eggs on Felix's roof? Tom and Jerri trusted him! They were loyal to him throughout their house hunting. How could Felix give away $10,000 of their money without even trying to negotiate?

The answer is easy. He was required to do so by law. Although Tom and Jerri were working with Felix, they never signed an agreement to hire him as their agent. In showing them houses, Felix was acting as a subagent of the listing broker on each house. In this role, his loyalty was committed to the seller, his *client,* even though he had never met that seller. He was required by law to disclose all the financial information he had been given by his *customers,* Tom and Jerri.

Got it? Here's the next puzzle.

Clark and Lois, the sellers, look at the contract and Clark says to Felix, "Hey, this is a great offer. We were just about to reduce the asking price to $190,000 because we've found another house that we want to buy."

"Yes, but don't tell *them* that!" says Lois. "If they'll go to $190,000, they'll go higher. Let's see what we can do. Tell them we'll take no less than $198,000."

Felix knows that $190,000 is probably on the high side of market value for this home. He also knows that, theoretically, both parties can come to an agreement at that figure. What does he say to Tom and Jerri? What would you do?

Felix calls Tom on the phone and says that Clark and Lois have countered with $198,000.

"That's terrible!" says Tom. "Do you think they'll take less?"

Now what does Felix do? He heard Clark say that they were about to reduce the *asking* price to $190,000. He also heard Lois say "Tell them we'll take no less than $198,000." Should he tell his loyal customers what Lois said even though he knows that it's a lie? Should he advise Tom and Jerri to make another, somewhat higher bid and test the "no less than" counter offer? Should he suggest that they bid the $190,000 figure they mentioned and stick to their guns? Or should he say, "I don't know at what price they'll sign a contract." What would you do?

Felix says, "I don't know what they'll take. But you mentioned $190,000, why don't you try that?"

He's hedging here by making a suggestion but not revealing the information he has been given by the sellers. It's probably legal.

Many agents, however, would have advised their loyal customers to go no higher than $190,000, saying something like "I think I can make a deal for you at that price." Working with a little flair, they would create lasting gratitude in these customers who, someday in the future, might find themselves looking for an agent to sell this same house. But in giving advice and implying that the deal could be made at that price, those agents would probably be breaking the law! Working as an agent of the seller, a salesperson is not allowed to disclose any financial information to the buyer unless he is given specific permission to do so. He therefore must keep the sellers' intended price reduction a secret. If he discloses that information and thus helps the buyers to get the house for $190,000 or less, he is acting in a dual agency capacity, which is prohibited by law unless both the buyers and sellers agree to it in writing.

You may be wondering why we're telling you this story. What has agency relationship and the question of dual agency got to do with the likelihood of your profiting from the S&L bailout?

A lot. This lesson in concepts is a big one. Whenever you're in the real estate marketplace, you must keep in mind that most of the brokers and sales agents you meet will be representing the *seller*. YOU MUST NEVER TELL THEM YOUR TOP DOLLAR FIGURE! Remember, you are the customer. The seller is the client. Except when . . . But that's the next section. Keep reading for an inside track on saving time and money.

BUYER BROKERS

Buyer brokers, or procuring brokers, as they are sometimes called, have been around for a long while. In the 1980s, however, a new awareness of the question "Who is my client?" and legislative action regarding client disclosure in many states stimulated spiraling growth in buyer broker activity. This growth was nurtured by some creative fee structuring and finally by somewhat grudging acceptance of the functioning of buyer brokers on local Realtor Boards.

Not too long ago, if you wanted to hire a buyer broker, you had to be willing to pay a hefty fee, often from 3 to 7 percent of the acquisition price of the property. In today's marketplace, however, most traditional seller brokers are splitting their fees in the usual and customary ratios with brokers who represent the buyers. (And remember, whatever is said about brokers here also applies, by law, to all their salespersons.) But we're getting ahead of ourselves. Let's go over what buyer brokers *do* before we tell you how to pay them.

WHAT YOUR AGENT WILL DO

Buyer brokers represent buyers. As the client of a buyer broker, you have hired a broker or one of his/her licensed salespersons to act in your behalf in procuring a property that is acceptable to you. You have thus created an agency relationship and you are entitled to the same fiduciary responsibilities as a seller who signs a listing contract: loyalty, obedience (except if asked to break the law), confidentiality, reasonable care, diligence and competence, full disclosure, and accountability for all money received or held.

Your ideal agent will:

1. seek out property;

2. pre-inspect property;

3. accompany you on property inspections;

4. help you to determine market value;

5. negotiate in your interests; and

6. follow through to closing.

Let's look at how these activities will affect your time in the marketplace.

1. Your ideal agent will seek out the kind of property you describe using all available sources. He or she will knock on doors, call bank officers who handle REO portfolios, make phone calls to government offices, check out notices of foreclosures, auctions, and tax sales, dig through tax assessors' records for the names and addresses of owners, and examine the local MLS files with a fine-tooth comb.

2. Your ideal agent will pre-inspect potentially interesting properties for you and report to you on what is observed. Since you will develop a working relationship with your agent, he or she will get to know your preferences quickly and can save you innumerable hours of "road time" by checking out properties. You will be shown only those that qualify under the guidelines that you establish. (A sample Investment Property Preferences Worksheet appears at the end of this chapter. You might want to use it as a written record of your objectives and your directions to buyer brokers, or in fact to any real estate professionals with whom you work.)

3. Your ideal agent will accompany you on your inspection of the prospective properties pointing out both positives and negatives in structure, location, and topography. He or she will also help you to obtain and inspect records of rent receipts and gather information on taxes and other expenditures tied to property ownership.

4. Your ideal agent will help you to determine probable fair market value by supplying information about recently sold comparables, community statistics, and recent political developments in the area such as proposed tax reassessments or rate hikes. He or she will also discuss with you the current zoning of the area and keep you informed as to what is generally being said about possible upcoming changes. You can ask your buyer broker to get community facts such as school and recreational information for you.

5. Your ideal agent will negotiate on *your* behalf. You will take on the role of Clark and Lois in the puzzles we asked you to solve above. But take warning! Real estate professionals are human and they want to make the deal. NEVER disclose your next negotiating move before the move you are now making is fully played out. For example, don't say: "We're offering $180,000 but we can go to $190,000 if we have to." Simply offer $180,000 and see what happens. And to repeat: NEVER disclose your top dollar figure. Even the most reliable agents may negotiate one way when they think a figure is all they are going to get as an offer, and differently when they know they have room to spare.

6. Your ideal agent will follow through on financing, inspections, and other contingencies in the contract. If you are extremely time-pressured you can hand these responsibilities over to your agent, but realize that you are giving up a good deal of control. We recommend that you allow your agent to assist in the work that precedes closing while you keep in close touch with what is being done and finally make all the decisions.

HOW YOUR AGENT GETS PAID

Before buyer representation came into vogue, most buyer clients paid their procuring brokers set fees or a percentage of the acquisition price out of their own bank accounts. You may still have to do that, but in today's marketplace, there are many creative payment schedules which may reduce the actual amount of cash that you pay out to nothing, or to a minimal retainer fee.

The Retainer: As compensation for the initial professional counseling, consultations, and research, most brokers require buyer clients to pay a set fee upon signing the buyer agency contract. This fee is usually in the hundreds of dollars (not thousands) and it is nonrefundable. The entire fee that is paid upon signing, however, is almost always credited against the brokerage fee when a property is actually purchased.

The Flat Fee: A flat fee for the buyer broker's services can be any amount mutually acceptable to you and the broker. It can be paid in a lump sum up front (not recommended) or paid with a portion on signing the contract to hire the buyer broker and the remainder at the closing when title to the property passes. If you choose to work with on a flat fee basis, be certain that your buyer-broker contract contains a clause stating that any commission paid to the broker by the seller of the property you purchase is credited toward payment of the agreed-upon fee.

The Commission: You can make an agreement with your broker that he/she will be paid by a commission based upon the sale price of the property you purchase. Most buyer brokers who work on a commission basis also require a nonrefundable retainer paid upon signing. The percentage of the sale price upon which the commission is based is always negotiable in theory, but currently, the most common arrangement is half the going rate on listing contracts. Which means that if most sellers in your area are signing listing contracts that agree to pay brokers 6 percent, you as a buyer will agree to pay the buyer broker 3 percent upon closing.

This half-the-going-rate arrangement works out well in the current marketplace because most seller brokers are willing to split their commission with buyer brokers. Which means that having your own agent will cost you nothing, or very little.

Bailout Specifics: In working with bailout properties, be aware that the RTC has agreed to pay commission to any licensed real estate broker who sells their property. This usually means they will pay your buyer-broker's fee. When working with lending institutions in conservatorship, your buyer broker may approach a bank officer handling REO that has not been listed. The bank, however, may refuse to pay commission on the property, which would mean that you must pay your broker according to your agreement if you decide to purchase it. A creative agent, however, might approach the bank officer saying that he/she has a client for the property and ask for a one-week open listing. If the bank agrees, and they often do, commission would be paid by the seller (which is the bank). You must be aware, however, that the broker will be acting then as a *dual agent,* working both for the bank and for you. This dual agency relationship must be disclosed and agreed to in writing by both parties (you and the bank). Now all this may sound troubling to you, but in the practice of working with lending institutions in conservatorship, it works quite nicely and will save you money.

HOW TO HIRE AN AGENT

Using a buyer broker is especially recommended if you are buying in an area unfamiliar to you, if you have minimal time to commit to hunting for your investment properties, or if you are somewhat new to the real estate marketplace. Not only can buyer broker representation save you time and money, it can also contribute a good deal of professional expertise to your investment decision. Remember, however, that the buyer-broker agent is your hired business associate, not your friend. Our cardinal rule still applies: YOU must watch out for your own money.

To use a buyer broker, you must *hire* a broker, and that means a written contract. There are many, many forms of contractual agreements being used currently, everything from handwritten notes on yellow legal paper to neatly printed "standard" contracts. In fact, there is no such beast as a *standard contract,* but there certainly are standard clauses that you want to watch for in any buyer-broker contract you may sign. Check for the following points.

The date. No document is legal without a date.

A retainer agreement. The contract should state the names of all the persons who are hiring the buyer broker and designate them as the

Client. It should state that the Client retains *[name of broker]* for the purpose of locating a property the nature of which is described below or another property acceptable to the Client.

Term of the agreement. Every agreement should be made for a specified length of time and name a definite termination date. A buyer-broker contract should also include a clause stating that the agreement may be canceled by written notice from the Client at any time. (You should understand, however, that you cannot avoid paying a commission by canceling your buyer-broker contract and then buying the property your broker located for you. Legally, if the broker's work was a factor in your successful purchase, you owe that broker the commission you agreed to pay.)

General nature, location, and requirements of property. Your contract should indicate the type of property you are seeking, generally acceptable locations, price range, and any other specifications and conditions that might affect a decision to purchase.

The retainer fee. The initial dollar amount paid to the broker should be named and the contract should state that the broker acknowledges receipt of that fee. It should state that the fee is a compensation for initial counseling and research and is nonrefundable. A statement should be included, however, that the retainer fee is to be credited against the brokerage fee if the broker's efforts result in the client's purchase of property.

The brokerage fee. The fee that the client agrees to pay as compensation for locating an acceptable property and negotiating the purchase or exchange should be named either as a stated dollar amount or as an agreed-upon percentage of the acquisition price. A statement should be included that this fee is due and payable at the closing and only if title to the property passes to the client. Without this clause, a buyer could be held liable for the brokerage fee if a property goes to contract but never closes because of faulty title or other problems.

Seller payment of commission. The contract should include a statement that if the seller pays a commission and the buyer broker shares in that commission, the amount of the compensation will be credited against the brokerage fee due from the buyer-broker's client.

Broker's obligations. A statement should be included that the broker and the broker's sales agents agree to use diligence in working to locate a property acceptable to the client and in negotiating the terms of the purchase contract. The broker and the broker's sales agents must also agree that they will act for the Client only and will not accept a fee from the Seller unless full disclosure of it is made to the Client before the execution of a purchase contract.

Signatures. Be sure that this agreement is signed by a broker of record in the firm. The signature of a licensed salesperson will not create an agency relationship. It should also be signed by all the buyers named as Clients. Addresses and telephone numbers should be included and the signature of a witness to the agreement can do no harm.

We have included a sample of a buyer-broker contract now commonly in use at the end of this chapter. If you have any questions about this agency relationship, however, we strongly recommend that you consult a local attorney. Be sure to choose one who specializes in real estate–related law. Bear in mind also that you can add or delete from any printed contract that you are offered.

HOW TO FIND A BUYER BROKER

You can't hire a buyer broker if you can't find one. But you're in luck because today you can find a buyer broker almost anywhere. In fact, any licensed real estate broker can act in the interests of the buyer. All you need is a contract that establishes the agency relationship.

Why did we say that you'd meet mostly seller agents in the marketplace?

Because seller representation is still far more common than buyer representation. Real estate brokers have been primarily representing sellers for over seventy-five years and change comes slowly in this industry. But change *is* happening. Many agencies now have both buyer and seller clients. This arrangement gets into trouble only when a buyer wants to buy a property listed by his/her broker. Then the broker becomes the agent of both the seller and the buyer, even if different sales agents are working with the seller and the buyer, and a dual agency exists.

But don't despair even if you find yourself in this situation. Dual agency is not illegal as long as everyone is aware that it exists and agrees to proceed under those circumstances. It's still much better than the inaccurate perception that led Tom and Jerri to confide in Felix.

If you'd like to work with a broker who represents only buyers, you'll be pleased to know that their number is growing rapidly. For names of firms near you, you can call the Real Estate Buyers' Agents Council (REBAC) in Denver at (303) 292-5454.

WHAT MAKES AN AGENT GOOD?

We do mean *good at the job,* you understand! But being good at the job of a real estate agent can require considerable skill in the art of being a good person. It also means becoming good at a lot of things that don't seem related to the profession, like being a good host or hostess, being a good tour guide, and being good at networking. We'll stick to five primary areas of evaluation that will help you find a good agent—good enough to sail you through the process of buying bailout real estate.

1. *Experience.* Americans like to root for the underdog and most of us like to give promising beginners an opportunity to prove themselves. However, when you're dealing with many thousands of dollars—your dollars—it's better to work with someone who "knows the ropes." The agent you choose should have at least three years experience as a real estate professional. If not, you'll have to be extra careful about watching for mistakes, both yours and your agent's, because they *will* happen no matter how careful, hardworking, and well-intentioned everyone is.

2. *Professionalism.* Above all else you want to work with a full-time professional. The chemistry teacher who sells real estate afternoons, evenings, and during vacations may be a very intelligent, persevering, and conscientious person, but he or she simply cannot keep on top of the rapidly changing real estate marketplace and also carry another full-time job. No one can, and invariably the moonlighter loses some effectiveness in both jobs. You, as the real estate client, also lose a

competitive edge and might just miss the opportunity of a lifetime because your agent was busy at another job when notice came round of a hot new listing.

Also beware the dilettante. This agent may have only one job, in real estate, but he or she spends only a scattered number of hours a week at it, showing up in the office from time to time with no definite schedule. These people are often less aware of what's happening in the marketplace than the hard-working individuals who are carrying two jobs!

Professionalism also includes on-going study. Formal classroom work might be cited by letter designations after an agent's name on the business card. GRI, for example, stands for Graduate, Realtor Institute. Or you might notice diplomas, certificates, and citations displayed on the office walls behind your agent's desk. Other status symbols are success designations like the Million Dollar Club and the President's Club, or professional community awards like Realtor of the Year. You don't earn your way into these designations by sitting on your hands.

3. *Specialization.* You not only want an experienced real estate professional, you want one with experience in the particular kind of real estate that you want to buy. Don't shop for a co-op apartment with an agent who has sold only suburban tract houses. Don't shop for commercial property with a residential specialist. And land? Well, some larger agencies are opening land-specialty offices just because it takes more than a little extra knowledge to do the best job in this field.

4. *Local Knowledge.* Ideally, your agent should live in the town where you intend to buy. Residence makes a person more sensitive to the rumors that are always in the air in every community: the talk about the school system, proposed highway construction, zoning changes, environmental concerns, and a long list of other goings-on. An agent who lives in the town, or at least in a contiguous town, can tell you how people feel about living there, can point out the neighborhoods where turn-arounds are just beginning, can show you through the most desirable areas and explain why people want to live there, and can help you immensely in determining probable fair market value for the property that interests you. He or she is also more likely to

know people who live in the community. Why is that important? As we've said, some of the best real estate leads come from people talking with people in social situations.

5. *Personal Characteristics.* It's important that you feel comfortable working with your agent. Of course you want loyal, faithful, and true along with intelligent, persevering, attentive, prompt, polite, and practical. Maybe thorough, creative, and hardworking too. But with all the "good" qualities in the world, an agent may still have a personality that clashes with your personality. Such a clash can prove disastrous, so take the time and make the effort to find someone that you can work with. There's plenty of stress built right into the process of buying and selling property. You don't need a personality conflict with your agent to intensify it. On the other hand, a good working relationship can smooth the way through some pretty rough times.

INVESTMENT PROPERTY PREFERENCES WORKSHEET

TYPE OF PROPERTY

(your name) *(your phone)* PRIMARY INTERESTS: ✔ WILL CONSIDER: ✘	Single-family houses	Multi-family houses	Condominium apartments	Co-op apartments	Apartment buildings	Land	Mixed-use property	Commercial property	Others
Enter ✔, ✘, or leave blank:									

QUALIFYING FACTORS (rate 1 through 5—5 is most important)

Condition									
Cost-to-income ratio									
Price									
Financing									
Location									
Quick resale prospects									
Conversion possibilities									
Rehab possibilities									
Expansion possibilities									
Tax considerations									

Comments and specifics _____

_____

_____

_____

_____

Price range: $_____

Financing preferences: ☐ conventional mortgage ☐ all cash
☐ seller financing ☐ minimum down payment
☐ government assisted ☐ equity sharing

AGENT EVALUATION CHECKLIST

(name of agent)

(name of firm)

(telephone number)

	Plus ✔	Minus ✘	
Full-time professional			Less than full work week
3 + years experience			Less than 3 years
Experience in your investment vehicle			Generalist or experience in other vehicles
Local resident			Lives at some distance from investment area
Continuing study			No study beyond license test
Awards and designations			No awards
Attention to detail			Inaccurate or careless
Organized			Disorganized
Prompt reply to questions			Unable to answer questions
Follows directions			Does not carry out requests or disregards directions
Takes initiative			Must be monitored
Inspires trust			Inspires wariness
Pleasant to be with			Unpleasant to be with
TOTAL PLUS POINTS			TOTAL MINUS POINTS

SAMPLE BUYER-BROKER CONTRACT

Retainer Agreement: The undersigned, _____,

hereinafter designated as Client, hereby retains _____,

hereinafter designated as Broker, for the purpose of exclusively

assisting Client to locate property of a nature outlined below or

other property acceptable to Client, and to negotiate terms and

conditions acceptable to Client for purchase, exchange, lease, or

option of or on such property. This agreement shall commence

this date and terminate at midnight of _____.

General Nature, Location, and Requirements of Property:

_____

_____

_____

Price Range, and Other Terms and Conditions: _____

_____

_____

Retainer Fee: Client agrees to pay, and Broker acknowledges

receipt of a retainer of $_____, as compensation for initial

professional counseling, consultations, and research. Said fee is

nonrefundable, but shall be credited against the Brokerage Fee

under paragraph 4, below.

SAMPLE BUYER-BROKER CONTRACT *(continued)*

Brokerage Fee: Client agrees to pay Broker, as compensation for locating property acceptable to Client and negotiating the purchase or exchange, a fee of (check one) \$_____, or _____% of the acquisition price.

Client agrees further to pay Broker as compensation for obtaining an option on a property acceptable to Client a fee of \$_____, and to pay Broker the balance of a fee of _____% of the purchase price in the event the option is exercised or assigned prior to expiration of the option.

Client agrees further to pay Broker as compensation for locating a property acceptable to Client and negotiating a lease thereon a fee of \$_____ if:

1. Client or any other person acting for Client or in Client's behalf, purchases, exchanges, obtains an option for, or leases any real property of the nature described herein during the term hereof, through the services of Broker or otherwise.

2. Client or any other person acting for Client or in Client's behalf, purchases, exchanges, obtains an option for, or leases any real property of the nature described herein within one year after termination of this retainer, which property Broker, Broker's

SAMPLE BUYER-BROKER CONTRACT *(continued)*

agent, or cooperating brokers presented or submitted to Client during the term hereof and the description of which Broker shall have submitted in writing to Client, either in person or by mail, *within ten (10) days after termination of this contract.*

In the event the Seller, optionor, or lessor pays a fee under a listing agreement, and Broker, with the consent of Client, is entitled and has agreed to receive any portion thereof, that portion shall be credited against the obligations of Client hereunder.

It is understood that Broker may cooperate with other brokers and their agents in an effort to locate a property or properties in accordance with this agreement, and may share fees with them.

In the event legal action is instituted to enforce the terms of this agreement or arising out of the execution of this agreement, or to collect fees, the prevailing party shall be entitled to receive from the other party a reasonable attorney fee to be determined by the court in which such action is brought.

Notice: The amount or rate of real estate commissions is not fixed by law. They are set by each Broker individually and may be negotiable between the buyer and the broker.

SAMPLE BUYER-BROKER CONTRACT *(continued)*

Broker's Obligations: In consideration of Client's agreement set forth above, Broker agrees to use diligence in locating a property acceptable to Client and to negotiate terms and conditions for the purchase, exchange, or lease of said property or for obtaining an option on said property, acceptable to Client.

Broker agrees that he will act for Client only and will not accept a fee from the Seller, optionor, or lessor unless full disclosure thereof is made to Client prior to the execution of an offer to purchase, exchange, option, or lease.

Receipt of a copy of this agreement is hereby acknowledged.

Date: _____ Time: _____

_____ Broker _____ Client

_____ Address _____ Address

_____ Phone _____ Phone

By: _____

[Adapted from Professional Publishing Corp. Form 100. Used with permission.]

CHAPTER 8

INSPECTING THE PROPERTY

Can you differentiate between an *ohm,* an *amp,* and a *watt?*

"A watt?" you say. "Uhhh. . . ."

Don't feel discouraged. We're not electricians either. But as a real estate investor you may recognize *joist, girder, bleedout, efflorescence, fascia, flue, jamb,* and *pilaster.*

Confused?

Yes, we are still writing in English, but it's construction English and we chose those particular words to illustrate our point. That point is: IN ALL PROBABILITY, YOU DO NOT KNOW EVERYTHING THAT YOU *ABSOLUTELY* NEED TO KNOW IN ORDER TO INSPECT A PIECE OF PROPERTY EFFICIENTLY AND EFFECTIVELY.

Property inspection is one of the big keys-to-success in the real estate marketplace. Nothing can change a property's profit-or-loss profile more quickly than discovering a major structural problem or a myriad of minor problems. Making that discovery after you've turned over your down payment money at the closing table and assumed title to the property is disastrous. So take heed of our next piece of advice: USE THE SER-VICES OF PROFESSIONAL PROPERTY INSPECTION FIRMS.

THE CASE FOR PROFESSIONALS

The fee for a professional property inspection varies according to the type and price of the property and the geographic area of the nation. Two hundred and fifty dollars to $300 is a pretty average price for houses; commercial and investment property is usually higher. A good inspection, however, is worth many, many times the fee. Let's look at what makes an inspection *good*.

EXPERIENCE

Choose a firm that's been in business at least five years and tell the people in the office that you want an *experienced* inspector assigned to your property. No amount of reading and study can achieve the intuitive sense of condition and quality that a person develops with experience. Even if you're a seasoned and frequent investor, you've probably inspected for purchase no more than ten properties a year. The professional inspector is likely to inspect one hundred or more properties a year. You just can't catch up to that kind of specialized experience.

PERSPECTIVE

Whenever you're looking at a piece of property that you think you want to buy, you're *involved*. And when you're involved, you see things. Sometimes you may see things because you want them to be there and sometimes you may see things as you want them to be even though they aren't that way at all. On the other hand, sometimes you may *not* see things because you don't want them to be there.

The professional inspector is not involved in your deal. He or she has nothing to lose or gain because of what's there or not there. This professional perspective is priceless. His/her rational judgment will help to keep your investment decision a good one.

METHODOLOGY

Most people who do their own inspections start in the basement or attic and work through each room. They run faucets, flush toilets, switch the lights, start the furnace, and metaphorically kick the tires. They think that they're doing a very thorough job, and almost always, they miss something, sometimes many things.

Unlike the typical buyer who's equipped only with a flashlight and determination, the professional inspector comes to the property with a clipboard holding an extensive checklist. The only spaces filled in on that checklist are those for your name and the address of the property you are considering. Completion or acknowledgment of consideration for every other space is required by the inspection firm. Merely by filling in the blanks therefore, the chances of missing an important evaluation factor are virtually eliminated.

In addition, experience acts as an override. As the inspector fills out the checklist, he or she uses the same methodology and walks the same route that has been walked through many other buildings at many other times. It's like playing a piece of piano music that you've practiced many, many times: you know immediately if you hit a wrong note, or if you skip a passage.

JUDGMENT STANDARDS

Construction materials, working systems, and appliances all have life expectancies. Professional inspection firms know the probable functioning time for construction and working systems in local climate conditions. As a part of the inspection process, inspectors will determine the age of the various systems and structures and tell you how much longer they are likely to last. "You'll probably need a new roof in three to five years" is the kind of warning that helps a prospective buyer to plot probable cash flow more accurately.

A WRITTEN REPORT

Many buyers who refuse to hire inspection firms wake in the middle of the night thinking, "Did I check the . . ." or "I wonder if that funny sound when the toilet flushed really was 'nothing' like everybody said." Going back the next day for a second look is embarrassing; not going back can be even more excruciating—and financially dangerous.

The written report is a wonderful soother of raw nerves and protector of delicate pride. You can read it over as many times as you need to. If there's a reference to something that's questionable, you can point out the passage to the real estate agent while you're making an appointment for another inspection with a plumber, electrician, carpenter, or whoever else might be able to render a more specialized opinion. You can even use the written report to negotiate a lower price than agreed to on the contract. (More about that in Chapter 10.)

A WARRANTY

For a small additional fee, many professional inspection firms will back up their written reports with a warranty. There's usually a deductible, much like medical or car insurance, but beyond that $100 to $250 figure, the warranty will usually pick up the tab for repairs to whatever goes wrong involving systems, structure soundness, and appliances. The warranty period is usually one year, although some longer warranties are available through some firms.

We believe home inspection warranties are well worth their price. Those first few years of ownership are always the tightest financially and a warranty could keep you solvent, not to mention its benefits in getting a good night's sleep!

WHAT THEY WON'T DO

The professional inspection will give you a detailed evaluation of the condition of the property. That's it. Don't ask the inspector if the price is right or if you should buy. That's your decision. *You* must answer the question, "Is this a good deal?" The information provided by the property inspection firm will help you.

SOME CONSIDERATIONS

Here are a few more facts, just in case you still aren't completely convinced that professional help in the property inspection process is absolutely essential. See how many times you can answer *yes* to the following DID YOU KNOW? questions.

1. Did you know that most RTC properties are being sold in "as is" condition? *As is* means that you get what's there. The seller makes no

promises. The water could be undrinkable, the foundation could be buckling, the ridge board and rafters could be rotting. Once you take title to the property, the problems are all yours.

We think, no, we *know* it's a good idea to be aware of as many of the problems as is humanly possible *before* you take title. In fact, in dealing with the RTC, you should have your inspection done before you submit your offer on a written contract to buy. (There are some other ways to work negotiating about condition with the RTC—see Chapter 10.)

2. Did you know that there are government programs called 203 K loans that will actually provide you with mortgage money to make necessary repairs that are identified before the purchase contract is signed? Under this program you can actually buy property with "nothing down"! More details in Chapter 12.

3. Did you know that in most cities and towns across the nation building codes require that a deck or porch have the vertical posts of a railing close enough together so that a child cannot get his or her head between them? If a previous owner added a do-it-yourself deck to his property, a nonconforming deck with wide spaces between the vertical posts and built without a building permit (this happens a lot), you, the new owner, would have to rebuild the railing, if someone complained. You could be sued if a child was hurt trying to squeeze between the posts on your "illegal" railing.

4. Did you know that old houses can change ownership and continue in use even though they don't meet current building codes? They are said to be "grandfathered" because they existed before the codes were written. If you bought one of these old houses and decided to make some improvements that required a building permit, did you know that you could be required to bring the entire house up to current code? The cost could be colossal.

5. Did you know that if you convert a building from one use to another (let's say residential to business use), you will be required to meet the building codes for the new use? This requirement could cost thousands in new exit doors, fire warning systems and sprinklers, plumbing, and landscaping.

Your property inspection firm will not answer all your questions as to your legal responsibilities in the property. But they can point out potential trouble areas and direct you to sources of information. Being forewarned in the real estate business is worth big bucks.

WHAT THE INSPECTOR WILL INSPECT

We strongly recommend that you accompany your inspector on the inspection tour of the property. Most inspection firms welcome buyer participation and a great deal can be learned from the conversation that transpires during the working time of the inspector.

Wear old clothes (you may have to do some crawling and climbing) and bring along your own flashlight and a pad and paper for making notes. If you are considering a property that may need extensive repair, you might also want to bring along a camera with a flash. The pictures you take might become powerful negotiating tools.

THE FOUNDATION

The foundation is what the house rests upon. It usually extends below or partly below ground level. A foundation can be carefully piled stones (many old foundations were and still are) or it can be a concrete slab, or at the other end of the spectrum a full, walk-out basement with a finished living space.

To prevent termite infestation and dry rot, all wood parts of a building should be at least six inches off the ground. In today's construction practices, when there is no excavation, a slab is usually used to accomplish this raising up. If you are buying a property built on a slab, have your inspector question the owner regarding its construction. A slab should be poured over a layer of crushed rock, and a permanent vapor barrier (usually a polyethylene plastic sheet) should separate the living area from the foundation. If the owner has no information on the construction, you can go to your town's Buildings Department. Ask what codes were in effect when the property was built. Unless some illegal construction occurred, your building will have met the building code requirements in force at the time it was built.

If you observe only hairline cracks in the slab, you probably don't need to be concerned, although you might mention them to your inspector. Major separations (big cracks) or extensive crumbling especially at the corners of a building can spell serious trouble.

A foundation that lifts a building eighteen to thirty-six inches off the ground is usually called a crawl space. If the lowest level of this space is the ground itself, watch out! When a crawl space is not floored with poured concrete, serious ventilation problems can result from the dampness of the ground below. Moisture can build up and eventually rot the joists (support beams for the floors of the living area). Trapped moisture in a crawl space can also send harmful ground vapor into the building.

Don't avoid inspecting the crawl space because it is uncomfortable and difficult. If it does have a dirt floor, be certain that there are ventilation openings at each corner and that they cannot be closed. If the crawl space is floored and heated, the venting is unnecessary.

If your building is built over a basement, the space from floor to joists will probably be seven feet high. Basements therefore are much easier to inspect than crawl spaces and most inspectors start there.

Most likely your inspector will first look for signs of water. Wet basements are a homeowner's nightmare and can often kill a prospective sale. Question the inspector if you see puddle-like, irregular stains on the floor or a white line at the same level around the entire foundation (could be a high-water mark). White fuzz growing on the walls is called efflores-cence. It's caused by moisture mixing with acids in the concrete and it indicates moisture behind the walls. Ask your inspector to evaluate this problem if you see it. Slight efflorescence is usually tolerable. Heavy can mean that you'll be paying the bill to have drainage tiles installed around the building.

Some home inspection firms do termite and radon inspections as a part of their package. In some areas of the country, however, these inspections must be done by specialized firms because lending institu-tions require their reports before they will write a mortgage. As you know, termites are wood-eating insects that can eventually destroy the infrastructure of a building. Radon is a colorless, odorless, tasteless gas with radioactive qualities. Long exposure to it can cause health problems.

If you are buying a single condominium or co-operative apartment, the home inspection fee can be structured in two ways. It can cover the apartment itself or it can also include an inspection of the common areas. Not all home inspection firms will do common area inspections but in all cases, you must get permission from the board of directors or at least from the superintendent of the building in order to do one. The warranties that can be purchased with home inspections do not cover common-area structures and systems.

"So why bother?" you may wonder.

Because major faults in the common areas (the need for new roofing, water problems in the basement, an antiquated elevator, for example) can send your monthly maintenance fee into the stratosphere. High monthly maintenance fees make resale more difficult and can even lower the value of a unit.

THE WORKING SYSTEMS

If the building you are buying uses well water, a potability test of the water will almost certainly be required. The mortgage lender will want to be sure that the drinking water is safe, since resale is virtually impossible without a source of safe water. Most inspection firms take the water samples, deliver them to a lab, and then include the results of the testing in their written report. In this age of environmental jitters, some lenders are even requiring potability tests when the water source is a municipal supply. And actually, it's not a bad idea.

Speaking of water, you mustn't forget to evaluate the hot water system. Find out what method of heating and storing hot water is used. How old is it? (Hot water tanks have a life span of ten to fifteen years. If they spring a leak while you're away on vacation, you might just return to a basement full of water!) Is the supply adequate for the type of occupancy you plan for the building?

Your participation in the inspection of the property's electrical systems will probably be confined to counting the outlets in each room and noting if the place uses circuit breakers or fuses. Your inspector will check the level of available power. If you plan to convert the building to commercial use, talk with him or her about the amount of electrical service you'll probably need. This information may not figure into negotiating but it will help you to determine if electrical work will be a factor in your cash flow considerations.

There are three main concerns about the heating system in a building. Is it safe? Does it provide enough heat? And how much does it cost? Ask your inspector for the answers to these questions. Heating evaluation is not a job for do-it-yourselfers.

Nor is plumbing, although virtually every prospective home buyer runs the water in the shower. Your inspector will check for leaks under all the sinks and around the toilets, but the real evaluation of the plumbing will be done in the basement. That's where the supply pipes can be seen.

Ask your inspector what kind of pipes are in use. Some old properties still have functioning systems with cast iron pipes. Buildup inside cast iron pipes reduces the water flow as the years go by, so you may only get a trickle from an upstairs faucet. You can test for cast iron by carrying a small magnet in your pocket. The magnet will be attracted to cast iron, but will not be attracted to copper pipes.

In some new construction, plastic piping is being used, especially for waste disposal pipes. Although plastic as a plumbing material seems to be working well, it is still too new to have been tested by long, hard, and sustained use.

Room air conditioners are often removed when property changes hands or they are negotiated as separate items in the contract. Central air conditioning is as complicated as heating and should be checked by your professional inspector.

Appliances that are to remain with the building (stoves, ovens, dishwashers, washing machines, dryers, etc.) are usually checked by the inspector to be certain that they are in working order. If your purchase contract reads that these appliances are to be in working order when the property changes hands, be prepared to recheck them during the day-of-the-closing inspection. (More about final inspections in Chapter 13.)

If you've ever been in a room when someone tried to start a fire in a fireplace that didn't work, or didn't work well, you know why we placed this paragraph under THE WORKING SYSTEMS. A faulty fireplace can fill a room and indeed a whole house with smoke. Have your inspector check the draft of each fireplace in the property. Also check outside to be absolutely certain that the fireplace is not pulling away from the house. This doesn't happen often but when it does, it's a major structural repair.

You may wonder why we've also included doors and windows under THE WORKING SYSTEMS. Well, they *must* work. Your inspector should check every window for ease of movement. Self-insulating (double pane) windows should be checked for the effectiveness of their seals, since these can become less than perfect as time goes by. What was then designed to keep the cold air out will allow it to flow in.

Doors should open and close freely. Note doors that stick, since they can be a sign of uneven settling, poor construction, or improper hanging. Or they might simply need to be planed down a bit.

FLOORS

Spots that creak on wood floors are common and usually not of concern. If all or some rooms have floor covering, ask your inspector to find out what's under the installed wall-to-wall carpeting. Much new construction uses plywood sub-floors, which means you're committed to carpeting as long as you own the property or to the high cost of installing new wood floors.

Tongue-and-groove hardwood floors are still the most highly valued floors, even if they are much worn and in need of sanding and refinishing. Tile floors in bathrooms (and sometimes in kitchens) should be inspected for broken tiles and missing grout.

As you walk through the house looking at the floors, look also at the baseboards. Moldings should not be separated from the floor. If there are gaps of a quarter inch or more, it usually indicates shoddy construction, the use of green lumber, uneven settling of the house, or a combination of all three.

WALLS AND CEILINGS

If you see diagonal cracks running from the corners of door jambs to the ceiling, the property has probably settled unevenly. Ask your inspector to evaluate the severity of the problem. It could be "nothing" and it could be the start of something big.

Popped nails and wallboard taping that can be seen through paint or wallpaper are aesthetic but not structural objections. Plaster walls should not be crumbling or dotted with unpatched nail holes. Plaster ceilings should not be lined with cracks. Plaster ceilings *can* fall down and you don't want to be the owner of one that does.

THE ATTIC

Your inspector should be agile enough to get up on the beams of the attic if necessary. Not all attics are completely floored but lack of a floor should not prevent an inspection because, like the basement, the attic is an area where much can be learned about the structure of the building. Your inspector will note the type, location, and amount of insulation that is visible. He or she will also shine a flashlight beam along the rafters and the ridge beam looking for irregular water stains which would indicate a leaky roof. Finally, there's the pest hunt. Squirrels, mice, bats, and birds sometimes live in attics. You do not want these guests!

THE ROOF

Whenever possible, an inspector will actually climb onto your prospective roof. He or she will check the shingles first. If a self-sealing asphalt roof is over fifteen years old, barren places where the granular mineral coating is worn away will indicate the imminent need for a new roof, even if there have been no leaks.

The inspector will also check your flashings. Now don't raise your eyebrows! Flashings are not rapidly waved raincoats, although they do function to keep the rain out of the house. The flashings on the roof are molded and shaped strips that act as barriers against water. They are installed at points where two roof angles meet or where something like a chimney or vent pipe protrudes through the roof. Flashings that look faulty can be resealed at a relatively small cost and may in fact be the reason for a leaky roof.

Gutters and downspouts are usually inspected at the same time as the roof. These structural additions are needed to control the flow of rainwater or melting snow from the roof. Most are made of aluminum today. You may, however, run across older properties with wooden gutters, which should be carefully inspected for rot. All gutters should be kept free of debris. Downspouts should be positioned so that the collected water is channeled away from the foundation of the building.

THE SIDING

The siding is what you see on the vertical plane when you look at the outside of a building. It might be brick, vinyl, aluminum, stucco, stone, wood, or (in the case of office buildings) glass. Your property inspector will check its condition and advise you as to how much time is probable before repair or special maintenance is needed.

PORCHES AND DECKS

Many porches and decks are added by homeowners doing-it-themselves. Your inspector, therefore, should check the structural soundness with extra care. The boards of a wooden deck should not complain if a 190-pound man jumps up and down on them.

THE LAND

Some home buyers are so focused on testing every system in the building that they forget to inspect the land. This is a *major* error. Problems on the land can cost many thousands of dollars, and some cannot be remedied. Drainage and grading, for example. Good grading takes water away from the foundation and helps to prevent wet basements. The best grading in the world, however, can't solve the basement water problem of a house built over a natural spring or in an area where the water table is very high.

Ask your inspector also if he or she knows what type of soil is common in the area. Sandy or gravelly soil usually has good drainage. Soil that is primarily clay will hold water and be difficult to drain no matter what you do.

The character of the soil and the lay of the land is particularly important if waste disposal in a building depends upon a septic tank. If that is your situation, have the property inspector or the real estate agent get information on the location of the septic tank, the dry well, and/or the leech lines. Leech lines are trails of gravel under the surface that lead the effluent away from the septic tank and allow it to drain into the land.

If your seller does not have information on the location of the waste disposal system, you may be able to get what you need at the Buildings Department of the town. Many municipalities keep records of building permits which also include the location of waste disposal systems.

If you are absolutely unable to locate records, walk the property, every inch of it. Look for "bleedout," which is a term for effluent from the system that is rising to the surface rather than draining into the ground. A bleedout area need not be wet on the day you see it. Watch for areas where gnats are hovering or look for particularly green lines through an otherwise sun-burned lawn. Take the time to do this inspection, since repairing waste disposal systems can be very expensive.

While doing your land inspection, try to have a copy of the survey in hand. (You can have the real estate agent ask the seller for it.) Walk the property lines and check for encroachments. Encroachments are buildings or parts of buildings belonging to your neighbors which extend onto *your* property.

If you find a suspicious tree house, doghouse, garden shed, or garage, check more carefully, even if you must pay for a surveyor. Encroachments make a property more difficult to sell and if they are allowed to remain for a certain period of time (the length of time is determined by statute in each municipality) the piece of land upon which they stand can revert to the owner of the building. This can be prevented without tearing down the encroaching building, however. More in Chapter 14.

HOW TO CHOOSE A PROPERTY INSPECTION FIRM

Do not ask your real estate agent to recommend someone. Most home inspection firms are reputable and reliable, but recommendation by a real estate agent who has a stake in the commission from the sale comes very close to conflict of interest. Think about it: you own a home inspection firm and you are often recommended by a particular real estate agent. If there are marginal questions about a property, will you phrase your report in a way that will make the buyer anxious and perhaps blow the deal? Or will you soft-pedal the information? Enough said.

A good place to get recommendations for a home inspection firm is your prospective lender. Banks want the properties upon which they hold mortgages to be in the best shape possible. They would urge an inspector to be especially careful and thorough.

You might also ask friends who have recently used an inspection service for evaluations of their firms. Or you can let your fingers do the walking and consult the yellow pages of your telephone book, looking for those advertisements that mention years in business and the availability of warranties.

If you want to hire an inspection firm for a house or other residential property, you can also call or write to the American Society of Home Inspectors. Founded in 1976, this trade group sets standards for the industry and will recommend member firms in the area where you plan to buy. They are at 3299 K Street, NW (7th floor), Washington, DC, 20007. Telephone: (202) 842-3096.

If you are buying commercial property, a large apartment building, land, or some other unusual investment, you might want to contact the American Consulting Engineers Council. They can recommend people in the specialty or specialties you need. Contact them at 1015 15th Street, NW, Washington, DC, 20005. Telephone: (202) 347-7474.

FIVE REASONS NOT TO BUY

1. Unsafe or inadequate drinking water.

2. A nonfunctioning or malfunctioning sewer or septic system.

3. Uneven settling causing structural stress or a buckling foundation.

4. Uncontrollable basement water problems.

5. A sagging ridge beam under the roof.

CHAPTER 9

THE POWER OF
A GROUP

Unless you live near Phoenix, Arizona, you probably haven't heard about Grove East, a development that was planned to be a lovely neighborhood of custom-designed homes in Mesa, Arizona. Because of the default of the developer, fifty-seven of the lots in the one-hundred-and-one-home subdivision reverted back to the lending institution that was financing the project. When the lending institution also went under, the lots became the property of the RTC.

"So there are fifty-seven building lots for sale in Arizona," you say. "That's *not* news!"

Not by itself. The news is that the homeowners who live in the already completed homes are fighting the RTC's efforts to sell the lots.

"How can they do that?" you ask. "These are legal building lots, right? The RTC has a right to sell them just like any other lots."

That's true, if they were planning to sell them just like any other lots. But the RTC is trying to arrange a package deal. Instead of marketing individual lots to individual home buyers (which is a *very* slow process), the RTC wants to sell in bulk. The Consolidated Office wants to find another developer who'll pay a lump sum for all fifty-seven lots and take over.

The current homeowners in Grove East are protesting not because they want to keep the vacant lots vacant but because the RTC plans to sell the bulk piece for about half of what the lots are probably worth if sold individually on the open market. (Appraisal figures can and do differ when estimating the market value of individual lots and estimating the market value of a tract of land.) If a savvy builder picks up the whole bundle of lots at a heavily discounted price, some homeowners feel that he might choose to build smaller, more affordable housing in order to sell more quickly. That possibility is disturbing because current residents foresee the homogeneity of the neighborhood being shattered and with it some portion of their property value.

The Grove East homeowners may or may not be right. But let's look at this deal from some other perspectives. Think of the RTC, under pressure to divest itself of some of its nonperforming assets as quickly as possible. Then think of yourself as a builder who needs land in order to work at his trade and make a living. Half-price lots in an area where the subdivision is approved and the streets and utilities are in! Bonanza!!!

As a smart businessman, you, the builder, would look at the demographics of the area, identify the foremost housing need of the next three to five years, and get right down to the business of filling that need. And if you're smarter yet, you won't leave the RTC office without talking about a deal to finance the purchase at favorable rates and terms. Meanwhile, you're thinking, "What a gold mine!"

"Sounds good for the developer," you say. "But I'm not a developer, I'm an investor. I'm looking for a place to put my money so that it will grow and multiply. And besides, I think these numbers are probably too big for me. Even if the developer only needs to put 15 percent down to buy this land, he's going to need working capital too. I think there's probably a lot of zeros after the first number in this deal! This is no place for the individual investor trying to make a few bucks in his spare time."

You're right! But this is an opportunity for a group investment deal. Group power may be one of the best ways to make money in the bailout. In its effort to dispose of property quickly, the RTC is actively exploring package deals. We recently heard of an investor in Jacksonville, Florida, who bought twenty REO condo apartments in one building for less than half their individual going rate.

In fact, if you're really a creative investor, there are likely to be some even bigger and stranger deals available in the near future. The RTC now has under consideration some co-fiduciary ventures. The idea on the drawing boards is to group selected properties into $500 million packages. RTC officials are talking about selling these at approximately a 20 percent discount (down to $400 million), offering financing, and (here's the catch) retaining a share interest in the possible proceeds of the later resale of the individual properties in the package. In other words, the RTC is willing to become a partner in the deal.

If $400 million sounds like an impossible amount of money, just remember that you don't have to have it, you just have to think about how you can get a share in it. All you really need is motivation, some expertise in working with the type of assets being sold, a group of people willing to invest, a good credit record, and ideally, a track record in successful real estate transactions.

"Hold it!" you say. "All you really need . . . Are you kidding? The list that follows your 'All you really need' is pretty stiff!"

Well, yes. But the nice part is that no one person has to have all of these attributes. If you form a group, it might include a developer, a previously successful investor, a property manager, a CPA, or a lawyer and a lot of people who work hard, save money, and pay their bills.

If numbers in the millions are still putting you off, you must remember that group purchases are not limited strictly to mega-deals. You can form a group to purchase a small apartment building, a working gas station, or a vacation home that you will share the use of in rotating weeks. If you've been hesitant about getting in on the bailout because you don't have a great deal of spare cash, group purchasing may be your ticket.

PARTNERSHIPS

A partnership can be two people or any number of people. The partners can be equal or unequal. And the association can be formed with a simple handshake or extensive legal documents. Your goal is to find the partnership form that fits your needs.

Most small-group partnerships are composed entirely of *general partners*. There is another partnership category called *limited partners*, which we'll discuss shortly (it's more complicated). Right now, let's look at what you buy into when you enter a general partnership.

General partners have personal liability for all the debts generated by the partnership. (If your partner decides to buy a yacht in the company name, you're just as responsible for payments as he is.) General partners also take an active role in the decision-making process of the business. In the event of the death, withdrawal, retirement, or insanity of a general partner, the partnership as originally structured is dissolved. A new partnership of the remaining members can be formed, however.

One of the chief advantages of the partnership is the pass-through income tax rules. In the eyes of the IRS the partnership is not a taxable entity. Instead, each partner assumes and reports his or her portion of income or loss (paper or otherwise) from the business. An apportioned share of depreciation and management/maintenance costs is also legal deductions, as is interest paid on the individual partner's share of the debt.

A partnership acts as a single party in the purchase and sale of real estate, although all of the partners' names may be required on purchase and sale contracts, deeds, etc. Within the partnership, individual members may have equal voting power or power accorded to the size of their investment. If everyone is equal, we suggest that you try to form your partnership with an odd number of members to forestall the paralysis and eventual discord of an equal number of people with opposite opinions.

A specific kind of partnership is the angel/worker arrangement. Let's say you and your cousin are excellent at renovation work but have little or no spare cash. Your dentist has a good deal of cash to invest, but no spare time. You can form a partnership to buy a group of run-down houses from the RTC. The dentist puts up the down payment and the working capital and may or may not take care of the record keeping, you and your cousin find the property, negotiate the deal, do all the work of renovating, and then market and sell the property. You split the profits. For the workers, this arrangement is an opportunity to invest in a real estate project with no money down; for the angel, it is an investment with the possibility of excellent return requiring minimal time and effort.

When this angel/worker arrangement is put together in big numbers, with a bank, insurance company, pension fund, S&L, or the RTC as the source of money, and with a group or company supervising the construction or conversion project, it's called a *joint venture*. Joint ventures are almost always general partnerships when you get past the legal rhetoric. The lending partner supplies the money; the working partner supplies the planning, vision, management, equipment, manpower, and labor. They split the positive cash flow, the tax benefits, and the profit when the property is sold. The split is divided according to whatever prearranged agreement they made.

The chief criteria for becoming a lending partner are the availability of money and the willingness to invest it. The chief criteria for qualifying as a working partner are a good track record in the kind of investment property you wish to buy and a good credit history.

But what about the rest of us, the small investors? Sometimes private partnerships (a group of coworkers both investing their money and working together) begin functioning so well as second-income businesses that the members want to give up their primary jobs and focus on the partnership. Nothing wrong with that. Except that many partners then think it's time to incorporate. This could work, but it could also be disadvantageous to your particular business. Be sure to get advice from an attorney and a CPA before you take such a step.

CORPORATIONS

Incorporating a business has advantages and disadvantages. The biggest disadvantage for the small business person is double taxation. The corporation is taxed on its profits and then the corporate stockholders are taxed on their dividends. Right behind double taxation, however, is the inability to pass losses along to stockholders.

"That doesn't sound like a disadvantage to me!" you say. "Why would I want to take on the losses of a business if I didn't have to?"

Because the losses are often on paper. Even in this post-1986 tax reform era, there are still depreciation benefits to owning real estate, especially for small investors. If you own shares of stock in a corporation that owns real estate, however, the corporation can deduct depreciation against its income, but *you* cannot. There is a form of corporate ownership that skirts this problem, however. We'll talk about it (subchapter S) just as soon as we tell you the *advantages* of becoming a corporation.

Once you form a corporation, you form an artificial person. That artificial person has the high profile, is identified as the "owner" or "landlord," and is responsible for the debts and liabilities incurred. You, the owners of stock in the corporation, have anonymity. No one ever need know who you are or where you live. You are also not responsible for the debts generated by acts of the corporation and you cannot be sued. And finally, one member of a corporation can sell his or her shares and leave the working group without dissolving the corporation, whereas one member's leaving the group would dissolve a partnership. Thus a corporate arrangement does give you liquidity and a certain amount of freedom.

SUBCHAPTER S CORPORATIONS

A subchapter S corporation acts like a corporation and is taxed like a partnership. It must not include more than thirty-five shareholders (husband and wife count as one shareholder), it must be a domestic corporation, it can have only one class of stock, only U.S. resident humans (no corporations) can be shareholders, and it may not own more than 80 percent of another corporation. In other words, an S corporation is a small business.

It is not taxed as a corporation; rather, each shareholder is taxed on his/her share of the profits as ordinary income. It may also pass along losses to its shareholders. In terms of real estate, however, rental income may be treated as a passive investment. Active investment exceptions would be a group of people who managed a hotel or motel, parking garages, equipment rental businesses, etc., where considerable service is required with the real estate holdings.

There have been whole books written on Subchapter S corporations and we obviously can't cover this business form completely here. If you are interested in exploring it further, you should consult with your attorney and a tax advisor. In most cases involving real estate investments, however, we recommend the limited partnership or the friendly syndicate as vehicles more appropriate and more advantageous to small investors and investor groups.

LIMITED PARTNERSHIPS

Limited partnerships are composed of a general partner or partners and any number of limited partners. General partners conduct the business of the partnership and have personal liability for all the debts of the partnership. The limited partners, however, have *no* say in the decisions of the business and are responsible for the debts of the partnership only to the limit of the money they have invested. Usually they cannot transfer their interest in the partnership without the consent of the general partners and they cannot continue the partnership without the general partners. Limited partnerships are taxed as partnerships.

Limited partnerships are a great way to buy real estate if you and a few friends have a good track record in real estate investment and you can convince a number of hands-off passive investors to support you in the purchase of a money-making investment. You must be cautious, however, and use competent legal advisors in forming your limited partnership because the Securities and Exchange Commission (SEC) regulates some limited partnerships and the Internal Revenue Service (IRS) is always there to check that your limited partnership isn't really a corporation and subject to corporate taxes.

HOW *NOT* TO BE A CORPORATION

The law says that a limited partnership must have no more than two of the characteristics of a corporation in order not to be taxed as a corporation. Let's look at the characteristics of a corporation and see how to avoid being considered one.

Centralization of Management. Since the general partners have complete control and the limited partners have no say, a limited partnership does qualify as having centralized management.

Limited Liability. If a corporation folds with a couple of million in outstanding debts, each shareholder loses only the price he or she paid for the shares. If a limited partnership folds, the limited partners also will lose only the value of their shareholdings. (The general partners must face the music, however.) Because of the limited liability of the limited partners, the corporation and the limited partnership are again alike.

Continuity. A corporation lasts forever, in theory anyway. The death or insanity of the CEO might cause something like an earthquake, but the position will be filled and the company will go on. In differentiating itself from a corporation, a limited partnership provides that in the event of the departure of one of the general partners, the limited partnership is dissolved. (It can be re-formed with a new list of general partners, however.) Point one in differentiating from a corporation therefore: the limited partnership does not have continuity.

Transferability of Ownership Interest. In a corporation you can choose to sell your ownership interest (shares) whenever you want. To fulfill the necessary second distinguishing feature from a corporation, a limited partnership usually requires that share interests cannot be transferred except back to the general partners or with the general partners' permission.

LEGAL STRINGS

The governing statute for limited partnerships is the Uniform Limited Partnership Act of 1916, as revised in 1976. The only trouble is that the act is not uniform in every state. Some states still use the 1916 version, others use the 1976 version, and many have added more than an idea or restriction or two of their own. Which means: if you're getting into this as a real estate vehicle, be sure to use a local attorney who is familiar with partnership law in your state.

The Uniform Limited Partnership Act requires that a new limited partnership make a public filing of a certificate of limited partnership that sets forth its name, the character, location, and term of its business enterprise, and the names of capital contributors and the profit share of the partners.

"Is that all there is to it?" you say. "Gosh, I could almost do that myself."

Don't even try. The procedure differs in each state and you could waste months going to the wrong department in the wrong building with the wrong forms signed by the wrong people. And you've still got to watch out for the SEC.

What have they got to do with your little effort to get a group together and make some money?

Well, if you cross a state line in marketing your limited partnership, the SEC can call you on the carpet for selling securities interstate. By law, if you want to sell securities interstate, you must register with the SEC and that procedure is both time-consuming (months) and expensive ($50,000 would be a very conservative estimate).

Now if you're just about to flip to the next chapter to see what else there might be for you, hold on a minute. It *is* possible to form a limited partnership with a minimal amount of legal paperwork. Also, you *can* make money through a limited partnership while contributing no money, only your time and talent. Keep reading.

Before we tell you how to avoid federal supervision, you must know that many states get into the act also. They oversee limited partnerships with so-called Blue Sky Laws. The supervising state agencies get their authority from the state's police powers, the laws being designed in theory to protect investors by requiring registration and disclosure of certain information in a certain format. Blue Sky Laws are nonexistent in some states, while in others they are demanding and exacting. Among those states with extensive legislation are: California, Illinois, New York, Ohio, and Texas.

Those are the snares and pitfalls. Now let us tell you how to make money in group investing while avoiding entanglements.

THE FRIENDLY SYNDICATE

There's no state in the union that prohibits a few friends from forming a partnership to buy real estate. And that's all you need if you want to buy a fixer-upper, or a four-family house, or perhaps a small business. But if you want to get into the seven-figure bargains in the bailout, you'll need more people and more structure. This is where the friendly syndicate comes in.

The friendly syndicate, your syndicate, is a limited partnership. To avoid the expense of registration and regulation it is essential to do the following:

- Limit your investor group to a small group of relatives, friends, and associates. People you know in some way, or who are friends of friends, or who share membership in a group with you. You can avoid SEC snooping if you keep the number under thirty-five. (Husband and wife count as one.)

- Form your syndicate and do business in the same state in which the property you want to buy is located.

- Make your offering of limited partnership shares only to residents of the state where you do business and where the property is located.

- Do not advertise your offering publicly. Make your presentations on a one-to-one basis, or at most to the number of people who can sit comfortably in someone's living room.

- Be absolutely certain that you do not break the laws of your state concerning fraud and equity.

Okay, now you have the structure and the rules, you're ready to make money. Let's follow Maximilian Smart through a deal. We'll be working with relatively small numbers here for the sake of clarity. You can add more zeros if you like.

Max has been watching a small waterfront motel on Florida's Longboat Key. It has been dwarfed by the new construction around it during the past few years and it generally looks a bit shabby. Room rent is among the cheapest on the island. Despite the magnificent location, there are virtually always vacant rooms available.

Three years ago, a group had bought the motel to try a time-share condominium conversion. They spruced up a model by converting the standard hotel room to a studio, with kitchenette. But the buying public didn't go for it. The marketing team sold a few units at below asking price and then quit. The lending institution took over. The time-share buyers were up in arms. They stopped mortgage payments, filed suit, and finally settled with the lender-now-owner to get out of the deal.

The lender then had a motel again and hired a management company to run it. They didn't choose too well, however, and maintenance and service went steadily downhill. The property was put up for sale for $1.5 million. Meanwhile it was losing money each and every month.

Then the lending institution that owned the motel failed also and went into conservatorship. Max knew the time was right for the deal he wanted and began to do some calculations. He figured he could purchase for $1,000,000—arriving at that figure because of the monthly loss reports and the desire of the lending institution to get rid of as much REO as possible before the RTC actually took over.

Max figured that he could turn the motel into a positive cash flow investment within a year while carrying a $500,000 mortgage. Knowing the development currently going on and with the demographic projections for the area in hand, he also estimated that he would be able to sell this oceanfront property for at least $1.8 million within two years, three at the most. So all he needed was $500,000 and a little something for the first round of fix-up costs.

Now Max is a well-known and well-respected real estate investor in the area. He runs an apartment management firm and actively invests in a variety of property types. He uses all of his expertise to put together a proposal to buy the motel.

Max decides to sell thirty limited partnership shares in the motel project at $20,000 each. That will bring in $500,000 for the down payment plus $100,000 for renovation and closing costs. He will not contribute any money of his own to the project, but he will take five shares in the limited partnership in return for his role as general partner.

In most limited partnership cases, the general partner gets something in return for his expertise and the responsibility of running the business and assuming liability. He might get an up-front fee and a portion of the operating income (called a free lease) or he might take a number of shares of ownership in the partnership (called a free piece). Or both.

Max is operating on the free piece principle. In taking five shares of the partnership without cost, he is getting the equivalent of a $100,000 investment in the property. When the profits or paper losses are divided, each shareholder will get 1/35 while Max gets 5/35. Because he is operating the motel, his losses from depreciation and such will not be considered as passive for tax purposes.

Once he has his group together with signed commitments, Max goes to the REO specialist at the lender/owner's office and begins to negotiate. To his surprise he buys the property for $900,000. Instead of restructuring his plans, however, he still takes out the $500,000 mortgage from the lender/owner. He now has an extra $100,000 to use in renovation which he is sure will increase the value of the property still further. He plans to sell in two years and dissolve the partnership, still aiming conservatively for the $1.8 million figure. If he gets it, his shareholders will get approximately $38,000 back for their $20,000 investment. Not bad, almost double. But Max, who invested nothing but his time, talent, and responsibility will get approximately $190,000. And if he does better than his conservative estimate, everyone gets a still greater return.

Yes, there is money to be made in the bailout. We figure that package deals and bulk sales are going to be around for another decade, maybe more. Plenty of time for you to get in on something that appeals to you. Start gathering your investor friends together. Form investment groups. Hold monthly meetings even if you haven't yet picked out a piece of property. Talk about what's new and what can be done. There will be tremendous strength in group power in this decade.

CHAPTER 10

NEGOTIATING IN THE BAILOUT

Don't believe everything you read in the newspapers. The RTC *will* negotiate. S&Ls in conservatorship will negotiate, even more. And private sellers will negotiate most of all.

At a meeting of the Advisory Board to the RTC in New York City, William Dudley, Director of Region 1 of the RTC, said his Consolidated Office managers had a "great deal of discretion to take offers way below appraised value." He pointed out that the RTC was losing money in carrying costs. "I don't believe that appraisals are an impediment to the sale," he went on, and then added that in his opinion RTC officials have "much more flexibility than people realize."

"Really?" you ask. Then you quickly add, "But *how much* will they negotiate? And exactly *what* will they negotiate?"

The RTC is a seller in the real estate marketplace and in that marketplace, *everything* is negotiable. Everything means price, closing date, who pays for the title search, title insurance and other closing costs, the condition of the property and who's responsible for fixing what, the extras like draperies and appliances that might or might not go with the building, date and conditions of occupancy, and even financing.

"How can anyone juggle so many different aspects of a deal successfully?" you may ask. "How does a buyer win at the negotiating game?"

It's a matter of attitude and approach. The key to negotiating the best possible deal (with the RTC or with anyone else) is the effective use of one of the most basic human interaction strategies in all the world. To help you to remember this secret of success, think of it as a formula: P^2. Yes, that's P squared.

What do we mean? Well, P^2 in the Bloch-Janik dictionary stands for *polite perseverance*. Which means: *don't lose your cool and do keep trying.* POLITENESS and PERSEVERANCE are powerful factors in the negotiating game. Whenever you're playing that game, think P^2: politeness multiplied by perseverance and perseverance multiplied by politeness.

Now they may laugh at our P^2 formula at MIT or Stanford, and we know it doesn't *exactly* fit any of the standard and usual rules for formulas, but it works. If you remember it and use it, you won't get lost in the marketplace and you can be a winner at the game.

Let's look at a detailed map of the negotiating terrain in this marketplace, along with some step-by-step advice on how to apply P^2.

HOW TO MAKE A DEAL

Just about everyone will tell you that a deal is a meeting of the minds. The seller comes down from his ideal figure and the buyer comes up from his "it's-a-steal" figure. The seller gives up more than he wanted to and the buyer gets less than he hoped for. But they agree to go ahead. Many real estate agents will tell you that the "perfect" deal is one in which both buyer and seller are screaming "PAIN!" or one in which both are beaming big smiles. Which is a nice best-of-all-possible-worlds thought.

In the real world, however, buyers want *almost* to steal the property, signing the purchase contract long *before* they reach the point of pain. Sellers want to beam all the way to the bank, counting the money they didn't *really* expect to get. Negotiating is the game they play to see who wins.

Investors are the athletes of the negotiating game and athletes warm up before they begin participating in their sports. Warming up in the negotiating game consists of three steps:

1. reviewing the negotiating process;

2. reviewing the specifics of the particular deal; and

3. deciding on a strategy.

Now this is no twenty-minute warm-up! It can take a good many hours. It *will* improve the effectiveness of your negotiating, however, and that can make a difference of many thousands of dollars in cash and extras. In anyone's book, "many thousands" is a pretty good rate of return on time spent.

So let's begin with a generic description of the real estate negotiating process, most of which can be applied to bailout properties. We'll then get into the specifics of bailout dealing in the next section of this chapter.

WHAT'S THE PROCESS?

Serious negotiating in the real estate marketplace always starts on paper. Talk like: "Whad'e'ya think they'll take?" or "Tell 'em I'll give 'em a hundred K" is nothing more than preliminary positioning. The first step in the process of buying a property, once you've decided that you want it, is to put an offer in writing. This can be done in two ways, through a nonbinding written offer, called (ironically) a *binder,* or through a completed and executed purchase contract. Each instrument is effective, if used properly and under the right circumstances.

Using a binder. A binder can have a lot of different appearances: scribbles on lined yellow paper, a typed letter, or a professionally printed form with the real estate broker's logo on it. It is used to discuss price, with the unstated understanding that everything else will be negotiated later.

A binder is usually most effective in the opening round of negotiations. You sign it and then turn it over to the real estate agent who is acting as the go-between in your negotiating process. You will also be required to give the agent a "good faith" check for $500 or $1000. Write this check to the real estate broker's trust account or name the broker and follow the name with the words "fiduciary agent." (Note: the check is written to the *broker* with whom your sales agent is affiliated. Do *not* make the check payable to the sales agent.) If no real estate broker is involved in the sale, the check should be made payable to the *trust account* of the seller's attorney, never to the seller.

To facilitate the forward movement of the negotiations and to protect yourself from legal webs, the binder should always contain certain information. Check for:

- The date (no agreement is legal without a date);

- Your name and the name of the seller;

- The address of the property;

- The price you are offering;

- Acknowledgment of having received the "good faith" deposit and specific notation as to the disposition of the money;

- A date by which a formal contract must be drawn and executed (usually within three or four working days);

- And, *most important,* a statement requiring that any contingencies to or conditions of the sale be set down in writing and executed by both parties.

For your convenience, we've printed a sample of what a binder might look like on page 155.

An offer made with a binder is a good way to start the price negotiations by showing the seller that you're serious enough to make the offer in writing and with a check. You can get a feel for the seller's attitude toward the price and negotiations in general from his/her response to the binder. When negotiations begin to close in on the purchase price, however, and other factors such as closing date, mortgage contingencies, condition, and the personal property to be included in the sale come into play, it's usually better to negotiate with a contract.

It's important that you realize that a binder does *not* take a property off the market. Its chief advantages are brevity and the facility of negotiating without commitment. Its disadvantage is lack of protection. While you are discussing details and splitting nickels, another buyer might come along and catapult the deal into a bidding war.

Using a contract. Do not sign a purchase contract until you've read Chapter 13. For the time being, however, remember that a fully drawn, formal contract is commonly used as the written document of a real estate negotiation. Unlike the binder, which focuses on price, the contract spells out all the factors in the deal. Your negotiating chips in any deal are price, closing date, occupancy, personal property included

SAMPLE BINDER

Memorandum of Agreement

The Seller of a house located at

_____

acknowledges receipt of $ _____ as a good-faith deposit on the above-described house from _____ (Buyer), hereinafter known as Buyer. The total price of the house is $ _____, and a formal agreement will be drawn and executed on or before _____ (date). If Buyer does not execute the agreement on or before above-mentioned date, then Seller shall keep the deposit as liquidated damages. If Seller fails to execute an agreement on or before the above-mentioned date, Seller shall return to Buyer the deposit as described above.

If an offer has been made subject to any conditions, those conditions shall be signed by both parties, attached to and made part of this agreement.

Accepted this _____ day of _____ (month), 19____ by

_____   _____
(Seller)   (Buyer)

_____   _____
(Seller)   (Buyer)

[*Note:* The binder money should be paid by check, made out to the "trust account" of the seller's attorney.]

in the sale, contingencies for property inspection, and contingencies for financing. These are all defined in the contract.

Pay careful attention to what is written on the contract form as it is being filled out for the first round of contract negotiating because, as a part of the offering process, you must sign it before it goes to the seller. If the seller accepts your first offer and executes that contract, you have made the deal described by the contract even if you had planned to make changes as the negotiations progressed. To give yourself space and to avoid getting trapped in a contract, always include the "jump out" clauses discussed in Chapter 13.

The counteroffer. The seller usually responds to the first offer by making a counteroffer. This is most often done by crossing out figures or statements on the binder or contract, writing in new ones, and initialing the changes. Some sellers, however, will insist on having the real estate agent draw a new document detailing their counteroffer. This response is often little more than a reverse form of the binder, focused primarily upon the price. Sometimes, however, the seller will initiate the drawing of a new contract to spell out not only the price he wants but also all the other terms of the sale as he would like to see them. The smart seller will insist that mortgage contingencies and all the other dates and details of payment be spelled out.

The buyer's response to the counteroffer. The change from binder negotiating to contract negotiating usually comes from the buyer on this second round. Now is the time to indicate your optimal closing date and name the extras you want with the property. Doing this in conjunction with the naming of a higher offering price makes these additional demands a bit more palatable.

The seller's second counteroffer. Many deals are made at the end of this second round, but theoretically, the rounds of negotiating can go on as long as there's someone to sign the papers. Each round requires some significant changes, some giving and taking that brings the two parties closer to a meeting of the minds.

These changes can be made in writing by scratching out and adding to the original contract, with both parties initialing each change. If the contract becomes hard to read, however, a new one should be typed with all the changes included. This new version becomes the new contract and it should be executed by both parties.

WHAT ARE THE IMPORTANT SPECIFICS IN YOUR DEAL?

Once you've completed the first phase of the warm-up and you're feeling comfortable with your understanding of the process of negotiating, you should focus upon the specific facts of your deal. This is the time to consider price, condition, cash flow, and any extras you may want to ask for. The possibilities, probabilities, and aspirations that you think through at this point can make a tremendous difference in how well your negotiations proceed and in how much you actually pay for the property. We've included a negotiating worksheet at the end of this chapter.

Money. How much you offer for a piece of property should be dependent upon how much it's worth. Use comparables, cost-to-income ratios, estimates of replacement cost, comparative tax assessments, an appraisal or appraisals, or whatever it takes to come up with probable market value. Then establish in your mind and on paper four possible purchase prices: your stealing-it price, your good-deal price, your just-below-market-value price, and your top dollar (which should never exceed your estimate of current market value unless the property is very unusual and has extraordinary potential for appreciation or for a radical change in income production).

The pace of the market. You should evaluate the pace of the market in your local area in order to map your negotiating strategy. In a market where property is turning over very rapidly, you should probably make your first bid fairly close to your estimate of market value. In a market where properties have FOR SALE signs on their front lawns for long periods of time, you can afford to make low first offers and inch the offering price up slowly, testing the staying power of the seller.

Extras and things. Before you make your first offer, you should make a list of all the items not attached to the property that you might like to have. Called personal property or chattel, this category includes the appliances, lawn furniture, window treatments, carpeting, etc., all of which can be written into a real estate purchase contract.

When you've completed a list, prioritize it. Then ask for the things you absolutely must have on the earliest round of negotiating. As you later increase the offering price, add more items. These new requests may well be refused, but by the third round or so, most sellers will give in at least to the items requested with the first offer.

Condition. You don't need to hire a professional property inspection firm to evaluate the condition of a building before coming to an agreement on price. Do your own inspection before you make your first offer and keep a careful list of potential problem areas, structural faults, or systems that you suspect need repair. Make some ballpark estimates of the cost of these probable repairs.

You will use this dollar-value list of potential problems in discussing property value. You may even be able to negotiate the completion of some repairs by the seller before you take title. Be sure that your contract is contingent upon a professional inspection of the property, however, since this is not only a jump-out clause but also a means of negotiating a still lower purchase price *after* the contract is fully executed.

Financing. Before you make an offer, you should know how much down payment you have and how much mortgage you can carry. This data will help you to determine the top dollar that you can afford to pay according to the qualification guidelines of the lenders you are considering. If this figure is below your estimate of market value for the property, you may want to calculate the pros and cons of accepting a second mortgage loan from the seller. If that's a possibility for you, we suggest that you take the figures to your accountant or financial advisor for a review before you make a commitment of any kind.

HOW DO YOU PLAY TO WIN?

Responsive listening is the insider secret of the real estate game. To practice it successfully you must know yourself and you must be sensitive to the words and actions of your adversary (in this case, the seller). Then you must use knowledge and intuition to your advantage.

About yourself. You've already decided on your price strategy by identifying your purchase price levels, the steal-it price, the good-deal price, and so on. Now gather together your other objectives. What are your ideal closing and possession dates? How flexible are these? Bring out your prioritized list of extras and your dollar-value rated list of negotiable repairs. Before you enter into each round of negotiations, review your lists and calculate what you can demand, trade, or offer to come closer to a deal.

About the seller. Try to find out from the real estate agent how badly the seller wants to sell. What is his motivation for selling? If he's already bought another house, you have a strong negotiating hand. Find out how soon he wants to close, then sweeten a very small increase in your offering price by moving the closing date closer to his ideal. Or hold out for a closing date far from what the seller wants until he lowers his asking price.

Generally, each time you offer more, ask for more. Or refuse to offer more money but offer something else the seller wants. To get a sense of *what* the seller wants, examine the listing sheet carefully, question the real estate agent, listen for clues in what's said and what's not said.

You do know one thing about the RTC. Like any other seller with a vacant property, this agency is motivated by costs. Carrying vacant properties reduces the return. REO account executives have the authority to consider carrying costs in their negotiating. The promise of a quick closing therefore might be a strong negotiating tool that could bring about agreement on a purchase price that's even lower than the 20 percent below appraisal minimum that has been written up as rock bottom.

Use time. Because it is a business, the RTC is unlikely to be affected by time play in making your offers. They will counter as soon as possible. You should reply to their counter as soon as it is convenient for you. When dealing with private sellers, however, the timing of your negotiations may become a factor. In a slow market, it's usually a good idea to let a day or two elapse between offers. In a fast market, negotiate hard on the heels of the last round.

Use comparables. Have the real estate agent explain to the seller what you think the property is worth and how you arrived at that figure. Of course, the "worth" figure you give to the agent may not be your actual estimate of current market value. It's simply what you think the property is worth. What's important is the documentation you present. Strong market documentation works equally well with the RTC, with home sellers, and with everyone in between.

Use length of time on the market. If a property has been long on the market, tell the seller it may be much longer before another offer comes along. Ask "Why do you think it hasn't sold yet?" You want to hear something like "Maybe the price is too high." Ask the seller to consider the cost of carrying the property while holding out for another offer.

Use condition as a negotiating tool. If the seller won't reduce his asking price further because of defects that you have pointed out, agree to pay a somewhat higher price if all the items you listed are repaired to your satisfaction before the closing date. This saves you money in the long run since you will be financing the cost of repairs over the life of the mortgage and you'll probably sell the property long, long before the scheduled date of the final payment.

Use the P² formula. Among the many aspects of polite perseverance are: Always be courteous. Never disparage the property. Keep cool. Negotiate rationally. Don't take no for an answer. Return again and again with slight changes in the contract, new suggestions, new insights into property value, new and creative suggestions for financing, or a little more of whatever it is the seller most wants.

DEALING WITH THE BAILOUT'S BUREAUCRATS

The business of running the government gets a lot of bad press in this country. Just say "bureaucracy" and Americans think of crowded offices run by despotic authority figures. The words that come to mind are *routine, regimentation, policy, procedure.* . . . And the overriding image is endless red tape.

Well, that's not far from the truth, but when working with the bailout's bureaucrats, you've got to see *beyond* the truth. As an investor, your odds of making money will increase if you try to separate the men and women you deal with from the bureaucracy in which they work. Remember that you're dealing with individuals who represent the seller (the seller is the RTC and your government). These people are not the sellers. They have no stake in the sale and in some cases their actions and decisions are governed by official policy statements. Also, they are almost always overworked.

As we've mentioned, the RTC was created late in the summer of 1989. Before its first birthday, it was holding and managing a larger asset base than General Motors! No one in the government was prepared for the immensity of the task at hand and as a result, there was much stumbling in the early months. Some of the people placed in positions of authority had little or no experience in the real estate marketplace. Early buyers had to negotiate with *and educate* bureau officials, often simultaneously.

The situation has improved considerably, but buyers still face the double pull of individual human beings and set policy standards as a part of every negotiating situation. This is not usually the case in the real estate marketplace, and the strangeness of the situation has made for awkwardness even on the part of experienced investors. At this point, the best advice we can give is to use the P^2 formula in all your RTC negotiations. Polite perseverance will take you places you never thought you could go and bring about results that everyone said were impossible to achieve.

THE RULES

Remember "read my lips"? As you write your income tax check, this year try to think of those words as a learning experience.

"What's the lesson?" you ask.

A lesson that applies to governments and organizations everywhere: RULES AND PROCEDURES ARE NOT CARVED IN STONE! Policies, procedures, even laws are changed and changed again to meet the needs of the times and changing socioeconomic situations. The bailout and the RTC is a part of our government and a part of life in our times, *not* an exception. Like everything else in our society, its rules, policies, and procedures will change, even though the principles of the real estate marketplace remain constant.

It's not knowing the current set of rules but the assurance of the timeless constancy of real estate principles that keeps the seasoned investor comfortable in any market. If a person understands the goals and methods of an investment discipline, he or she can work with whatever changes in policy and procedure happen to come about.

The following RTC policies are current as of this writing. They will certainly play a part in shaping the future direction of the agency, but some of them may be changed by the time you are ready to make your deal. So read through them, understand them, and then check with bailout officials or your local attorney for the current status of each category.

Price. By law, the price of an RTC property is determined through appraisal. These appraisals stand apart from what the original owner paid for the property and from what the original lender saw fit to lend on the property. The appraisals are an evaluation of current market value in current condition. But remember, appraisals are educated guesses. True market value is not determined until a buyer buys.

So, like every other real estate seller in the country, the RTC must set an *asking* price. According to current policies, agency officials are allowed to set that asking price at a figure of their choice between the appraised amount and 110 percent of the appraised amount. At this time, they are not required to make public the appraisal figures, which means that some negotiating space is probably included in every asking price. Just like the deal you make with the couple who owns the small house around the corner, the only way you're going to find the bottom-dollar price on an RTC property is to start your negotiating low and work up.

In several states described as "distressed" in terms of their real estate markets (Texas, New Mexico, Colorado, Oklahoma, Louisiana, and Arkansas), properties can be sold as soon as they come onto the market at 95 percent of appraised value. In other states, they can be sold at 90 percent of appraised value.

"Hold it!" you cry. "We're in this to make money. We want to buy property *at least* 15 percent below market value. Now you're telling us we can't do that with the RTC. So why bother?"

Don't be dismayed. The RTC wants to sell these properties and they have already set up a system to reduce prices until they find a seller. It involves time. After a residential property has been on the market for four months or a commercial property for six months, the RTC can sell below its 95 percent or 90 percent guidelines. Asset managers can then sell 15 percent below appraised value. After another three months, they can take another 5 percent off.

But be aware that these numbers are not absolutely rigid. A printed statement of Oversight Board policy states: *"However, the RTC will consider the sale of a property below the normal threshold values if properly substantiated in accordance with its procedures. Many factors should be considered when considering the adequacy of an offer versus the appraised value of a property. These include length of the previous marketing period(s); previous offers received; opinions of brokers as to the value of the property; the cost of holding the property, in terms of actual and opportunity costs; the risk of vandalism; and local conditions or trends of real estate sales."*

So you *can* negotiate! Remember, however, that just because the RTC can sell at a lower price does *not* mean that they must reduce the asking price. In dealing with the RTC therefore, it is absolutely essential that you know how long a property has been on the market. And marketing time includes the length of time a property was listed for sale while its lending institution was in conservatorship, that is, *before* the RTC officially took control of the property. Time on the market therefore is a key to your negotiating strategy.

Let's look at a hypothetical example. Imagine that the RTC has listed the little house on the corner of Sunnybrook Road for $99,999. Neither you nor the real estate broker who has the listing knows that the appraisal figure for the property was $91,000. If Sunnybrook Road were located in one of the states that limits the bottom line on sales to 95 percent of appraised value, the RTC could accept an offer of $86,450. If the house were in any other state, they could accept $81,900.

The property needs some paint and elbow grease but otherwise is in good shape and you estimate that if you could buy it for $70,000 you could sell it easily within a month for $78,000. What should you do?

Check all the numbers twice and then make an offer of $63,000.

No, no one will laugh. Once you get your offer in, you should wait. If you're worried that you'll lose the property, don't worry. Instead, on whatever form you choose to use to convey your offer, you will state that you wish to be notified of any other offers that are made on the property. Now you're in on the deal and you know that the RTC can lower its minimal selling price once the property has been on the market for four months.

Don't worry about your bid being forgotten. It is a good idea to call from time to time to check status and touch base with the asset manager, but your bid is important. RTC officials see competitive bidding as the optimum way to determine maximum market value on their properties. They will be keeping careful records of who's bidding on what.

You should check with RTC officials to be certain that you have the correct current time guidelines for sale price reductions. Ask "Exactly how long has this property been marketed?" Three to four weeks before the selling price change goes into effect, you make another offer of $65,500 on a contract. Let's look at the numbers. Remember, the property is still listed on the market at $99,999.

After four months on the market the RTC can reduce the selling price to 85 percent of appraised value. Now they can legally sell the Sunnybrook Road house for approximately $77,300. Still not what you want but you're getting closer. The RTC makes a counteroffer of $79,000 to your bid of $65,500.

Another two months go by. The RTC has reduced the asking price on the property to $84,800, but no one has snatched it up. You check again on the rules and discover that they can legally sell at a price reduced by another 5 percent within another month. (That's three months after the original 15 percent allowed reduction.) Using rough figures, you know that the RTC can price at 110 percent of appraised value. So you guesstimate the appraisal price by reducing the asking price by 10 percent. You get a ballpark figure of their rock bottom after the prescribed time lapse on the market, by taking 20 percent off the figure you estimate to be the appraised value.

Playing with the numbers, you believe that the RTC can sell for $72,800 and you come up with an offer of $67,300 two weeks before the final price acceptance reduction goes into effect. If you're patient and you keep in touch with the people in the deal, you'll get a counteroffer of approximately $73,000.

Okay, this is $3,000 over your ideal purchase price. Is it worth the effort? It could be. Try making your offer at $70,500 and then negotiate to have the RTC pay all closing costs including title insurance.

Point out that carrying the property another two or three months could eat up the difference between your bid and theirs. Meanwhile, recognize that closing costs will usually exceed $3,000. Even at $71,500 or $72,000, this looks like a go-ahead situation to us.

One of the most important of all the things to remember in dealing with the RTC is that, unlike many private-sector sellers, they are not out to make a killing and they have no emotional interest in the property. They just want to get the properties SOLD. Many of the appraisals are already below what the properties originally sold for or were financed at. These appraisals reflect a market that is bottoming out and are therefore already a good deal. If you can get rather well below the appraisal figure, you may be approaching the proverbial *steal*.

Letters of intent. The RTC will not accept the conventional binder as a negotiating document. They will, however, work with a letter of intent, especially with higher priced commercial property.

"What's a letter of intent?" you ask.

The RTC is working on a form they'd like everyone to use. Until it's ready, however, your attorney can supply you with an acceptable format. The letter of intent allows you to negotiate price without committing to a contract. Once a purchase price is agreed upon, you'll get a letter back from the RTC saying that they are prepared to accept your offer of $_____. This means it's time for a contract.

"Well, the government is finally doing something right," you say. "What a great way to negotiate. You can find the bottom dollar without commitment!"

Right, except for one problem. Neither your letter of intent nor the RTC's letter of reply will take the property off the market. Until you have a contract of sale, another buyer can move in on your deal, *legally*. Which is why we suggest that a letter of intent be used only to establish initial contact with the people in charge at the local RTC office. When you begin to approach purchase price, use a contract.

Contracts to purchase. Once the buyer and the RTC sign a contract, the property comes off the market. This does not mean, however, that you're in a deal that you can't get out of. The RTC will work with most usual and customary real estate clauses. This means you can write in safety nets to your deal.

We'll discuss contracts in detail in Chapter 13. For the purposes of your negotiating, just be aware that your contract to purchase can be dependent upon financing, a professional inspection report (even though the first RTC guidelines dictated that everything be sold "as is"), and the approval of an attorney of your choice. The attorney approval clause can get you out of a deal if you discover that it's keeping you awake all night.

Your contract with the RTC should be just as specific as the contract you would sign with an ordinary seller. It should state what's included and not included in the sale and who pays for what closing costs. (Payment of closing costs, by the way, is a negotiable item, even with the RTC.) It should also name a closing date, which may or may not be a point of negotiation.

Time. Current law states that the RTC must reply to your offer within thirty days. That's not a bad reply time when the purchase of a multimillion-dollar hotel/resort is being considered but it's abominable for negotiating on residential property. As we write this, however, officials at the RTC have informed us that the reply time for residential property is being changed to five days.

Sealed bids. At a recent Sonny Bloch seminar, a disgruntled investor told a tale of RTC woe. He had found a property he wanted and had negotiated a satisfactory price by using letters of intent. He held up a letter of response from the RTC that began, "We are prepared to accept your offer of . . ." Then he told us that he might lose the property and he didn't think the RTC was acting ethically or legally.

It seems that while he was negotiating and before he transposed the acceptable offer in his letter of intent to a contract, three other offers came in on the property. Since the property was legally still on the market, each of these offers had to be addressed.

A private-sector seller would probably have encouraged a bidding war, especially with *four* prospective buyers. Instead, and in an attempt to be fair, the RTC instructed all four interested parties that it would accept sealed bids on a specified date. Whoever made the highest bid would get the property.

This is perfectly legal. It also makes a good case for doing your serious negotiating on a contract.

THE PEOPLE

The process of negotiating involves people. No software, no system, no machine can do it. And wherever there are people, there are complexity, variety, intensity, laziness, dedication, rivalry, and all the other aspects of humanity with which writers have filled the bookshelves of the world. That's what makes negotiating such a slippery challenge. You can never be sure what you'll encounter. You must always be prepared for everything and anything.

Even the most carefully constructed policy manual in the most tightly organized bureaucracy cannot control the thoughts and acts of the people who work in the bureaucracy. If you want to work with the RTC, therefore, you must learn to work with its people.

Don't expect perfection. Expectations have a tremendous effect on our emotional responses. When we expect one thing and get another, we often get angry, or frustrated, or so disappointed that we quit. Nothing could be more detrimental to success in the real estate marketplace than the grand entrance of these negative emotions into a deal. Winning investment strategies are planned and executed by the head not the heart.

To remain rational throughout your dealings with the RTC, do not expect everything to go perfectly. Oh, don't get us wrong, you *should* have a schedule that describes exactly what perfect progress should be, but you must work toward it, not expect it.

Again, people are the key. Be absolutely certain that you get to know the names of the people working on your deal, then maintain control by applying gentle pressure. For example, if you don't get a response on time, call and ask how things are going. If there's an important paper to be delivered, hand-deliver it yourself and ask to meet the *person* to whom it is addressed. This need only take a minute, but a handshake goes a long way. If you can't meet the person, call the day after you deliver the paper and ask to speak with him or her. Then ask that person if what you delivered was what he/she needed or if there's anything else you can do. Bear in mind: *polite perseverance.*

When things do go wrong, follow a three-step program to set them right. First, find out what happened. Second, find out who was responsible and why. (Don't jump to conclusions and don't get angry. There may be extenuating circumstances. Polite perseverance and an attitude of "let's make this right together" could win you an ally on the inside!) And third, make a plan to accomplish your goals and work through the plan (with polite perseverance, of course).

Stroke and stand firm. Working is hard, especially working in a bureaucracy. There's always too much to do, there's too much paperwork, there seems to be a web of potential entanglements in every envelope that is opened, recognition of work well done is hard to get, and blame usually comes in the large economy size. A friendly voice on the phone, a person who remembers your name and asks how you are before addressing the business at hand can brighten an oppressive day.

Try a little "schmooze" as they say in New York. Find something good to say before you launch into what went wrong. You'll be surprised at how much more helpful people are.

On the other hand, working with a bureaucracy can be a trying experience for the person who's not a part of the organization. It's easy to lose your way, to find yourself tucked into an unobtrusive corner, and sometimes to get stepped upon. Don't let that happen to you. Remain active. Stand up for what you know are your rights. Follow everything through to its completion. And do all of that with polite perseverance.

DEALING WITH THE OTHER REO OFFICIALS

As we said earlier, there are excellent deals to be had by digging out the REOs of lending institutions in conservatorship. If you choose to venture down this avenue to wealth (and we think you should), you'll be dealing with another kind of bureaucracy. It'll be a bureaucracy that's smaller and more concerned with itself, but it will still be a bureaucracy peopled with men and women who control their particular domains.

Most often you'll find that the bureaucrats in S&Ls in conservatorship are operating under one of two mind-sets. Whichever predominates, it will effect your negotiating experience. Just for fun, we've named them: Get-with-the-program and Denial.

In a Get-with-the-program situation, the people in charge of the S&L's REOs are anxious to move them. They want to get rid of these nonperforming assets before the RTC takes over operation of the S&L or, sometimes, to *keep* the RTC from taking over. When dealing with such people, emphasize quick closing. Negotiate not only for price but also for in-house financing at rates that are below the going market figures. Be aware that you're unlikely to meet anyone from the RTC while dealing with an institution in conservatorship, since most departments will still be run by its original staff.

In a Denial situation, the S&L may be in conservatorship, but its employees (or at least the person in charge of the REOs) is conducting "business as usual." In the good ole days before the bailout, many S&Ls tried to keep their REOs under wraps. It was considered bad publicity to let the public know that their friendly corner bank had foreclosed on property because of nonpayment, also known as bad debts. Getting information on REOs was often tough and took perseverance that sometimes stretched the concept of politeness to the breaking point. Some REO officials even tried to hold on to the properties, not only refusing to negotiate but also denying the very existence of the properties.

Today, when an institution goes into RTC conservatorship, it is encouraged to sell its REOs. If you come across officials in the Denial mind-set, however, you do have recourse to some powerful help. Although you may not be dealing with anyone from the RTC directly, the RTC does have control over the functioning of the institution. If you're not getting cooperation, if your bids are being ignored, call the director of the Consolidated Office of the RTC for your area. (See Chapter 5 for a list.) With a little polite perseverance, you can get official pressure applied to the S&L and you should be able to make a deal quickly and to your liking.

Your dealings with REO officials need not be limited to employees of the RTC or officials of S&Ls that are in conservatorship, however. Even the healthiest lending institutions have REOs from time to time. To negotiate for these properties, get to know the officials in charge. Then use all your skills and knowledge to get the best possible deal. Depending on the policies of the lending institution, you may do very well, or you may hit a wall. If you find that you are getting nowhere, stop wasting your time. There is no government authority to which you can appeal. Leave and go on to more profitable pastures.

One of the best ways to get really great deals from S&Ls in conservatorship or from healthy lending institutions with a bit of REO lying about is to make package deal offers. For example, if an institution owns the ten remaining condominium apartments in a conversion attempt that went broke, you can often get amazingly low purchase prices by buying all ten. If you're thinking that you don't have financial resources of that magnitude, consider forming a group for the investment. More about this in Chapter 9.

DEALING WITH MOTIVATED SELLERS

When buying property from individual owners, property not related to the bailout, you'll find all the above information helpful, but there is one strategy that is more important than all the others. *Find out what the seller wants.*

The amount of negotiating space varies all over the lot among home sellers and emotions creep into most of their responses. You can increase your negotiating effectiveness by making an effort to define the seller's primary motivators. Be aware that price is not always the first consideration. Closing date may be of utmost importance. Or financing. Or the condition of the building. Or something that seems entirely irrelevant to you, like having a "nice" new owner for the property. So be nice.

BE PREPARED TO WALK

The willingness to walk away from a negotiating situation that is not going well is an important factor in the creation of a good many happy millionaires. Always set a top limit on the amount you're willing to pay for a property. Then don't go over that figure unless you have new information that justifies changing it. Remember: there will always be another deal.

EXTRAS
(check appropriate box)

	1st round (must have)	2nd round (would be nice)	3rd round (could use)
carpeting			
draperies			
appliances			
furniture			
fireplace fixtures			
lighting fixtures			
room air conditioners			
water purifier			
closet organizers			
attic fan			
garage door openers			
lawn furniture			
gardening equipment			
tool shed			
playhouse			
doghouse and/or run			
recreational items (pool table, exercise equipment, etc.)			
Others:			

(continued on next page)

PROBLEMS TO BE REPAIRED
(check appropriate box)

	1st round (must be done)	2nd round (will need repair soon)	3rd round (may need repair)
roof			
wet basement			
plumbing			
wiring			
exterior painting			
interior painting			
bathroom fixtures			
kitchen cabinets			
kitchen appliances			
floors			
ceilings			
windows			
driveway			
landscaping			

PROFESSIONAL INSPECTION FINDINGS
To be renegotiated after inspection is complete.

☐ Termites ☐ Radon ☐ Water ☐ Drainage ☐ Structural Soundness

NAILING DOWN THE SALE
A Program of Negotiating Tools for Buyers' Eyes Only

Address of property: _____

PRICE

Steal _____ Bargain _____ Good Buy _____

ABSOLUTE TOP DOLLAR _____

CLOSING DATE

Your ideal _____

Your quickest possible close _____

Your longest possible close _____

Seller's probable ideal _____

First round date _____

Second round date _____

Third round date _____

TRADE-OFF DATE FOR MAJOR PRICE REDUCTION _____

CHAPTER 11

AUCTIONS

In November of 1990, $300,000,000 (that's 300 million dollars) worth of RTC-owned real estate was scheduled to hit the auction block. It was to be the first world auction for Uncle Sam and his Resolution Trust Corporation and it was *not* going to be conducted in a tent by an auctioneer in shirtsleeves. The auction site was a posh hotel in Miami. Bidders were not expected to fly to Florida to participate, however. The entire auction, complete with slide presentations, was to be broadcast live, via satellite, to approximately 11,000 prospective buyers in ten major U.S. cities and in London and Tokyo.

Are you feeling badly that you weren't invited? You shouldn't. We weren't invited either. And, more important, the auction never took place. The government blamed the auction company and the auction company blamed the government. Meanwhile Uncle Sam still owns properties and a new auction site in Dallas is being discussed.

When the first international auction does take place, its inventory will be almost exclusively million-dollar-plus, income-producing properties for which the RTC has clear title. Prospective bidders will be required to have in hand a cashier's check for somewhere between $50,000 and $500,000, depending upon the property that they plan to bid upon. And that cashier's check is only the initial deposit on the earnest money!

If you're beginning to feel the impulse to skip the rest of this chapter and go on to something that might be *really* important to you, please don't. The RTC may hold several million-dollar-plus auctions before the bailout is over, but it's almost certain that they will also hold a good many auctions for residential property in price ranges that ordinary Americans can afford. The prospects for condo, co-op, vacation home, and time-share sales are especially good. And the *Federal Register* of August 31, 1990, states: "The RTC is giving serious consideration to using a structured auction process that responds in full to the mandates of the affordable housing provisions of FIRREA, and at the same time, allows for expedited sales of single-family and multi-family property."

Besides upcoming RTC auctions, there's also plenty of other real estate auction activity going on *right now* all across the nation. The procedures and principles of buying at auction are exactly the same whether the seller is the RTC, a developer, a mortgage corporation like Fannie Mae, or a healthy lending institution selling off its REOs. So take a few minutes to learn about auctions. There may be a real bargain waiting for you under the gavel.

WHY HOLD AN AUCTION?

Auctions pop up around the country whenever the real estate market slows down. They are a means to clear out inventory for developers and to clear the books of nonperforming assets for lending institutions. Even some private sellers use them as a means to stimulate a sense of time pressure when a market is so slow that no pressure exists. Sometimes the marketing of properties in a closed room filled with competitive bidders actually brings in more money than the property could possibly command on the open market, and it brings that money in quickly. As a prospective buyer, you must be aware of this auction mania and take care that you don't let yourself get caught into impulse bidding that will contribute to the seller's profit margin.

Besides the usual sellers of foreclosed properties and overbuilt housing, there is now an old government department commanding new attention on the auction scene. You probably guessed. It's the Treasury Department. They must sell at public auction the real estate and other possessions that it seized from drug dealers and certain other serious offenders. Municipal, county, and state governments also holding more auctions in an effort to reduce surplus property they have gathered through abandonment or nonpayment of taxes.

HOW DOES AN AUCTION WORK?

Real estate auctions are conducted by auctioneers or by licensed real estate brokers acting as auctioneers. With the exception of on-site auctions for large condominium communities, they're rarely held outdoors under a tent like the church-fair antiques auctions you might remember. Today's real estate auctions are usually held in hotel meeting rooms or in auditoriums. The auctioneer does stand on a raised platform up front, but he doesn't need to shout. Today he has a microphone, excellent lighting, climate control, and, very often, video technology. At some larger auctions, slides of the property being sold are projected on a screen behind the auctioneer, sometimes videotapes are shown between bidding sessions, and descriptive color brochures are virtually everywhere.

Participants are given placards or "paddles" with numbers printed on them. A prospective buyer holds up his number to make a bid. Meanwhile assistants, sometimes called "ring men" and usually dressed in identifiable suits with the equivalent of red carnations in the buttonholes, roam about the audience, ostensibly to help the auctioneer identify bids. Very often, however, they also encourage bidding. They might look right at you and say something like, "Can't you beat that by $500?" or "Don't lose this great investment over just a few thousand dollars!"

As part of the hype, successful bidders are sometimes identified with WINNER! buttons or stick-on labels. Whether singled out or not, however, they are required to turn over deposit monies and sign purchase contracts and financial qualification papers before leaving the auction premises.

There are several types of sales formats in today's auction marketplace. Before you take the time to attend an auction even in a learning-not-buying mode, you should recognize them and be prepared to evaluate the proceedings accordingly. Let's go through the list.

ABSOLUTE AUCTION

In an absolute auction, there is no minimum bid required and the property *will* be sold to the highest bidder regardless of the price. Many buyers think absolute auctions are their best chance for a steal and this type of auction usually brings out the largest number of participants.

Some property certainly is "stolen" at absolute auctions. Sometimes, however, the frenzy of bidding actually boosts purchase prices above what the seller could expect to get on the open market.

ABSOLUTE AUCTION WITH A MINIMUM BID

This variety of auction protects the seller against the "steal" but still entices prospective buyers with the possibility of excellent deals. In an absolute auction with a minimum bid, the seller sets a price below which the property cannot be sold. That price is usually where the bidding starts. The property will be sold on the day of the auction if anyone offers the minimum bid or higher.

RESERVE AUCTION

The reserve auction is sometimes couched in advertising that uses lines like "subject to confirmation by the seller." There is no printed minimum bid, but the seller reserves the right to accept or reject the highest bid of the day. Which means you, the winning bidder, may or may not have bought a piece of property.

Usually, there is a specified waiting period for confirmation of the sale by the seller. Forty-eight hours is common. You probably won't "steal" a property at a reserve auction, but if the seller needs to sell, you may still get a very good deal.

MIXED AUCTION

A common practice in today's marketplace is the mixing of absolute auction property and reserve auction property. Developers with long lists of unsold units have found that the absolute auctions bring out the best crowds. They therefore use headlines like NO MINIMUM BID— PROPERTY WILL BE SOLD TO THE TOP BIDDER as a leader, auctioning a limited number of their units at whatever price they will bring. The remainder of their properties, however, are auctioned with a reserve.

Does it work? Yes indeed! You see, the prospective buyers are already there, gathered together in a room, and most of them keep bidding even though the seller has taken back the right to say NO SALE!

POOLED-UNIT AUCTION

In the pooled-unit format, properties of similar size and style (almost always within the same housing development, condominium community, or co-op apartment building) are grouped together. When you bid in a pooled-unit auction, you are bidding to buy *one* unit from among the group on the block. Whoever makes the highest bid gets first choice among the units in the pool. The next highest bidder gets second choice, etc. Sometimes, however, the bidding is begun again after the highest bidder makes his choice. The highest bidder in the second round then gets first choice of the remaining units.

HOW TO FIND AUCTIONS

You can get information from the RTC about the time, place, and inventory of their upcoming auctions by calling the Assets For Sale number (800) 431-0600, or the General Information number (202) 416-6940. Information on local auctions by developers or government agencies is advertised in local newspapers. You can also get the names of auctioneers in your area by telephoning the National Auctioneers Association at (913) 541-8084. Their mailing address is:

The National Auctioneers Association
8800 Ballantine
Overland Park, KS 66214

Once you know who's operating in your area, call the auction companies individually and ask to be placed on their mailing lists. Since the RTC, developers, lenders, and many local and national agencies usually use private auctioneers to conduct their auctions, you'll be getting an extra chance at being notified, just in case you miss the advertisements in the newspapers.

If you're interested in bankruptcy sales (usually business property), we have printed the names, addresses, and telephone numbers of regional United States Trustees for bankruptcy at the end of this chapter. These people handle auctions for the nation's Chapter 7 bankruptcy sales.

Neither Chapter 11 nor Chapter 13 bankruptcy sales are pertinent to real estate.

For information on the auction sale of property seized in law enforcement activities, you must contact either the U.S. Customs Office or the National Asset Seizure and Forfeiture (NASAF) Office of the U.S. Marshals Service. You can write the Customs Office at:

U.S. Customs Office
Post Office Box 17423
Gateway I Building
Washington, DC 20041

NASAF maintains regional offices. For your convenience, we've listed these addresses at the end of this chapter.

HOW TO BECOME A BIDDER

Unfortunately for beginning investors wishing to learn about auctions, you can't just walk into the room where an auction is to be held, sit down, and wait for a chance to raise your hand and bid. The risks are just too high for the seller, not to mention the expense of providing space and auction facilities. As a representative of the seller, therefore, the auction company will maintain some control over the bidding by allowing only "serious" bidders to bid. Admission to the auction room is usually limited to preregistered participants and their guests. (The number of "guests" is often limited to one or two per participant.)

From the process of registering to the moment of walking away with an executed contract in your pocket, an auction is not quite as simple as its advertising would lead you to believe. Let's look at the process.

GET A BROCHURE

The very first step in becoming a bidder is to get the written material describing the properties for sale and the format of the auction. Do this well in advance. The brochure will tell you time and date, the type of auction (absolute, reserve, etc.), the conditions of the sale, the amount of deposit required, and any special financing and title insurance information that is being offered. Most important, it will list the properties that are to be auctioned.

Developers' auction brochures will often include color photographs, floor plans, and lists of appliances and extras such as carpeting that are being sold as part of the real estate. Foreclosed and repossessed property sales and other auctions may only list the addresses of the properties with a brief description. You will have to make your own list of what's included and what's not and have it verified before the sale.

From the information in the brochure, you will be able to make a preliminary list of the properties you might bid on and sometimes even begin to plan your auction strategy. (More about that strategy in the section below titled HOW TO PROTECT YOURSELF.)

REGISTER

Plan to be at the auction site about an hour before the scheduled start time. At the registration desk, you'll be asked to fill out the usual name/address papers and then you'll be asked to show your deposit money. Deposit money can be cash, certified check, cashier's check, or in some cases, a pre-approved personal check.

We recommend that you use a certified check made out to yourself. You can safely leave this with the registration officials. If you do not buy property at the auction, you will simply take it back at the end of the day and redeposit it in your own checking account. If you do buy property, you can endorse the certified check over to the seller or the auction company.

Dealing with cash is risky. More than one wallet or briefcase has disappeared while a bidder was focused upon the action of the auction. Cashier's checks are safe if they are written payable to you but they represent money already withdrawn whereas the certified check leaves the money safely in your account until you endorse it. Personal checks are fine, but not all auction houses will accept them and those that do will insist upon pre-approval.

At the registration desk, you'll be assigned an auction number. Usually, you'll also be given an auction placard or paddle with that printed number. Don't lose it! You are responsible for the bidding done with that number.

THE ACTION

Inside the auction room, the auctioneer will ask for bids, calling out each bid that is made and asking for more. If you raise your paddle, you have bid. Watch for the ring men/women. Sometimes eye contact with one of them and a nod from you will be your signal for a bid.

Once the highest bid is reached on each piece of property, auction company staff will take down the buyer's number and confirm his/her name, address, and the description of the property that has just been purchased. At this time, *you* should ask *them* for a price and property confirmation also. Get the information in writing and have the staff person initial it. This will avoid later discussion about *how* much and *which* apartment.

If you are a top bidder, you will be asked to sign a purchase contract on the spot. If your attorney is with you, he or she should review the contract before you sign it. If you don't have an attorney present, add a clause to the contract to the effect of: *This agreement is subject to review by the buyer's attorney within three working days of its date. The attorney may void the contract for any reason and all deposit monies will be returned to the buyer.*

Before you leave, you will also be required to sign the certified check over to the seller or the auction company as trustee. Usually, there is a statement in the contract that defines how and when the remainder of the purchase money will be paid. An earnest money deposit of 10 percent is usually required. You will be asked to bring in whatever additional funds are necessary beyond your current deposit check within three to ten days.

HOW TO PROTECT YOURSELF

The biggest danger at an auction is allowing emotional response to overrule rational thought. Acting on impulse is so easy; after all, it only takes a moment to raise that paddle. And the hype is so stimulating: the fast, continuous talking; the sense of immediacy (it's now or never!); and probably most of all, the knowledge that your rivals are right there in the audience with you.

Those investors who bid safely and get the best deals are usually the men and women who spend time doing the necessary preparation work before the auction and then come to the selling arena armed with knowledge, rational restraint, and the emotional distance to know that this is *not* their only chance at a great deal. We've put together a list of ten MUST DOs to help you to become one of these best-deal people.

1. KNOW VALUE

As we've been saying all along, a primary factor in all successful real estate trading is knowledge of local property values in general and the probable market value of the particular piece of property in question. If you see an auction advertised with a minimum bid and your research leads you to believe that the minimum is just slightly below current market value, you might as well stay at home. Local property value information will save you a lot of time, not to mention money.

To estimate the property value of auction-eligible pieces that interest you, you can and should use all the guidelines and techniques we mentioned in Chapter 4. If you are still uncertain, pay for a professional appraisal. The several hundred dollars that it costs could save you several thousand.

2. CHOOSE SEVERAL PROPERTIES

Don't put all your eggs in one basket, so the saying goes. Unless you are attending an auction to buy one specific property and that property only, you should make a list of the properties that are appealing investments and rank these in order of your preference. Make notes after the ranking as to why you feel one is worth more or is more desirable than another.

Having a list of several acceptable properties will keep you from getting into emotional bidding as you see *your* dream property being chased by someone else. It will also help you to shift focus and keep the heart palpitations down.

3. INSPECT ALL OF YOUR PROSPECTIVE BUYS THOROUGHLY

Most auctioned properties are sold "as is" on the day of the auction. After the purchase contract is signed, there's no negotiating over the leaky roof that you missed on your sunny-day inspection. Or the leaky basement. Or the bad-tasting tap water.

If you are serious about buying at auction, it's usually a good idea to pay for professional inspections, including termites and radon, before you decide upon your top dollar figure. We know what you're thinking: Good gosh! There are four properties that interest me! Four inspections! That will cost me over a thousand dollars. Yes, and by buying at auction, you should save *at least* ten times that much off the market value of a property that you buy.

The professional inspection will also help you to determine the cost of fix-up before resale is possible. This figure should be calculated into your decision upon a top dollar bid. And finally, the inspection will help you to determine the probable life expectancy of the working systems and structural elements of the property. If you are buying rental property, this information will help you in calculating your cash flow.

4. EXAMINE ALL PERTINENT DOCUMENTS

One of the things that makes the purchase of real estate more complex than buying shoes is the amount of legal paperwork involved. If you plan to buy a condo or co-op apartment, you should carefully examine the offering prospectus (for a new unit) or the last two years' financial statements (for a resale in an existing community). Also take the time to read the by-laws and the house rules for the community. Be absolutely certain that you can live with these rules because they're very hard to change. Among the chief considerations are children, pets, smoking laws, parking privileges, the right to rent the unit, use and cost of recreational facilities, and age restrictions on owners or tenants.

If you are considering occupied rental property, ask to examine the record books, paying special attention to rent receipts, taxes, and maintenance costs over the past two years. This information is every bit as important as the inspection in determining probable cash flow. Be aware that the greatest rental-property bargain in the state is no bargain if units stand empty and rental income cannot cover expenses.

If you are considering a single-family home, get information on taxes; heating costs; sewer, water, and waste removal costs; and the requirements and costs of any memberships in so-called neighborhood associations.

If you are considering land, be sure to get an accurate survey, information on zoning, and whatever is available on percolation tests and environmental problems or restrictions.

5. DETERMINE YOUR ABSOLUTE TOP DOLLAR

This auction top dollar figure is even more important than your negotiating top dollar. You must decide on a number for each of the properties that interests you and then resolve that you will not exceed that number. Write it in red. The red number may shout STOP! to you. See it as a signal to keep your brain in gear.

6. COMPILE YOUR STOP! CARDS

Get some 3 × 5 index cards, one for each of the properties that interests you. At the top, identify the unit. On the next line, print your top dollar figure in red. Below that make a list of plus and minus points about the unit and finally note what you think is the probable market value. The market value figure should be well above your top dollar auction figure. If you have any doubts about your market value figure, ask yourself, "Could I sell this property within two months at this price?" Your goal is to buy far enough below that market value price so that you could sell the property the day after you buy it. That day-after-you-buy-it price should be your top dollar.

Keep these index cards in your pocket or purse. As each of your prospective properties comes on the block, take out its card. Keep it in the palm of your hand and look at it again and again. Remember, you must not go above the number in red.

7. PREQUALIFY FOR FINANCING

Most auction sales are not contingent upon the buyer obtaining financing. In other words, if you can't get a mortgage, you lose the 10 percent earnest money deposit!

To protect against this, talk with some mortgage lenders or mortgage brokers about the amount of debt you can carry and about the probable amount of loan to value financing available on the properties in question. (More about this in the next chapter.)

Some auctions advertise that financing can be arranged at the auction site. Don't relax and say *Great!* You should still check on how much you can carry and where to get the best rates. Sometimes the interest rates and terms offered at the auction are excellent; sometimes they're an outright rip-off. You'll be able to tell which only if you do some investigating before you go.

8. WATCH FOR SHILLS

It may not come as a surprise if we tell you that not everything in the world is as nice and proper as it appears to be. There are thieves, and charlatans, and stooges among us and sometimes they show up in the real estate marketplace. On the auction floor, the stooges are called "shills" or sometimes "straw men."

These are people placed in the audience by unscrupulous sellers. Their sole function is to force honest buyers to bid higher for the properties they want. You'll see them bid whenever there's a quiet moment. You'll also see them become quiet whenever the action gets hot.

If you see the same person bidding on many properties without ever winning his or her bid, you have probably identified a shill. Not all auctions have shills in the audience, but if you strongly suspect that one or more are controlling the bidding, just leave. This is a no-win game and not worth your time.

9. READ THE CONTRACT

Every single word. Buying property is a major commitment, not to be entered into lightly. The best safety net is the attorney-review clause we mentioned. If you don't want to risk the auction house's refusal to accept that clause and your necessary walkaway, you might go to the agents handling previews of the property a week or so before the auction and ask for a copy of the purchase contract that is to be used. Take this blank contract to your attorney and discuss it. If there are changes that he/she thinks necessary, ask the auction company or the real estate broker handling the property to arrange them with the seller beforehand.

10. CHECK YOUR STATE'S CONSUMER PROTECTION LEGISLATION

A number of states have legal *recision* periods. Call the real estate commissioner's office in your state and find out if there is such consumer protection on the books.

When a state has recision legislation, consumers can change their minds about a purchase if they notify the seller *in writing* within three to fifteen days (depending on the state's law) after signing a contract. You do not have to give any explanation for changing your mind. It's a good idea, however, to have your lawyer draft the letter to get you out of the contract and to send it by registered mail with a return receipt required.

BEHIND-THE-SCENES BUYING

Whenever an auction is advertised, some buying and selling occurs that is never seen on the auction floor. You may or may not be interested in this nonconforming buying but you should know that it exists and realize that you can use it if the situation is right.

BEFORE THE AUCTION

Some buyers go out to inspect a property before the auction and fall in love. They feel that they just must have one of the units and they can't bear the thought of risking it on the auction block. They think: *What if someone else wants it just as much as I do? The bid could go up and up! And I could lose!*

If any piece of property is that important to you, you should consider trying to negotiate a sale price before the auction date. You'll probably come close to paying market price, but at least you won't be driven higher by competition and you won't lose something you want very badly.

THE RIGHT OF FIRST REFUSAL

But what if you decide to risk it at the auction and someone does outbid you for the unit you want? Don't give up. People do change their minds and mistakes do happen. You might still have a chance at it.

Most auctioneers keep a list of the unsuccessful bidders on each property. If you want to stay in the game to the very last inning, tell the auction staff that you would like a right of first refusal on the property. Then have your lawyer put the request in writing the following day and get everyone to execute the agreement. "Everyone" is the seller and you, the second-in-line buyer.

A right of first refusal is a legal document which guarantees that you will be given the chance to buy the property *under the same terms as the successful bidder* in the event that he/she either cannot meet the contractual obligations or simply has a change of mind. Or perhaps heart.

AFTER THE FACT

Occasionally, when property is selling far below what the seller expected, that seller will withdraw units from the auction. If your selected properties are among those withdrawn, you can still approach the seller after the auction and make an offer. You are now negotiating in the usual manner. You may be surprised, however, at how good a deal you can make. Just be sure to keep your estimates of market value and your top dollar price in your mind. And leave your emotions outside the room.

BANKRUPTCY SALES—UNITED STATES TRUSTEES

United States Trustee
Old Custom House
1 Bowling Green
Room 534
New York, NY 10004
(212) 668-7663

United States Trustee
Boston Federal Office Building
10 Causeway Street
Boston, MA 02222
(617) 565-6360

United States Trustee
60 Park Place
Suite 210
Newark, NJ 07102
(201) 645-3014

United States Trustee
Strom Thurmond Federal
 Building
1835 Assembly Street
Room 1108
Columbia, SC 29201
(803) 765-5886

United States Trustee
421 King Street
Room 410
Alexandria, VA 22314
(703) 557-0746
(Note: this is a suboffice
of the S.C. regional office)

United States Trustee
1418 Richard Russell Building
75 Spring Street, SW
Atlanta, GA 30303
(404) 331-4437

United States Trustee
113 Saint Claire Avenue, NE
Suite 200
Cleveland, OH 44114
(216) 522-7176

United States Trustee
U.S. Courthouse
46 East Ohio Street
Room 258
Indianapolis, IN 46204
(317) 226-6710

United States Trustee
U.S. Courthouse
Room 505
110 South Fourth Street
Minneapolis, MN 55401
(612) 348-1900
(Note: this is a suboffice
of the Cedar Rapids, Iowa,
regional office)

United States Trustee
Columbine Building
Room 300
1845 Sherman Street
Denver, CO 80203
(303) 844-5188

United States Trustee
Custom House
701 Broadway
Room 313
Nashville, TN 37203
(615) 736-2254

United States Trustee
175 W. Jackson Boulevard
Room A-1335
Chicago, IL 60604
(312) 886-5785

United States Trustee
Federal Office Building
911 Walnut Street
Room 800
Kansas City, MO 64106
(816) 426-7959

United States Trustee
Transportation Center
425 Second Street, SE
Room 6750
Cedar Rapids, IA 52401
(319) 364-2211

United States Trustee
Texaco Center B
400 Poydraf Street
Suite 1820
New Orleans, LA 70130
(504) 589-4018

United States Trustee
700 Louisiana
Suite 2610
Houston, TX 77002
(Note: this is also
a regional office)
(713) 653-3000

United States Trustee
U.S. Courthouse Room 9C60
1100 Commerce Street
Dallas, TX 75242
(214) 767-8967

United States Trustee
320 North Central Avenue
Suite 1000
Phoenix, AZ 85004
(602) 379-3092

United States Trustee
10 U.N. Plaza
McAllister Street
Suite 300
San Francisco, CA 94102
(415) 556-7900

United States Trustee
Federal Building
Room 3101
300 North Los Angeles Street
Los Angeles, CA 90012-4790
(312) 894-6387

United States Trustee
Wells Fargo Bank B
101 West Broadway
Suite 440
San Diego, CA 92101
(619) 557-5013

United States Trustee
Park Place Building
1200 Sixth Street
8th Floor
Seattle, WA 98201
(206) 442-2000

NATIONAL ASSET SEIZURE AND FORFEITURE OFFICES OF THE U.S. MARSHALS OFFICE

NASAF
606 U.S. Courthouse
101 West Lombard Street
Baltimore, MD 21201

NASAF
Federal Building Annex
77 Forsyth Street, SW
  1st Mezzanine
Atlanta, GA 30303

NASAF
244 U.S. Courthouse
300 Northeast 1st Avenue
Miami, FL 33132

NASAF
1416 J.W. McCormick
  and Courthouse Building
Post Office Box 1146
Room 407
230 South Dearborn
Chicago, IL 60604

NASAF
231 West Lafayette St.
645 Federal Building/
  Courthouse
Post Office Box 2869
Detroit, MI 48231

NASAF
Room 1171
210 Building
210 North Tucker
St. Louis, MO 63101

NASAF
Room 465 Federal Building
1961 Stout Street
Denver, CO 80294

NASAF
2104 U.S. Courthouse
515 Rusk Avenue
Houston, TX 77002

NASAF
1258 Federal Building
300 North Los Angeles Street
Los Angeles, CA 90012

NASAF
880 Front Street
1-S-1 Federal Building
San Diego, CA 92188

CHAPTER 12

A SHORT COURSE IN FINANCING

At a consumer-information seminar held in June of 1990, Philip Jones, a Senior REO Specialist for the RTC, said that 80 percent of RTC properties are sold for all cash.

Do you feel as though someone just put a pin in your balloon?

"All cash!" you think. "No one buys *anything* in the real estate marketplace for all cash. Well, there go my chances at the RTC, whoosh. Maybe there's still a *healthy* S&L in the area with a few pieces of REO they want to sell . . ."

Don't rush off. When sellers in the real estate marketplace (and the RTC is a seller) say they will sell only for all cash, they don't mean that you have to bring a suitcase full of $50 bills to the closing. The "cash" usually comes from at least two sources: a down payment check withdrawing funds from the buyer's savings or checking account and a mortgage loan.

You can get an inside track in the race to buy particularly desirable RTC properties by arranging for mortgage financing before you even sign the contract. Or you can make your contract contingent upon your being able to get financing. Or you can get financing through the RTC if no other loan source is available.

Whatever your choice, you must become familiar with the words, acronyms, and systems of the financial arena. We can give you an introduction here, but to assure yourself of the best possible terms you should talk with several loan officers at nearby lenders, a mortgage broker or two, and if you have any doubts at all, your attorney.

MORTGAGE ALPHABET SOUP

Let's start with some definitions of the acronyms, jargon, and unfamiliar English words that real estate agents, bankers, and sometimes even attorneys throw around as though everyone *should* know them by heart. You don't have to memorize these—just take the book along and place it quietly on the desk of whoever is interviewing you. You may be surprised at how often you'll catch that person's eyes darting over to see if the title can be read upside down. You may even get treated a little more carefully.

MORTGAGE

You don't give up title to your property when you take out a mortgage loan, you simply secure the loan by giving the *mortgagee* (the lender) the right to take title if you do not make agreed-upon payments. When you do this, you are the *mortgagor*. To get title, the lender must *foreclose* on the loan. Foreclosure is a process that can take many months in most states. You, the mortgagor, still own the property during this process (the property is said to be *in foreclosure*) and you can rescue it by making the payments that are due, refinancing with another lender, or selling. Once a property is *foreclosed,* its title reverts to the lender, and you no longer own it.

TRUST DEED

A loan based on a trust deed is not a mortgage because you can't pledge as security property you don't have title to. But it feels like a mortgage and it acts like a mortgage. The real difference is in foreclosure proceedings. There are none. Since you never actually have the title in your name, you can lose the property in lightning swift strokes if you fail to make the payments on time. Sometimes as little as ninety days!

Trust deed loans are common in the south and west. The *deed,* which is the legal instrument that grants title to the property, is held by a third party (not the lender and not the buyer/borrower), usually the title insurance company or the escrow company that handles the closing. You, the buyer/borrower, are called the *trustor*. The title holder (who'll turn title to your property over to the lender if you don't pay on time) is called the *trustee*. And the lender is called the *beneficiary*.

SECOND MORTGAGE OR SECOND TRUST DEED

A loan that stands second in line for payoff if the borrower defaults. A second mortgagee can collect funds only after the entire remaining *principal* (money owed) of the first mortgage or trust deed has been paid out. The risk to the lender is therefore greater and interest rates for secondary financing are usually somewhat higher.

INTEREST

The fee charged for the use of money. It is usually expressed as a percentage of the principal to be paid annually. In rounded-off numbers: If you borrowed $100,000 (the principal) and your interest rate is 10.75 percent, you will pay $10,750 interest in the first year. In the second year, however, you will pay slightly less for the use of the money, since interest will be computed on the remaining principal after making a year's payments. This process of paying off the principal gradually over a stated period of time is called *amortization*. A thirty-year mortgage will be amortized over thirty years unless you sell the property and pay off the balance of the principal sooner.

FIXED RATE LOAN

A mortgage loan with an interest rate that will not change for the entire life of the loan.

ARM

The acronym for Adjustable Rate Mortgage. The interest rate on this type of loan can be changed at agreed-upon dates, every six months, year, two years, three years, or five years. The amount of change allowed is tied to a national index such as Treasury Bills. A good ARM in the consumer's eye-view will have a maximum amount of change per adjustment period.

For example, most loans cannot increase by more than two percentage points at each adjustment date. A good ARM will also have a cap which limits the *total* amount of interest rate change over the life of the mortgage to four or five points above the original figure or to a named maximum, such as 14 percent.

TERM

The life span of the mortgage. With a self-amortizing loan, you will have paid out the principal at the end of the term, usually fifteen or thirty years. When other types of mortgages come to term, however, you may still owe money.

BALLOON

With a *balloon* mortgage, you make payments as though you had a very long term but you must repay whatever principal remains on a mutually agreed upon date, which is always much sooner than the date upon which your payments would fully amortize the loan. With a 10/40 balloon mortgage, for example, you make payments that would amortize your mortgage in forty years, but you agree to pay the lender the entire remaining principal at the end of the tenth year. This is not a recommended financing instrument unless you are absolutely certain that you will be selling well before the principal-payment date of the balloon.

STRAIGHT MORTGAGE

The borrower pays interest only for the entire term of the mortgage. When the loan comes due, the entire amount that was originally borrowed must be repaid. Most straight mortgages are written for short terms (between three and ten years) and most are instruments used in seller financing.

THE CALL

A call in a mortgage is usually written in the smallest print. It gives the lender the right to demand payment in full either on certain dates during the life of the mortgage or in the event that the borrower is late in making scheduled payments. Be absolutely certain that there is no provision in the documents that you sign that would allow your lender to call your mortgage on named dates for no good reason. Nonpayment of the monthly amount agreed to *is* a good reason, however.

DUE-ON-SALE CLAUSE

A clause that makes your loan nonassumable by a future buyer of your property. If your mortgage loan has a due-on-sale clause, it must be paid off when title passes to another party. The new buyer must get a new mortgage. However, if your mortgage loan does not have a due-on-sale clause it is *assumable,* which means a buyer can pay you your equity and take over payments and responsibility to the lender. But don't rely on the absence of a due-on-sale clause to guarantee that your mortgage is assumable. Have assumability written into the documents. (And have your attorney check the wording.) An assumable mortgage, even an ARM, is a plus factor in selling, since it can save the new buyer considerable cost in loan origination fees and points.

POINTS

Ironically also called *discount* points, this is a fee charged by a lender and payable before closing to make the loan more lucrative (to the lender). One point is 1 percent of the principal. A fee of three points on a $100,000 loan will cost you $3,000. Sometimes the borrower must pay a portion of the agreed-upon points in cash when the loan commitment is signed, with the remainder being paid at the closing. Sometimes the points are just deducted from the amount of cash you actually get from the lender. For example, on a $100,000 loan with three points, you would only get $97,000 at the closing. That's where the word "discount" comes in. You can get around this problem by borrowing enough money so that you'll come out with what you actually need after the discount points have been deducted.

LOAN ORIGINATION FEE

Another charge to be paid before closing. This is supposedly levied to cover the lender's administrative costs, actually it also helps to make the loan more lucrative. The loan origination fee may be a named amount, $250, for example, or it may be a percentage of the principal. Not all lenders charge loan origination fees. Don't confuse this with the *loan application fee,* however. Application fees are smaller and must accompany the application form.

LOAN-TO-VALUE RATIO

Loan-to-value ratio determines the amount of down payment required to obtain the mortgage loan. If a lender will loan 80 percent of the value of the property, you must come up with a down payment of 20 percent. Of course, you may make a larger down payment. Usually, the loan-to-value ratio is tied to the purchase price, but occasionally the lender's appraisal will come in below the purchase price and you'll be required to put down more cash in order to close the deal.

FHA

Not a magic spell. FHA stands for Federal Housing Administration, a departmental arm of HUD which is the cabinet-level Office of Housing and Urban Development. For many years the letters FHA have been synonymous with "low down payment mortgages" to millions of Americans. As little as 5 percent down in fact. The FHA accomplishes this lending miracle safely by *insuring* loans, not by actually lending the money. The buyer pays a small monthly premium for the insurance. You can get FHA insured mortgage loans through most of the traditional lending institutions in your community.

VA

The Veterans Administration, newly named the Department of Veterans' Affairs (DVA). You can still get 100 percent home financing with a VA loan, in theory anyway. Like the FHA, the VA does not actually lend the money. It guarantees the loan to the financial institution that holds the mortgage.

PMI

Generally used to refer to private mortgage insurance. This insurance from private enterprise will also enable buyers to purchase with minimal down payments. Sometimes the insurance premium that the buyer must pay drops off after a certain percentage of the original principal is paid back. *Note:* one of the largest vendors of private mortgage insurance is named PMI. This has nothing to do with what they sell, they say. PMI just happens to be the initials of the founder and president of the company.

FANNIE MAE

The Federal National Mortgage Association. This is the largest member of the secondary mortgage market. Primary lenders such as banks and S&Ls sell the mortgages they write into the secondary market. FANNIE MAE has become so powerful during the past decade that its qualification guidelines set the standards for mortgage loans at the vast majority of lending institutions. Even officials of the RTC say that any buyer applying for financing from that agency will have to meet mortgage qualification guidelines set by FANNIE MAE.

GETTING A HOME MORTGAGE

The information required on a home mortgage loan application is quite different from what's required on an application to finance an investment property. With the exception of multi-family houses, your primary residence doesn't usually produce income. The lender therefore wants to be assured that you'll be able to make the scheduled payments (and continue to eat, etc.) with the income you earn each year.

"What are they worried about?" you ask. "They've got our down payment money and/or the mortgage insurance and if we don't pay, they get our house!"

Yes, but foreclosure is expensive. And, as we've said, lenders do *not* want to carry REOs. If you can't get a mortgage loan elsewhere, the RTC will arrange financing. But even *they* want at least 15 percent down payment and they want some assurance that you'll be able to make the scheduled monthly mortgage payments. And you can't really blame the RTC on this one, they're trying to unload this property, not recycle it!

So buying a home from among the bailout inventory may indeed be a steal, but you're still going to have to hunt for mortgage money just like everyone else. Your goal should be to get the best possible financing, efficiently and painlessly. To that end, we've compiled a list of ten questions you should ask prospective mortgage lenders.

1. *What types of mortgages are available for this property?* The loan officer should discuss with you FHA, VA, fixed-rate loans, ARMs, and any creative programs available like the Graduated Payment Mortgage (GPM) or the Growing Equity Mortgage (GEM). If you don't understand something that's rattled off in passing, stop the conversation and ask for an explanation. Getting a mortgage is a business deal, make sure it's a good deal for you.

2. *What are the current interest rates for each type of loan?* You may be surprised at the difference in rates for different types of loans. Beware "teaser" rates on adjustables that will surely go up at the first adjustment period. If you are considering an adjustable, be sure to have all the options explained, including rate hike caps.

3. *How long a term can we get with each type of loan?* Sometimes loans written for a shorter term (say, fifteen years) carry lower interest rates than long-term loans. The most common term for a home mortgage is currently thirty years. But because the amount of monthly payment is crucial to many buyers, some lenders are now talking about writing loans for longer terms. Monthly payments on a forty year mortgage would be lower than those on a thirty year mortgage.

4. *What is the loan-to-value ratio (minimum down payment required) on each type of loan?* Answers to this question will help you to determine exactly how much cash you'll need. How much cash you *have* will also be a primary factor in determining which property you can buy.

5. *What guidelines does your bank or S&L use for loan qualification?* This question is just as important as the down payment question because a lender will not lend money unless you can show that the monthly payments are within your comfort zone. Currently, the most common qualification guideline is an income-to-long-term-debt ratio. A ballpark figure, subject to change at any time, is that the total of your long-term monthly payments (housing expenses,

car loans, large outstanding credit card balances, alimony, and child support) should not exceed 36 percent of your gross monthly income. If two or more people are buying a home together, all incomes will be considered in establishing qualification.

6. *Are points being charged? Are they different for different types of loans?* Points represent money you must pay out-of-pocket. If you're short on down payment money, you may want to choose a loan with a slightly higher interest rate but no points. If you plan to own the house for a short time only (less than five years) definitely try to avoid points. The extra interest you pay on a *no point* loan will take several years to equal the up-front fee you would pay in points to get the lower-rate loan.

7. *What are the other fees involved in getting financing at this lending institution?* The lender is required by law to disclose all fees to you. Ask about application fees, loan origination fees, appraisal fees, credit check fees, bank attorney review fees, and the all-encompassing: *anything else?*

8. *How long will it take to get a decision on our application?* You'll probably get a "Well, about . . ." type answer from the loan officer but at least you'll have an idea. The length of time allowed for a mortgage contingency is an important part of a home purchase contract.

9. *Will the interest rate be fixed in the loan commitment?* In times of unstable interest rates, some lenders try to make a mortgage commitment without an interest rate commitment, hoping that the buyer/borrower will accept the going rate at the time of the closing. Don't accept this. Instead, try to get a commitment for a maximum interest rate which includes a statement that if going interest rates should be lower on the date of your closing, your loan will be written at the lower rate.

10. *Based upon the information we've given you on this application, do you think we qualify for a mortgage loan from your bank?* With a personal computer at hand, a loan officer can usually answer this question pretty accurately. If the answer is a hesitant "Well, I'm not

exactly sure. There may be some problem with . . ." you might want to consider saving yourself the application fee and looking elsewhere.

Every business deal has two sides. While you're looking at what the lender has to offer, the lender will want some information about what you have to offer. Be prepared with facts and figures regarding the following ten items.

1. The full names of each of the buyers.

2. Employment information for each buyer. You'll need statistics on job title, how long employed, salary, and the name of a supervisor or company department where employment can be verified.

3. The number of your dependents. The bank wants to know how many people are living on your income.

4. Other income. Bring along a list of all your sources of money including commissions or salary from a part-time job, rental income from investment property, child support payments, and other investment income.

5. Your assets. Take the time to make up a list of stocks, bonds, life insurance policies, retirement funds, real estate that you own, rare coins, oriental rugs, Renoirs, and anything else that has monetary value.

6. Your debts. The lender will want this list broken down to individual commitments with credit card numbers and loan account numbers. On long-term debts like car payments, the lender will want to know how many more payments are due.

7. The address of the property you are buying. Sometimes they'll also ask you for a description of the property. We've found it helpful to bring along a copy of the listing sheet that the real estate agent gave you.

8. The probable purchase price. If you've already made the deal, you'll know this number. If not, give the banker your best guess at where you'll probably make a deal. He or she will not be involved in the

negotiating. If you have appraisal information on the property, bring that along too.

9. Property taxes. Your prospective lender will need the amount of local taxes to calculate your probable monthly payment.

10. The amount of money you plan to use as a down payment. This and the price are the keys to calculating exactly how much of a mortgage loan you'll need.

GETTING INVESTMENT
PROPERTY MORTGAGES

Although your income and credit history may designate you as a good lending risk, they won't carry nearly as much weight on an investment property mortgage application as they do on a home loan application. Once you step into the investment arena, lenders become much more interested in gathering facts about the property that you want to buy.

Why? Because investment property produces income and income pays the mortgage. And (more important from your perspective) because smart investment property buyers ask for nonrecourse mortgages.

A nonrecourse mortgage limits the debt obligation to repayment from the property that is mortgaged. Unlike a home mortgage, it is not a personal obligation. If you cannot make the scheduled payments, you will not be personally liable. The lender's claim will be limited to the real estate upon which they hold a mortgage and its rents.

Some lenders do try to add a personal liability clause to investment property mortgages. You should refuse to accept this, always, even if it means that you must look elsewhere for financing. Some lenders will also try to include a due-on-sale clause. Try to avoid this addition, since the property will be easier to resell if the mortgage is assumable. A due-on-sale clause, however, is not necessarily sufficient reason, of itself, to walk away from an otherwise advantageous financing agreement.

When comparison shopping for investment property financing, you should ask exactly the same questions as the home mortgage shopper. Loan officers will also ask you all of the questions listed above *and:*

1. *What is the current income from the property?* They will probably want figures for at least two years.

2. *What are the operating expenses?* You'll be asked about property taxes and insurance costs, so be sure to get this information from the seller.

3. *What is the condition of the building? Have there been any recent renovations? Are any major repairs pending? Do you plan to renovate or remodel?* The lender is trying to anticipate large cash expenditures and calculate whether or not you have sufficient resources to handle them.

4. *What is the length of the leases in the building?* In other words, how long can you count on the amount of income the property is now showing? In residential rental property, leases are usually short (one or two years) whereas in commercial rental property, leases can be very long (sometimes twenty-five years or more).

5. *What kind of leases do the tenants hold?* This question is not pertinent to residential property. In commercial leasing, however, there are various lease arrangements ranging from a net lease to a net, net, net (triple net) lease. The more nets in the lease type, the more expenses of the building will be paid by the tenant (even including property taxes in the triple net version). If you are dealing with commercial leases, you should have your own lawyer. No exceptions!

MORTGAGE BROKERS

If you are pressed for time or are feeling overwhelmed by the complexity of today's mortgage financing, you might want to consider using a mortgage broker. These trained professionals act in a capacity much like that of a travel agent. They find out what you, the buyer/borrower, want and need and then they find the program and lender that best suits those needs. Sometimes you'll get a better deal than you could possibly get on your own, almost always you'll be saved a lot of time, talk, and legwork.

Most mortgage brokers are paid a commission by the lender with whom they place your mortgage. Occasionally, there is also a small fee to the buyer.

Sometimes real estate agents will recommend mortgage brokers with whom they are familiar. If no one has been recommended to you, you might call several mortgage brokers on the phone and interview them. How long have they been in business? Do they charge a fee? What financial services will they take on? Ask for references. You want the mortgage broker to give you the names and phone numbers of satisfied customers. And ask for trade group affiliations. There are two: the Mortgage Bankers Association and the American Institute of Mortgage Brokers. Membership does not guarantee quality, but it does mean the broker has made a professional commitment.

SPECIAL DEALS

Believe it or not, some factors in a mortgage are negotiable. Especially when dealing with S&Ls in conservatorship, you should go after lower interest rates, longer terms, assumability, the stretching of qualification guidelines, lower down payment requirements, and anything else you and your attorney might think up to make the financing more lucrative *for you*. Remember: when it comes to financing, you won't be offered anything if you don't ask for it.

There are also some special deals available that require not only asking but also some rather aggressive, polite yet persevering, and sometimes almost visionary effort. Are they worth it? People who use them usually answer with an unqualified *yes!*

SHARED EQUITY

Shared equity is a mortgaging arrangement for home buyers who can qualify for the monthly payments but don't have the down payment money necessary to buy a home. It's also usually a good investment for a parent, relative, or merely someone who wants a no-work, no-responsibility money-making opportunity. It does work, but *DON'T* enter into this arrangement without a written agreement drawn by a lawyer.

The key to success is to find a property (house or condo) that can be purchased below market value and is likely to appreciate. The investor then makes the down payment while the home buyer agrees to live in the home and make the monthly mortgage, tax, and insurance payments and maintain the property. When the property is sold, the investor gets his down payment money back, plus 50 percent (or whatever split has been arranged) of the profit.

It's usually a good idea to include a buy-out clause in the event that the home buyer does not want to sell and decides to stay in the property beyond the five- to seven-year maximum usually written into the shared-equity agreement. In such a case, the home buyer would have the property appraised at current value and then refinance.

Let's say the property originally cost $100,000. Mom and Dad, as shared-equity participants, put down $15,000. Five years later, the kids decided they wanted to stay. Their incomes had gone up and so had the value of the property. The appraisal came in at $147,000.

With private mortgage insurance, "the kids" could now get a mortgage in the amount of $132,000. After paying off the old mortgage of just under $85,000 there would be $47,000 in cash. Closing costs would be deducted and Mom and Dad would get their $15,000 back plus half the appreciation which would probably be close to another $15,000.

Not bad. The investors doubled their money in five years and the home buyers have a home, a mortgage they can afford, and enough left over to buy a new car. And during the five years, the investors did nothing and the home buyers had a home of their own.

Equity sharing became popular in the 1980s when appreciation was red-hot. It may not work as well in a flat market unless the property to be purchased is chosen very carefully and negotiated to a price well below market value. It also has some tax questions that are still being debated by the IRS. If this mortgaging option appeals to you, we strongly recommend that you consult with a tax accountant as to the most advantageous structuring of the arrangement for tax purposes.

203 K

There's a little-known and much underused program insured by HUD and available through conventional lenders that will allow home buyers or investors to purchase one- to four-family houses in need of repair with no down payment. You must have a good credit rating and you will be judged by standard qualification guidelines, but if you qualify, this is a great program. Here's how you do it.

1. Find a property that is structurally sound but in need of repairs. Sign a contract to purchase it subject to obtaining HUD 203 K financing. (You can get a list of local lenders working with the program from your nearest HUD office.)

2. Get *written* professional estimates for the cost of repairs that must be done.

3. Take these estimates to a professional appraiser and hire him or her to do an appraisal for the estimated value of the property when the improvements are complete.

4. Take your plans, estimates, appraisal, and purchase contract to the lender you select and apply for a HUD insured 203 K mortgage.

HUD will base its insured mortgage amount not upon the price in your contract, but upon the appraised value when renovations are complete. There are limits on how much they will insure, however, and there are strict inspection policies so that HUD can be certain you are doing the work you promised. Eligible expenditures include windows, stairs, walls, floors, roofing, wiring, plumbing, solar energy installations, room partitions, modernizing baths, kitchens, electric service, energy conservation, air conditioning systems, expanding living area, and adding apartments.

The 203 K program is a great way to buy property with nothing down, but it is not a program for the flat broke. There are up-front costs that cannot be avoided. The earnest money, for example, which could be as much as 10 percent of the purchase price. Yes, you can borrow this money, but remember it will cost you interest. And then there's the fee for the appraiser. You can probably get the cost-of-repair estimates done without charge, or for small fees. But you've also got closing costs and attorney's fees to pay.

These out-of-pocket costs are about the same as in most property purchases, and you'll get the money back once the loan is in place. We just want you to be aware that you'll need some cash backup even in a "no down payment" program.

STATE SPONSORED LOW INTEREST MORTGAGE PROGRAMS

From time to time, states offer mortgages for first-time home buyers at below market rates with minimal down payment requirements. These programs are funded by state-issued tax-free bonds and they come and go, almost in a flash. Currently, negotiations are going on between state agencies and the RTC to provide financing for the RTC's affordable housing inventory.

If you think that you may qualify, call the appropriate state office. They go by different names in different states but it usually reads something like Housing Finance Agency, or Mortgage Financing Agency, or Housing Finance Corporation. Whatever your state's office is called, get on their mailing list. And watch your newspapers too because mailing lists are sometimes slower than press releases. When a program is announced, drop everything and run. There are usually long waiting lists and the money usually runs out before the end of the list.

If you're not one of the winners of the low-interest mortgages, just don't give up. If you miss one issue, have your name put on the list for the next one. Meanwhile, keep looking for a good deal and don't focus only on the state supported programs. Look into the other available programs or seller financing. If all else fails, leasing with an option to buy can work in the private marketplace.

CHAPTER 13

THE PURCHASE CONTRACT

They couldn't believe it! But it was really happening. Dick and Jane Smith had grabbed a dream. Three years ago they had passed on an ocean-view condo because they couldn't get a mortgage. Every lender they approached had said *No*. The Smiths simply couldn't afford the monthly payments, even if they had put every spare penny into a down payment toward the $385,000 price tag that the developer insisted upon, absolutely firm.

And today, here they were holding a fully executed purchase contract with the RTC as seller for the *same condo,* at a purchase price of $272,000. They had found their chunk of gold in the S&L volcano! They were in heaven! Life was great!

Heaven lasted for two days and then turned *unbearably hot* during a conversation in the locker room at the YMCA.

"Sorry you lost the condo, Dick."

"What?"

"The condo. I heard about the Japanese investor."

"What Japanese investor?"

"You mean you don't know? Cindy's cousin works at the RTC office. A Japanese investor came in yesterday and offered them the full $300,000 asking price on that unit, cash and no contingencies. My brother, Jack, has a real estate license and he says that the RTC has to accept. The deal meets all their requirements with an immediate close too. Too bad for you, though. I heard you got the price down pretty low."

Dick wrapped a towel around his waist and called his lawyer from the phone in the locker room. He was so anxious and angry, he could hardly get the words out in sequence. What the lawyer said in reply changed a lot of his attitudes. There was some comforting reassurance, there was some added pressure, and there was a new idea.

Once a contract is executed by both buyer and seller, it's a firm deal. *Unless* the buyer withdraws because any one of the contract contingencies cannot be met. The Smiths' condo purchase was contingent upon their being able to obtain a mortgage. The lawyer explained to Dick that the forty-five days specified in the contract as the time limit to get a mortgage commitment had taken on new meaning. The deal now hinged both on getting a mortgage and on getting it by a certain date. Yes, Dick could ask the RTC for an extension of the mortgage contingency cutoff date if he applied for the mortgage immediately, and if through no fault of the Smiths, the lender didn't reply within the time limit. But the RTC did not have to grant the extension, since there was no automatic extension clause in the contract.

During the forty-three days remaining in the mortgage contingency clause, however, Dick's deal was safe, the lawyer said. The Japanese investor could pace up and down outside the offices of the RTC if he wanted to but he could not buy the property unless the contract between Dick and Jane and the RTC was officially terminated and the earnest money being held in escrow was returned to the Smiths.

If Dick and Jane were determined to get that particular apartment, they would have to make every effort to be certain that work on the mortgage application progressed quickly and smoothly, or . . . Then the lawyer made a surprising suggestion. Had the Smiths been considering any other condos? If they had had several apartments in mind, they might try to find out the name of this Japanese investor and offer to assign their contract to him.

"Why ever would they do that?" you ask.

Because they could make $28,000 for doing almost nothing. When you assign a contract, you give (or sell) your position as buyer, with all its rights and obligations, to another party. If the Japanese investor was willing to pay $300,000 for the condo, why shouldn't he pay $28,000 to the Smiths and $272,000 to the RTC. This kind of dealing is more common in the real estate marketplace than most inexperienced investors and home buyers realize. It is made possible by the terms of the contract.

Legally, a contract that does not specifically forbid the right of assignment is considered assignable. If you are interested in this road to extra pocket money, however, we suggest that you consult with your lawyer about getting the right to assign the contract written in. If you choose to go ahead on the premise that assignment is not expressly prohibited, as the Smiths did, you may run into some resistance, legal and otherwise. Whichever approach you choose, be certain that you have a competent attorney draw up the assignment agreement between you and the new buyer. This is not a playground for amateurs.

But let's get back to contracts that actually result in acquiring the property. Whether you are buying a home or a property that's strictly for investment, you should try to make your purchase contract contingent upon as many factors favorable to you as possible. Contingencies almost always work to the buyer's advantage. The contingency is an "I'll buy your property if . . ." clause: *if* I can get a mortgage, *if* an engineer says it's in good condition, *if* you'll throw in the living room draperies, *if* the land has good drainage, *if* I can get my house sold, etc. We'll give you a sample of commonly used contingencies in just a bit. First, however, let's look at what must be in a contract to make it delineate the basics of your deal clearly and to make the deal airtight, so airtight that a much better offer made the next day cannot break in.

CONTRACT NECESSITIES

Don't let anyone ever convince you that the piece of paper he or she is holding a pen over is a "standard real estate contract." There is no such thing. Each and every contract is unique and almost anything can be written in or deleted. There are, however, some standard clauses in most real estate contracts. These may appear in any order in the contract you are being asked to sign and their wording may differ slightly. Just check this list item by item against what you find in the contract. Do this yourself, whether you use an attorney or not.

In many parts of the nation, attorneys rarely participate in real estate closings. We both feel strongly, however, that attorney review of a real estate contract is very advisable. To paraphrase the American Express commercial, *Don't buy a home without it.* Or any other kind of real estate either!

The following are the necessities of every real estate purchase contract.

1. *The date.* Every contractual agreement, of any kind, must be dated to be legally enforceable.

2. *Names.* Be sure that the full, legal names of all the buyers and all the sellers appear in the contract. Do not use nicknames. Men should include "Jr." when appropriate and women should usually include their maiden name if they are married.

3. *The address of the property being purchased.* A street address is usually sufficient with an apartment number or unit number included if you are buying a condo or co-op. Don't forget the name of the municipality. Many neighborhoods have nicknames that should not be used as property identification in a contract. For example, a mutual friend of ours lives in Liberty Corner which is an area in a town commonly called Basking Ridge (that's the mailing address too), but the real name of the municipality is Bernards Township. A contract to sell her home should give the address as "Bernards Township." Many real estate agents and most lawyers also include the block and lot number on the municipal tax map as further identification.

4. *The purchase price.* The amount of money upon which there was a meeting of the minds. It must appear in the contract.

5. *Closing date and place.* A closing date and the place where it will take place must be *named* in the contract, but in reality date and place are often changed. Closings can take place in a lawyer's office, a branch office of the mortgage lender, a title company office, an escrow agent's office, a real estate agent's office, or any other mutually agreeable place. The date is usually considered approximate and can be altered by days or weeks.

If the contract identifies the date as *of the essence,* however, the closing must take place on that day. If you, the buyer, do not close on the date named, you could lose your deposit money and the property could be sold to another party. If the seller does not close on the specific date, he could lose the sale with the buyer walking away escrow deposit in hand, or the seller could be faced with a judicial order for *specific performance* which means *perform as directed in the contract* and usually carries significant financial penalties for each day of delay.

If your contract does not identify the closing date as essential to the contract, it still could be made essential at a later date. A legal notification that *time is of the essence* can be served to either party. Usually at least two weeks' advance notice before the essential date is required.

Occupancy of the property is usually tied to the closing date, either in the same clause or in the one immediately following. Most often, occupancy is *upon passing of title,* which means the property should be empty and ready for you to take possession on the day of the closing. If there are other specific agreements regarding occupancy, they should be carefully delineated in the contract. For example, one type of occupancy agreement concerns leases that survive the sale in a residential or commercial rental building. Another common agreement is seller holdover. When the seller wishes to remain in the property for some time after the closing, a per diem rental fee should be named in the occupancy clause. If you want an unoccupied property, be sure that the fee is high enough to encourage the seller to move as soon as possible. Financial pain has a way of motivating people.

6. *Deed.* Your purchase contract should name the type of deed that is to convey title. We're going to talk more about deeds in the next chapter, but for now be aware that a warranty deed is a guarantee of clear title whereas a bargain and sale deed promises nothing. (Checking for clear title is one of the reasons you pay a title insurance company. More about that also in the next chapter.)

7. *Escrow.* The contract should state how much earnest money will be held in escrow and by whom. Among the likely candidates are closing agents, title companies, attorneys, and real estate agents.

All escrow monies must be held by a third party fiduciary agent in a special trust fund which cannot be commingled with the normal operating funds of the company holding it. These accounts do pay interest, however, and your contract should state who gets the interest, the buyer or the seller. Many contracts state that the interest is to be split equally between them.

8. *Closing costs and adjustments.* Sometimes who pays what closing costs is a part of the contract negotiations. If that was the case, the agreement that was reached should be written out in the contract.

    "Adjustments" refers to the apportionment of taxes, sewer use fees, water, community membership fees, even oil left in the oil tank. Get it in writing that everything will be adjusted equitably as of the date of closing.

9. *Signatures.* Signatures on a purchase contract need not be notarized but they must be in ink and they must be original signatures on each copy. In other words, if there are seven copies of the purchase contract, each buyer and seller must sign *all seven*.

    We like to see addresses and telephone numbers included under the signatures both in order to identify the participants more fully and to facilitate contact if necessary.

10. *The real estate commission.* This is not really an essential of the contract but naming the amount of the commission and who is to pay it can same time-consuming arguments at the closing table. The names of the selling and listing broker should be recorded. If the amount of real estate commission was reduced during the negotiating process, be sure to name the exact dollar amount that is to be paid, not simply a notation like 4½ percent of the purchase price.

CONTRACT CONTINGENCIES

The following are some buyer protection clauses that are important in protecting your money and your purchase interest. Check the wording carefully in the contract for your purchase and be *certain* that the dates that are named are within your comfort zone.

1. *Attorney review clause.* We think this is absolutely essential. By including an attorney review clause, the buyer can "jump out" of a contract that may have been entered into on an emotional high

without sufficient rational evaluation. Or a buyer could get out of a contract upon realization that the price he agreed to pay was higher than market value, even if this realization came two days after the contract was fully executed.

Remember also that some states have consumer protection legislation that will let you out of a contract for a specified time after signing for any reason or no reason. Other states, like New Jersey, make the attorney review clause a mandatory part of all real estate contracts.

The attorney review clause should state that the contract is subject to the review of the buyer's attorney who may reject the contract for any reason. It should also name a time limit for this attorney review period (usually three to five working days) and state that a rejection of the contract must be made in writing.

2. *Clear title.* Your contract should be contingent upon the seller being able to deliver clear title. This is especially important when dealing with RTC properties because many of them have title problems or liens against the property. Title clouds must be cleared before closing, unless you agree to take these on in return for a much-reduced price. This is risky business, however. Do it only after careful consultation with a competent attorney.

3. *Mortgage contingency.* Unless you have enough cash to pay for the property in a bank account somewhere (or under your mattress), you'll have to get a mortgage. If you have a mortgage contingency clause in your purchase contract and for some reason you can't get the mortgage that you need, you'll get your earnest money back. Otherwise, you could lose it all.

The mortgage contingency clause should state how much mortgage money you need. It should also break down exactly how you're planning to pay the purchase price and at what intervals. Usually this clause is several lines long, listing the numbers for each entry in a column that adds up to the total purchase price. The lines are:

Earnest money accompanying this contract _____

Additional funds to be deposited in the escrow account within ten days

of the execution of this contract _____

A first mortgage in the amount of _____

Additional cash to be presented at the closing in the form of a certified

check _____

Total purchase price _____

Most mortgage contingency clauses today state that the buyer will make earnest efforts to procure a mortgage and will accept a mortgage at the prevailing rate of interest. As an added protection to the seller, some contracts state that if the buyer does not make mortgage application, the real estate broker can do so for him.

One of the most important parts of a mortgage contingency clause is the cut-off date. Try to find out from your prospective lender how long most applications are currently taking and then give yourself two extra weeks.

You can also give yourself a little additional insurance by including a clause that automatically extends the mortgage contingency for 30 days if the delay in reply is the fault of the lender. If you don't have this clause in your contract and it looks as though your lender will be late, have your attorney draw up a short letter of agreement stating the time extension and have both parties sign it.

4. *Condition of the building.* When the RTC first embarked on the sale of its REOs, it stated that all properties were to be sold "as is" which meant no purchases could be conditional upon a professional inspection. The difficulty of that rule has become apparent, however, and it is changing. Try for the same inspection clauses with the RTC as you would with any private seller. Each of the following contingencies should be stated as a separate clause in the contract.

Professional inspection of the property should be done within five working days of the date of the contract. If the report reveals structural defects or nonworking systems, you can walk away from the deal, insist that the seller fix what's wrong, or renegotiate the price to take into account the cost of repairs.

Termites are active in all fifty states, although they are rare in Maine, Alaska, and some other northern states. Your purchase contract should be subject to a professional termite inspection. If termites are found in the building, the contract should state that they will be exterminated at the seller's expense and all damage repaired to the buyer's satisfaction. Or if you prefer, you can renegotiate the price by the cost of the extermination and repair and have this work done after the closing. Some lenders, however, won't give a mortgage until a termite problem is cleared. Most termite extermination companies do give warranties. If the seller won't pay the few additional dollars for this added protection, you, the buyer, should do it.

Radon is a colorless, odorless gas that occurs naturally in the ground and makes its way to the surface. It is usually most concentrated therefore in closed basement areas. If the property you want to buy tests above accepted limits, the radon contingency clause should provide for correction of the problem. Sometimes the seller pays the entire cost of installing an air exchange system, sometimes the cost is split between buyer and seller. Whichever you agree to, have it written into the contract *before* the radon test is done. You can also go even further and make your contract contingent upon a satisfactory radon test.

Drinkable water is essential. The contract should be contingent upon the availability of uncontaminated tap water.

A clause stating that maintenance of and liability for the property remains with the seller until closing should be included in every contract. In other words, if lightning strikes, you can walk away from the deal or you can insist that the seller put the property back into the condition it was in when you signed the contract.

It should be agreed in your contract that the property delivered at the closing will be in broom clean condition. "Broom-clean" doesn't mean spotless, but it does mean free of rubbish, unwanted furniture and appliances, and reasonably clean. Be certain that this is understood. If the seller does not comply, have funds held in escrow until the rubbish is removed or deduct the cost of removal and cleaning from the purchase price paid at the closing.

The right to inspect the property on the day of the closing is absolutely essential. Be certain that it is written into your contract. If you find something that is different from what you saw on the day you signed the contract, something that is not working, or something about which you have a serious concern, you can arrange to have enough money to cover the repair, if it is necessary, held in escrow until the question is resolved. Or you can simply delay the closing, although this usually upsets everyone, including the lender, the lawyers, the title company, and most of all the seller. We've included a day-of-the-closing inspection checklist for you in the next chapter.

5. *Personal property.* The personal property that you negotiated to have included in the deal should stay with the property.

Upon reading that sentence you may be thinking that we're getting a bit simplistic.

"Of course!" you say. "If you negotiate that something stays, it stays."

Not always. People do strange things when money becomes a part of the picture and sometimes lawn furniture, appliances, draperies, etc., "accidentally" go into the moving van and disappear to some location four states away.

Have you ever tried to get something back from someone who has moved across state lines? Going to court is your only recourse, and when two different states are involved it's unbelievably complex. It's also usually not worth the cost and trouble and the buyer takes the loss. To be certain that doesn't happen to you, list everything that is supposed to stay in or with the building in the contract. Then check off each item on your day-of-the-closing inspection.

6. *Sale of your current home.* Home buying would be less risky if the purchase of the new home could be contingent upon the sale of the old. Sellers in California and some of the western states have come to accept this contingency in their contracts. The rest of the nation has

been more resistant, but a slow real estate market has prompted some lenders to write contingencies in their mortgage commitments that require a contract on the "old" house before they'll write a mortgage loan for the new. Such a clause essentially delays the closing on the new house until the "old" one has a contingency-free purchase contract on it.

For a buyer, a contingency that makes purchase dependent upon a firm contract for the sale of an "old" home is a fine safeguard. The RTC will not hear of it, however. Or at least not as of this writing. Lenders in conservatorship might be more lenient. Private sellers in a slow market can sometimes be convinced.

NO STANDARD CONTRACT

As we write this, the RTC is working on a standardized contract form. Which is lovely, so long as you remember that there is *no standard contract* for the purchase and sale of real estate anywhere. Nor should there be.

You can use the form provided by the RTC or any real estate broker *and* you can change it. Words, phrases, or clauses can be deleted. Words, phrases, or clauses can be added. If you want to add a large amount of material, for example, a list of all the items of personal property (stove, carpeting, etc.) that stay with the real estate, you can add an *addendum* to the contract. (An addendum is any addition, but it usually refers to an added page.) Just be certain that everyone involved in the purchase/sale initials the bottom of the page.

Many buyers become anxious at the thought of signing a real estate purchase contract. They look upon it as a complex commitment that holds the possibility of legal webs and financial entanglements. Which is true. But that's looking at the hole when you could be looking at the donut.

Your purchase contract can be an exquisite means of protecting *your* legal and financial interests. We strongly recommend therefore that you do not sign a contract unless it contains an attorney review clause or unless your attorney reviews it prior to execution. Once you have that executed contract, you're on your way to property ownership. The property you have chosen is legally *off the market,* but not quite yours yet. That will happen at the closing.

CHAPTER 14

CLOUD-FREE TITLE

We won't be the first to compare buying real estate to a roller-coaster ride. It's almost a cliché. But clichés get to be clichés because they mean something. They usually begin as a new insight that everyone understands, everyone agrees with, and everyone begins to use to describe certain feelings or situations. And then the insight becomes a cliché.

Well, the roller-coaster ride cliché is a great description of the real estate buying process. There's the long, slow climb up the first and highest peak (looking for the right property), there's the scary descent (negotiating), then there are the smaller climbs and dips and wild turns (contracts, inspections, financing, and contingencies), and finally the last turn and the satisfying coast back to the platform (the closing).

The final coasting may be the easiest part of the ride, a time when you are gathering yourself together and relaxing a bit, but remember, you can't get off the roller coaster until your car arrives at the platform and comes to a stop. In just the same way, you can't take title to a piece of real estate unless you have a closing. This chapter will help to make that last part of your real estate ride more comfortable and, we hope, safer.

We'll go through some legal terminology and a few other facts you must know in order to approach the closing table as an educated buyer. Then we'll help you through the closing process, step by step.

TAKING TITLE

Taking title is simply taking over ownership of the property. But because every piece of real estate borders on other pieces of real estate, is a part of a neighborhood and a municipality, and is a symbol of wealth and status in our land, taking ownership is not simply a matter of signing your name. There are things to watch for and watch out for.

WHAT'S A CLOUD?

A *cloud* on a title is an outstanding claim, which, if valid, would impair or affect the owner's rights and holdings in the property. Although clouds might result from many different acts, title problems generally fall into two types: encroachments and encumbrances.

ENCROACHMENTS

An *encroachment* occurs when a building, a part of a building, or any kind of obstruction that is owned by someone else intrudes upon your land. It is a cloud upon the title if the intruder thinks he or she has a right to the land that you claim is yours. Most encroachments can be cleared up by having a survey done and then negotiating with the offending party.

There are two obvious solutions. The piece of land being encroached upon is sold to the encroacher. Or the encroacher is required to remove the building part or obstruction on your property. A third, less radical solution, however, sometimes keeps neighbors more neighborly. The encroachment can be acknowledged and the bit of land can be leased from the rightful owner for a small annual fee. This could be $1 if the encroachment is a doghouse or a children's playhouse on the back corner of your property. Or it could be thousands of dollars if ten feet of the width of a two-hundred-foot-long commercial driveway is actually on your land.

Encroachments are not uncommon in the real estate world but they are usually resolved without going to court. The bigger problem is encumbrances.

ENCUMBRANCES

An *encumbrance* is a claim, lien, charge, or liability that is attached to a piece of property. It will diminish the value of the real estate in question. Sometimes an encumbrance must be cleared before title passes, sometimes it passes with title.

Judgments, mechanic's or materialman's liens, unpaid taxes and utility bills, a divorced spouse's claim, and an heredity estate claim against the property are all encumbrances that must usually be cleared before title passes. Easements, however, usually pass with the deed.

An *easement* is a right of way. It gives one party (the party could be an individual, a group of individuals, or a utility company) the right to cross over the property of another. In the case of utility companies, it may also give them the right to dig up the property in order to service buried pipelines or other equipment. Easements for private individuals are usually driveways to landlocked lots. Private individuals and community groups sometimes hold the right of way to cross private property on a path to a facility or space shared by a community such as a beach, a lake, the riverfront, or open land intended as greenspace.

If you choose to buy a house with the gas line for the town buried in the backyard, be sure to negotiate for a lower price than that commonly being paid for properties free of this encumbrance. Every future buyer of your property will look at the dotted lines showing the gas line easement on the survey, and hesitate a bit. The property therefore will be somewhat harder to resell and may bring a lower price.

THE TITLE SEARCH

Before you can work out what to do about an encroachment or an encumbrance on a piece of property that you want to buy, you've got to know about it. So how does a prospective buyer find out about potential title problems?

You have a title search done! Insist on this. Some title insurance is actually issued without a search. You want to have a search done and you want to see the report. Your attorney can make the arrangements.

A title search will cost you a small cash outlay, but it's worth the money for the security. This is especially true in dealing with RTC properties and other foreclosures which historically have a larger number of title problems than conventional real estate sales.

THE SURVEY

Many mortgage lenders insist that a new survey be done when a property is sold. Others allow a simple affidavit of no change. Usually if the survey is no more than three to five years old, the owner can turn it over to the new buyer with a notarized statement that he/she has made no changes in the buildings or property lines.

A survey will show pictorially any encroachments that might be on the property. It will also show the siting and shapes of the buildings.

TITLE INSURANCE

Most mortgage lenders require title insurance. Title insurance, however, does not guarantee clear title. Rather it insures that the holder of the title insurance policy will be repaid for any loss sustained because of defects in the title. "Loss" might be court costs to fight a claim by a divorced spouse or it might be the cost of moving a driveway when the deed you got from the builder showed it to be on your land and, in actuality, a corner of it was on your neighbor's land.

In the vast majority of cases, the buyer pays for title insurance. It is available through your attorney or through the closing agent for the property, sometimes at a discounted rate if you ask for the attorney's discount. The actual cost of title insurance fluctuates but it is usually expressed as a percentage of the amount you insure. You will probably be encouraged to insure the full purchase price, but you can elect to insure only the amount of the mortgage. (A slight risk here, but the amount of risk is somewhat dependent upon what the title search shows.)

Just to give you a ballpark figure to work from (and remember, these numbers change all the time), a typical title policy might cost from ½ to 1 percent of the first $50,000 and ¼ to 1 percent of the remaining amount to be insured. You can actually call title companies to get their rates, but there is rarely a significant difference. Our experience has been that a good attorney, one on your side, can usually get you the best deal.

Some RTC properties have had serious title problems. No one at the RTC has said that the organization will pay title insurance, but then again, as of this writing, no one has said they won't. This is a point worth negotiating, especially in a property that has been in trouble.

For your own protection, you should do a little checking on your title insurance policy. Get a copy of the policy at least five days before the closing date for the property. Then request a copy of the unsigned deed before closing. Compare the legal description on the title insurance policy with the legal description of the property on the deed. They should match *exactly*. If they don't, contact your attorney or the closing agent immediately.

An efficient way to check title policy description against the deed is to use the method writers use to check galley proofs against their original manuscripts. It takes two people. One person reads aloud slowly from one document, saying each word and each punctuation mark; the other person follows the text in the other document, word by word.

When you get your title policy, you may see a listing headed EXCEP-TIONS. These are the items needed to clear title on that property before you take over ownership. They might include back taxes, liens from creditors, unpaid water bills, or a sewer assessment that has payments scheduled for another three years.

Most of the exceptions should be paid off before the closing and you should demand good evidence that this has indeed been done. If anything is not cleared to your satisfaction, have the money in question held in escrow until the matter is cleared. One exception might be certain municipal assessments, such as sewer lines. In some cases, the new owner agrees to take over the remaining payments.

THE DEED

A deed is the legal instrument that transfers title to property from one party to another. It is always in writing. A handshake might be an agreement, but it is never a deed. There are, however, several kinds of deeds. The three that follow are the most common.

WARRANTY DEED

A warranty deed states that the grantor (the seller) guarantees good title and will protect that guarantee (the buyer) against any claims. It is the very best kind of deed. Ask for it. You may not find your seller (or his attorney) agreeable but you won't know unless you try. And don't be intimidated by the size of the RTC. Treat them just like any other seller. Ask for a warranty deed. You may need it if the property has been in trouble!

Note: A warranty deed does not mean that you shouldn't have a title search or buy title insurance. The seller may guarantee something, but sometimes guarantees are hard to collect.

BARGAIN AND SALE DEED

A bargain and sale deed conveys property from one owner to another for a stated purchase price. There are no guarantees regarding title. (Which is why you have a title search and buy title insurance.)

BARGAIN AND SALE DEED WITH COVENANT VERSUS GRANTOR'S ACTS

This deed does not guarantee clear title but it does guarantee that the grantor (seller) has done nothing to adversely affect the title. It's probably the most common type of deed in use today.

CC&Rs

Sometimes certain specifications for use are written into a deed. Once this is done, they pass from one owner to another and are said to "run with the deed." Generally there are three types: covenants, conditions, and restrictions, commonly referred to as CC&Rs.

Covenants are promises: *The owner agrees to keep the sidewalks free of snow and ice.* Conditions border on threats: *If the owner cuts down the pine trees at the back line of the property, one-quarter of the acreage reverts to the town.* Restrictions usually govern use and building size: *No building on this lot shall be more than two stories high.*

The RTC plans to put restrictions into the deeds of multi-family apartment buildings that it sells under its affordable housing mandate. The restrictions will maintain rents on specific apartments at levels deemed affordable for low and moderate income families.

THE CLOSING

If a purchase contract is a meeting of the minds, a closing is a meeting of the bodies. Everyone involved in the sale gets together at an appointed time in an appointed place and shakes hands, reads and signs papers, and passes money from one to another. The secret of a good closing is preparation, and that includes knowing how much money you'll need, how to bring it to the closing table safely, and what other documents you may need.

HOW MUCH CASH?

In 1974, the federal government made life a little easier for real estate buyers. That was the year of RESPA, the Real Estate Settlement and Procedures Act. Under the act, both parties to a real estate transaction must be given notice of exactly what costs are going to be paid by each party and the amount of those costs. Usually, you can get your completed RESPA form (and there *is* a standard form) two days before closing.

But the arm of RESPA reaches much farther than the few days before closing. Under the act, a lender is required to give you a *good-faith estimate* of settlement costs and a copy of the Housing and Urban Development (HUD) booklet entitled *Settlement Costs* within three business days of the time you sign the written loan application. The lender must also give you a list of the documents and services that must be presented or completed before the closing. Check off each item as you have it completed and then check again to be sure it will be at the closing or that you will be bringing it with you.

Look for the following entries under the *borrower's* column. The numbers there will tell you how much money to bring to the closing table.

Loan origination fee. Remember, this is not the application fee. It is money you are paying for the privilege of borrowing.

Points. A part of the points due is sometimes paid upon signing of the mortgage commitment. You'll see the remaining amount listed under the *Loan Discount* category. Plan to bring this amount with you in your cashier's check because it will be deducted from the amount of your mortgage loan. For example, if you were borrowing $100,000 and you still had one and one-half points to pay, your check from the bank would be in the amount of $98,500.

Credit report. Sometimes you are asked to pay this upfront with the mortgage application fee. Be certain that you aren't billed for it twice.

Lender's inspection fee. This is usually the fee for the lender's appraisal. In new construction, however, it is indeed an inspection, sometimes several inspections during the course of the construction process.

Mortgage insurance application fee. This applies only if you are getting a low down payment mortgage that requires insurance. If you have a hefty down payment, be sure that this line is blank. Mortgage insurance is usually paid as a percentage of the remaining principal added to the monthly payment.

Assumption fee. Applicable only if you are assuming the mortgage already in place on the property.

First interest payment. Many lenders collect the first interest payment in advance and then send you a payment booklet within thirty days.

Hazard insurance premium. Better known as homeowner's insurance. Some lenders insist on paying the annual premium themselves, collecting the money from the homeowner. If you ask, however, you may be able to convince the lender to allow you to make your own homeowner insurance payments. If this is the case, the lender will require that you bring a signed affidavit from your insurance company saying that you have taken out and paid for a full year's policy.

Reserves. Most lenders want to pay the property taxes just to be certain the house doesn't go into tax sale. They require therefore that from six to nine months' taxes be kept on deposit at their office. The reserve will be collected at the closing and then you will pay one-twelfth of your annual tax bill with each mortgage payment. Try to negotiate with your lender to pay you interest on the money they are holding. It *is* your money after all.

Even better, you can try to negotiate the right to be responsible for paying your own taxes. This is usually granted only to buyers with a down payment of 50 percent or more, but there's no harm in asking.

Lenders who are making your hazard insurance payments for you will also require a reserve against the premiums. Sometimes a full year's reserve, while you make monthly payments toward the next year's premium. If you can't arrange to pay for your own insurance, try to get interest paid on this money being held.

Adjustments. The RESPA statement should include exactly how much you owe for oil in the tank, prorated water bills, etc.

Pest inspection fee. Unless the lender arranged for and dispatched the termite inspection company, you will have paid them on the spot. No payment should be required at the closing. This square should be blank.

Recording fees and transfer taxes. These vary according to the municipality, county, and state that you're in. The exact amounts should be named, however.

Title insurance. The entire one-time fee is to be paid at the closing. It usually runs several thousand dollars.

Title search. Usually listed as a separate charge from your attorney's fee.

Attorney fees. There may be a lender's attorney review fee even if you use your own attorney. Your attorney's fee can usually be paid by personal check, but be sure of this before the closing day.

Survey fee. Survey fees are usually paid directly to the company doing the work. In some cases, however, they may be paid out at the closing.

Balance due on the purchase price. The big number. This is the amount you're to bring to the closing beyond the money that's being held in escrow and the mortgage loan that's been promised to you.

Once you get the RESPA statement, check that all the fees listed are accurate. Then add them up. Now you will need to get a certified check or a cashier's check for that amount. Have the check made payable to you, yourself. Why? Because if something goes wrong and the property doesn't close you can simply redeposit the check. Nothing lost. If nothing goes wrong, you can endorse the check over to the closing agent.

It's often a good idea to get your cashier's check made out for a few hundred dollars more than you calculate you will need. Just in case you encounter some unexpected costs. If your check is for more money than you need, your closing agent will be happy to write you a check for the change.

DOCUMENTS YOU'LL NEED

You won't be required to bring all of the following yourself. Just make certain that someone has them and that they'll be at the closing. Otherwise annoying delays are almost inevitable.

Contract and mortgage commitment. You don't have to lay your copies out on the table, just bring them along in case there's a question.

Hazard insurance policy. Be certain you have the policy or a letter from your insurance agent stating that it has been paid and its terms. Most lenders won't allow the closing without it.

Pest inspection report, radon report, home inspection report. Again, you may not need to lay these on the table, but it's a good idea to have them with you.

Identification. If you're from out of town and unknown in the area, the closing agent or the attorneys for the lender may ask for identification. A driver's license might suffice but a passport would be better.

CLOSING CHECKPOINTS

To make what-to-do and what-to-bring as easy as possible, we've compiled a checklist for you. Happy closing!

1. Check to be sure everyone involved has the same date, time, and place.

    Address: _____

    _____

Time and date: _____

    □ Seller □ Lender □ Your attorney □ Real estate agents

2. Do you have your good-faith estimate of settlement costs and your HUD Settlement Costs booklet? □ Yes □ No

3. Notify utility companies and arrange for meter readings.

	Change of account notification	Meter reading scheduled
Electricity		
Water		
Gas		
Oil company		
Telephone		
Post office		
Security office in a condo or co-op community		

4. Do a careful day-of-closing inspection. Check appliances and working systems:
   □ Dishwasher □ Oven □ Stove
   □ Garbage disposal □ Water heater □ Furnace
   □ Air conditioner □ Humidifier □ Attic fan
   □ Garage-door openers □ Sump pump
   □ Lawn sprinkler system □ Smoke alarms □ Doorbells
   □ Burgler alarm system □ Broom clean □ Refuse removed

5. Check you personal-property-that-stays list from your contract. Be sure everything is on the premises. If movers are still at work while you are closing, you may want to remove the items that stay if you have a convenient place to keep them. If not, gather them into one room labeled with a sign that tells the movers they are NOT to be loaded into the van.

6. Bring to the closing:
   □ Purchase contract   □ Your checkbook with extra cash
   □ Certified check   □ Home inspection report
   □ Hazard insurance policy   □ Termite inspection report
   □ Personal identification   □ Radon inspection report
   □ Mortgage commitment
       letter

7. Be sure that all the keys to the property will be brought to the closing. Have your real estate agent check with both the seller and the seller's listing agent for keys.

CHAPTER 15

COLLECTING YOUR PROFITS

Monopoly was a favorite game in our childhood households. We both loved the scramble to buy property and then the joy, tinged with a malicious grin, of collecting rent from anyone who happened to land on our spaces. It didn't take us kids long to realize, however, that the real money was not in collecting rent, but in *selling*!

What negotiating, trading, sulking, and persuading sessions we had. The best times were in holding the odd property a fellow player needed to complete his set. Prices got to ten and twenty times the original purchase price, sometimes with a railroad or a utility company thrown into the bargain. We understood the secret of the game: *selling put cash in your pockets*.

So it is in the real world too. But to have something worth selling, you first must buy and buy carefully. That takes time, talent, skill, perseverance, and all the knowledge we've been writing about. Selling is the reward, a time for you to collect your profits. It too must be done carefully, however.

WHEN TO SELL

Some investors have a hard time selling. Putting their properties on the market is a little like putting the family jewels up for sale. If you tend in this direction, remember why you got into real estate investing in the first place. To make money, right? Well, *sale time is money-making time*! The only question left is *when*?

IN A CLIMBING MARKET

When properties are selling in days rather than months and new listings have lines of prospective buyers at the door, selling fever often hits investors. And no wonder! Selling in a hot market could bring in optimum profits. The opportunity is almost irresistible if you're moving out of the area or if you want to get your money out of the real estate investment marketplace. The proverbial seller's market could be the time to take your money and run (or book a world cruise).

But if you're in the middle of a price spiral, and you intend to sell one property at maximum profit in order to buy another, watch out. Because of the hot market, you may not be able to find another investment property that fits your guidelines for a "good deal." Then the market would be appreciating while you stand about holding bags of money that you want to invest. Now don't misunderstand, there are good deals available in a hot market, they just take longer to find.

When the pace of the market is very fast, we recommend that you identify the property you want to buy before you sell the property you own. You may be able to do this by signing a purchase contract contingent upon the sale of your current property or you may be able to negotiate an option.

When you take an option on a piece of property, you pay an agreed-upon amount of money for the exclusive right to buy a property at a named price during a named period of time. You are not required to buy, however. Often, if you exercise your option and do buy the property, the money you paid for the option is applied to the purchase price. If you don't buy during the option period, you lose the price you paid for the option, but that could be a minuscule portion of what it would cost you to carry two properties if you signed a purchase contract and then were unable to sell your old property at the price you anticipated. On the other hand, having the new property held for you while you get your old property sold, is usually well worth the price of the option.

If you can't get an option, tell the seller of the property you want to buy that you are interested and ask that seller to contact you if another interested party makes an offer. Do not negotiate price, however. Just say that you have a property to sell and you can't talk price until you see how much it will bring. Then put your property on the market. If you get an acceptable offer, sign the contract but be sure that it includes a five day attorney review clause for you, the seller, as well as for the buyer. During those five days, negotiate on the property you want to buy. If you come to an agreement on price, don't forget to put the attorney review clause in that contract also. Then if your deal on the property you're selling falls apart, you can jump out of the deal on the property you're buying. If nothing falls apart, you've got yourself a relatively risk-free two part deal.

IN A SINKING MARKET

Everything moves much more slowly in a sinking real estate market and most investors get very nervous. Few have the courage to sell. Ironically, a sluggish market may be the very best time to collect your current profits and set up a situation for even greater profits in the future.

The first step is to make your property particularly desirable, either through decorating and maintenance or by attractive pricing. If you bought well, you should have a great deal of price flexibility within your comfort range. While your property is for sale, look around for the very best deals, usually the properties of sellers who *must* sell. When you get a contingency-free contract on the property you're selling, go out and negotiate the very best deal with the sellers you've identified as having the best properties and the greatest motivation to sell.

If the property you sell is strictly an investment property and you sell it before you find an appropriate replacement, you can put the cash into a CD until you find another money-making steal. If you are living in your investment, however, try to negotiate a distant closing date (six months or so) in order to give yourself plenty of time to pick and choose your next home from among the many properties available in the slow local market.

CHANGE OF HEART

Maybe you thought you'd like landlording when you bought the twenty-unit building three years ago but you've since changed your mind. Maybe a nice hands-off investment like a REIT or some second mortgages has more appeal now. Or maybe you've done really well with the two four-family houses you own and would like to sell them off and use the funds to buy the garden apartment complex you heard was for sale.

Moving from one investment vehicle to another is a common reason for selling property. We do suggest, however, that you have contracts of sale on the vehicle(s) you're getting out of before you jump into a new one. Also ask yourself why you're getting out. What in the old vehicle displeased or disturbed you? What in the new vehicle appeals to you?

But perhaps you're moving. Leaving the area is more like a change of plans than a change of heart. And it is a good reason to sell investment property, since most real estate is best managed from close proximity. If market conditions are not appropriate for a sale, however, and your investment has a positive cash flow, consider hiring a professional management company. You can always sell next year.

Sometimes a change of heart is pure necessity. You simply need the money that's invested in the property. No need to feel guilty about selling. After all, you put that money in to make money and that's exactly what you've done!

MAXIMUM APPRECIATION

Many investment properties have an upward spiral of appreciation for a period of time and then level off. This is particularly true of handyman specials, contracts for unbuilt condominium apartments, turn-around apartment buildings, newly converted mixed-use buildings, renovated small strip malls, condominium conversions, and the kind of hammer and nails conversions where you transform a carriage house or a firehouse into a home. Usually when the remodeling is done, the units are sold, or the rents have been raised and the building is at capacity, it's time to sell and move on. There's sure to be another creative investment waiting.

WHAT'S IT WORTH?

Before you put any piece of property on the market for any reason, you should have a very good idea of its market value. Because you were once a wise buyer, however, you know that estimating market value is not a sport strictly limited to the pros. Get onto the field and use your knowledge and your instincts.

USING CMAs

Comparables were the key to estimating market value when you were looking to buy residential property and they play a major role in estimating market value in residential selling also. You can get them, along with a professional service known as a Competitive Market Analysis (CMA), from your local real estate agents.

Real estate firms need listings. Without listings they have nothing to advertise. To get them, therefore, they make every effort to present their services to the prospective home seller.

In order to tell you about his/her firm (and try to get you to list with that firm), an agent will come to your home, take a tour with you, bring out comparables, and do a competitive market analysis. A CMA measures your house or apartment against similar houses or apartments that have sold recently. The goal is to come up with a probable selling price.

If you invite three to five agents from different firms into your home and have each do a CMA, you will have an excellent idea of probable market value. Be aware that in this process you will be offered the opportunity to list your property. Don't sign anything! And don't feel sheepish about getting these CMAs done for no fee. Those agents want your listing and the CMA along with a talk on "how we'll market your property better than anyone else" is their sales kit. You are giving them a chance to present their wares while you are also gathering invaluable information.

If you don't want to spend the time it takes to talk with several agents, you may want to get a professional appraisal of your property's value. This will cost you several hundred dollars, however, and it may not be as accurate as the consensus of five CMAs, since it is just *one* professional opinion.

CAPITALIZATION RATE

Income-producing properties, both residential and commercial, are more difficult to evaluate in terms of fair market value, since comparables are far more scarce. So how do you get the numbers you need? You might try estimating value by changing roles and using a buyer's technique.

Many savvy buyers use capitalization rate as a guideline for the price they should pay. With current tax laws, high-priced financial advisors are suggesting the use of nine times net income as a guideline.

If you assume a buyer is using this guideline and your net income is $50,000 a year, you can expect that a buyer will think $450,000 a fair price. Add from 10 to 20 percent (depending on the pace of the marketplace) for negotiating space, and you have a starting point for your asking price.

HIGHEST AND BEST USE

Estimating the value of raw land is one of the most difficult tasks an appraiser must face. One guideline, however, is to check the zoning laws to see what the maximum income-producing use might be for your land. Then compare your land with the going price for land being used in that way. If tax assessments are current and relatively accurate, you might check the land value assessment for properties that have been developed in ways consistent with the possibilities for your property.

TAKING A STAB AT IT

Very often the right price for a property is affected by the goals of the seller and the mood of the marketplace. If a seller wants to sell quickly, the price will be lower. If the market is slow but the seller has plenty of time, he may try out a higher price first and lower it later. In a fast-paced market, the tendency is to price high and see what happens. It's very easy to reduce the price once it's set, but almost impossible to increase it.

PROPERTY PREPARATION

"Sayings" abound to remind us to make judgments based upon quality rather than appearance. Such rules to live by include: "Don't judge a book by its cover"; "There is no trusting appearances"; and "Beauty is only skin deep."

But, funny thing! Publishers spend millions on cover design, car manufacturers count on buyers trusting in appearances, and the American beauty industry is practically the backbone of the national economy. So what's the real message in our society? *Appearances count.* Say it over and over again as you get your property ready for market.

RESIDENTIAL INTERIORS

Not only does appearance count on the interior, neatness counts too. Your aim is a lived-in look that's sparkling clean and without clutter. Have we created an oxymoron? Maybe. But that *is* what sells houses and condos. Let's take a room by room tour which we'll pepper with bits of advice.

The foyer. Keep this as spacious as possible. If you have a foyer table, consider a vase of flowers. Some sellers put property description sheets on the foyer table also. We prefer the dining room or kitchen where there is more space for a group to gather around and discuss what they see on the description sheets or the survey.

If there is a coat closet in your foyer, empty it of everything except a few coats. Bulging closets look small and put ideas of "not enough storage space" into the heads of prospective buyers.

The living room, family room, or great room. These rooms should look comfortable and inviting but never cluttered. Try taking some furniture out. Plants add a nice touch. Don't have a fire burning in the fireplace for each prospective buyer unless you want to spend a lot of time cleaning up the ashes as soon as that buyer leaves. Otherwise the next buyer gets a whiff of dead ashes, and that is *not* a selling point. If you want to highlight your fireplace, buy some white birch logs and stack them on the grate. A basket or vase filled with eucalyptus branches will also add the hint of an appealing odor to the air.

If the carpeting is worn in the center of the room, consider buying a light-colored area rug (9 × 12 is usually a good size and easy to get). Placing this in the center of the room will draw the furniture into a conversational area and draw attention away from the old carpet. Or, if you're lucky enough to have hardwood floors and they're in good condition, tear up the carpet and have the floors refinished. Hardwood floors have become a hot selling item of late.

The kitchen. Paint the ceiling. Kitchen ceilings have a way of turning gray which makes the whole room seem darker. No buyer will notice that you've recently painted your ceiling, they'll just think how nice and bright your kitchen is!

Clear the countertops, including toasters, coffee makers, mixers, recipe books, and all the other clutter of everyday life. It may be unreal, but buyers want to see clean countertops. They seem bigger that way.

Clean the insides of appliances, ovens, and cabinets. Put down new shelf paper and organize your cans and foodstuffs neatly. We know, none of this has much to do with the value of the property, but buyers will open ovens, dishwashers, kitchen cabinets, and broom closets. Those prospective buyers must not be put off by accumulated grease and grime or by precariously stacked canned goods.

The dining room. Some sellers like to set the table as for a dinner party to give the room an elegant look. This often works quite successfully. A lovely centerpiece of flowers (real or silk) in the center of the dining table can be just as appealing, however. Do turn on the dining room chandelier. The light adds a gracious touch, particularly if you have a beautiful chandelier. (It doesn't matter if the chandelier doesn't stay with the property, light it anyway!)

Bathrooms. Clean! Everything should gleam, with no grime between the tiles or elsewhere. Just before going on the market is a great time to change the shower curtain. And you're not wasting money. You can take the curtain with you. If you have cabinetry around the bathroom sinks, be certain to clear the insides of accumulated debris. Also check for leaks in the trap of the sink. Most serious buyers look under the sink and leaks make them very nervous!

Bedrooms. Empty closets and corners as much as you possibly can. A good storage place is under the bed, no one ever looks there. And keep the shades raised; sunny is a plus in bedrooms.

Everywhere. Have the windows cleaned; you'll be surprised how much bigger everything looks. Be sure all carpets are well vacuumed. Touch up chipped woodwork with a coat of paint. Wash handprints from the walls.

Be aware of smells. These have a subliminal effect. If you own a cat, be absolutely certain the litter box is cleaned daily.

Garage and basement. Remove clutter and cobwebs. Be sure all the light bulbs work; you don't want any suspicious dark corners.

CURB APPEAL

Studies have shown that buyers who don't like the exterior appearance of a property often refuse to go inside, much less buy. So increase the curb appeal as much as possible.

If the house needs painting, paint it. Surveys in *Practical Homeowner* Magazine show that a paint job can return ten times its cost in increased property value. Pay special attention to the front door which should be in a contrasting *and* welcoming color.

Keep foundation plantings well trimmed. That goes double for your grass. (Weeds don't look so much like weeds if they're kept cut.) Prune dead branches from trees. Remove all lawn ornaments. (Some buyers like them and some don't. But the ones who like them may not like yours, so in general, it's better not to have any.) Keep toys, bicycles, your teenage son's pink hearse, and your boat and trailer out of your driveway. You do not want this area to look crowded!

WHAT YOU DON'T SEE

Every buyer worries about the structural soundness of the building and the working condition of its systems. If you want to speed your sale along, have a professional home inspection done *before* you put the property on the market and buy a home warranty plan that guarantees the inspection for a year or more.

A recent Gallup poll shows that eight out of ten prospective buyers surveyed considered a home warranty an important part of their next real estate purchase. And a six month study in a major metropolitan area showed that homes with a warranty sold on average about 60 percent faster than homes without a warranty.

PAPERWORK

We've found that a property description sheet, often formatted in a style similar to the local MLS sheets, helps to identify your property in the minds of prospective buyers. Leave these on a convenient table along with copies of the survey, if you have it. If you're selling a condo or co-op, you might also make up a brief summary of house rules and by-laws. A few words about why you like the community never hurt either.

MONEY-MAKING PROPERTIES

Just about everything said about residential properties applies to investment properties also, except that you do not have as much control. Tenants can be a problem. You must arrange for showings with them in advance and you must encourage them to present the premises with its best face forward. The promise of a month or two free of rent (after the property is under contract but before closing) in return for cooperation can work wonders.

When selling investment property, you must also have your books and other records up to date and ready for inspection. Income and expenditures play an important role in determining the offers you will get and in the way you respond to those offers.

HOW TO SELL IT

Not more than a decade ago there were only two commonly used ways to sell a piece of real estate, by owner or through listing with a full-service broker. Today, you can still sell *by owner* but your choice of brokerage services has expanded tremendously. Let's take a look at property marketing in the 1990s.

BY OWNER

When selling your property without the help of a broker, you must realize that you are now competing in a marketplace peopled by professionals with state-of-the-art equipment. Real estate offices have had MLS for decades. Today, they also have computers that can retrieve lists of "just right" properties in minutes, hunt out mortgages, and call up the appropriate comparables, to mention only a few functions. Many agents have car phones and paging systems. Property advertising is no longer limited to newspaper ads in the classified section. Whole pages are filled with pictures, radio spots describe the bargains, and some agents make videotape presentations on local television.

So who's going to notice your flyer on the supermarket community bulletin board or your four-line ad in the solid-print classified section of your local newspaper?

Many, many people. While most transferees house hunt with a real estate agent, local home buyers and investors often seek out for-sale-by-owner properties. They are usually in search of a better deal or want the first crack at whatever is new on the market. You, as a seller, must attract their attention and then market the property professionally.

Now don't let that put you off. "Market the property professionally" does not require a degree from Harvard, folks. It just takes some knowledge sprinkled with common sense and careful preparation. You start your marketing work *before* you put an advertisement anywhere.

Directions. One of the most common reasons for no-shows among house hunters is poor directions. People get lost and decide, "It's probably not worth it anyway!"

To avoid this prospective customer loss, prepare fool-proof directions and leave a printed copy near each telephone extension. Read the directions *slowly* to each caller and then ask that caller to read them back. Say something like, "Could you read those back to me now just to be sure I didn't leave anything important out?" Of course you didn't leave anything out! You're reading. What you really want to know is "Did you get it all down?" But if you ask that question, virtually every caller will swear they have every traffic light in place even if they've run off the envelope back where they started writing and onto the used napkin from the kids' lunch.

To compose your direction information sheets (and this applies to commercial property as well as residential), start with a street map of your town. Mark four major landmarks or road intersections that everyone in town would recognize if a stranger were to ask, "How do

I get to . . ." Now in four different colors mark the best routes to your property. Best need not be shortest. It goes without saying that you should avoid directing your prospective buyers past the county sewer treatment plant.

Once you have the map marked, you'll need the help of a driver. Go out in the car to each of the four points with a notebook in hand. Then drive each route writing down directions for the red route, the green route, etc. Get odometer readings, traffic lights, and landmarks down exactly. If you do a good job, your prospective buyers will arrive at your door saying, "Well, it certainly is easy to get here!"

Your Sign. You do need one! Any real estate agent will tell you that calls generated by a sign are hot. The person is motivated and already likes the outside of the property and its location.

Keep your sign simple. Use the same wording on both sides: FOR SALE; your phone number; and "by appointment only." You can buy stick-on, weather-proof letters at your local stationery or crafts store.

Hammer the sign into the ground near the curb, *perpendicular* to the road so that it can be read by cars passing in either direction. If you are selling a condo or co-op or a commercial property where there is no lawn for display, put the sign in a front-facing window.

Your Flyer. If you want to compete with the professionals, you must make a description sheet for your property. Many sellers successfully copy the format of the MLS, others prefer a more creative approach with pictures and comments. Whichever you choose, don't forget:

- the address of the property;
- your name(s) and phone number;
- property description;
- taxes;
- the asking price.

Newspaper Advertising. Keep it simple. You shouldn't try to compete with the professional advertising. Prospective buyers look for and read FOR SALE BY OWNER ads even though they may seem lost among the print.

When you write your copy, be sure to include the number of bedrooms, the number of bathrooms, the neighborhood, and most important of all, the price. Studies show that there are fewer responses to advertisements that do not include price. If your property has some special feature, a view, a screened porch, proximity to a railroad station, mention it but don't get into lengthy purple prose.

Showing. As you conduct prospective buyers through your property, ask as many questions as you answer. *Where are you folks from? How long have you been looking for a place? How many children do you have?* Questions like these may seem like small talk, but actually they are an excellent means of gathering information you can use later in the negotiating process. Keep a notebook. Get the names and phone numbers if you can and jot down all the information you gather while showing.

It's usually a good idea to have two people in the property while it's being shown. Violence is rare in owner-sales, but it can occur. If you can't have two people at home, arrange to have a friend call during the showing time with a call back from you scheduled when the house hunters have left.

Facts and Figures. Whether you are selling a home or an investment property, you will need to have the essential facts at hand. Block and lot number, assessment, taxes, survey, heating costs, condo community information, rent receipts, and other expenses.

Don't put this information out for any casual walk-through, however. Just keep it in a drawer that's handy. You'll know when someone is interested enough to pull it out.

Your Attorney. If you sell your property without a broker, you really should have an attorney, selected before you put the house on the market. The attorney will hold escrow funds and can be the someone you need to talk with when you want to buy some thinking time during negotiations.

BY BROKER

To hire a broker you must sign a contract, usually referred to as a listing contract. There are three main types.

Exclusive Right To Sell. You give the broker the exclusive right to sell your property. If, during the term of the listing contract, you sell it to an old friend from high school or even to your mother-in-law, you owe the broker a commission. The broker, however, may make arrangements with other brokers to act as his subagents (the rationale behind multiple listing). The exclusive-right-to-sell is the most commonly used listing contract. Not coincidentally, it gives the most protection and power to the broker you hire.

Exclusive Agency. You give the broker the exclusive right to act as your broker (he gets a piece of the commission if another agency actually sells the property) but you reserve for yourself the right to sell the property to someone who has not seen it through the efforts of a real estate agent. If you sell to your Aunt Jane, for example, you do not pay a commission. Some Realtor Boards allow exclusive agency listings to appear on their MLS.

Open Listing. This may be written or oral; we highly recommend written. In an open listing situation, you agree to pay the broker a commission if he or his sales agents sell your property. You reserve the right to sell it yourself, however, and to hire any number of other brokers to represent you. This is a whoever-gets-here-with-a-buyer-first-gets-paid situation. It works best in a very fast market.

Most sellers agree to pay an open listing commission of half the usual and customary rate, since there are no advertising costs involved and the commission is never split with another agency. Some sellers use open listings successfully after an exclusive listing expires. Since many agents are already familiar with the property, the seller simply says, "Okay, boys and girls, whoever works the hardest gets paid." Needless to say, open listings are not popular with brokers.

Payment for services. How much do you pay a real estate agent? The answer twenty years ago was "Six percent of course." Not anymore. In the first place, the law of the land states that there can be no price fixing, every contract is negotiated between seller and agent. There have been for years, however, customary and usual amounts. But even these guidelines are breaking down as sellers select from the broker buffet.

Traditional Broker. A traditional broker is not paid until the property closes. They will advertise, show the property, negotiate the sale, and follow through to closing. The usual commission is 6 to 7 percent, although some traditional brokers are working for 5 percent.

Discount Broker. There is an ever-widening variety of discount plans available to the public. Essentially, most discount brokers charge a fee, paid up front and nonrefundable whether the property is sold or not. Some charge an up-front fee, plus a commission of 2 or 3 percent when the property is sold.

Most discount brokers will advertise your property, take calls, and make appointments, but in most cases, they will not show the property. Conducting prospective buyers through is the responsibility of the seller, although special arrangements can sometimes be made for agented showings at an additional fee. Fairly often, sales agents working for the discount broker will become involved in negotiating and in finding a mortgage. Some discount brokers list their properties on MLS, many do not.

Multi-option Broker. These are the new guys on the block. They offer the seller a selection of programs ranging from a sign for the front lawn, to some advertising and call answering, to full service. The seller chooses and pays appropriately. Switching from one plan to another is quite easy, however. A multi-option broker may act like a discount broker or a traditional broker, depending upon the service you choose. Most multi-option brokers are members of their local Realtor Boards and the MLS.

SELLER NEGOTIATING

Before you negotiate as a seller, you should go back and reread Chapter 10. You see, a good part of successful seller negotiating is understanding buyer negotiating. In fact, you can use all the same guidelines and tactics, with reversed perspective.

Successful seller negotiating is mostly a matter of changing roles. Instead of the suitor showing up with roses (and money), you are now the party being sought. You have the prize. Like the Victorian lady, you must wait to be asked, but you have the immense power to say No or Yes.

Use your knowledge and power carefully and you'll come away with a handsome profit. Then you can buy yourself a Mercedes, cruise the Caribbean, or perhaps, just perhaps, go back into the bailout bonanza and pick yourself another piece of winning property.

We wish you all the very best!

APPENDIX 1

DIRECTORY OF HUD FIELD OFFICES

Region I

Jurisdiction: Connecticut, Maine, Massachusetts, New Hampshire, Rhode Island, Vermont

Boston, Massachusetts Regional Office
David T. Forsberg
Regional Administrator—
Regional Housing Commissioner
HUD—Boston Regional Office
Thomas P. O'Neill, Jr.
Federal Building
10 Causeway Street
Room 375
Boston, MA 02222-1092
(617) 565-5234
(FTS) 835-5234

Hartford, Connecticut Office—(Category A)
William Hernandez, Jr.
Manager
HUD—Hartford Office
330 Main Street
Hartford, CT 06106-1860
(203) 240-4523
(FTS) 244-4523

Manchester, New Hampshire Office—(Category B)
James Barry
Manager
HUD—Manchester Office
Norris Cotton Federal Building
275 Chestnut Street
Manchester, NH 03101-2487
(603) 666-7681
(FTS) 834-7581

**Providence, Rhode Island
Office—(Category B)**
Casimir J. Kolaski, Jr.
Manager
HUD—Providence Office
330 John O. Pastore
Federal Building
  and U.S. Post
Office—Kennedy Plaza
Providence, RI 02903-1745
(401) 528-5351
(FTS) 838-5351

**Bangor, Maine
Office—(Category D)**
Richard Young
Supervisory Appraiser
HUD—Bangor Office
Professional Building
Casco Northern Bank Building
23 Main Street
Bangor, ME 04401-4318
(207) 945-0467
(FTS) 833-7534

**Burlington, Vermont
Office—(Category D)**
William Peters
Chief
HUD—Burlington Office
Federal Building
Room B311
11 Elmwood Avenue
Post Office Box 879
Burlington, VT 05402-0879
(802) 951-6290
(FTS) 832-6290

Region II

Jurisdiction: New York, New
Jersey, Virgin Islands

New York Regional Office
Dr. Anthony Villane
Regional Administrator—
Regional Housing Commissioner
HUD—New York Regional
Office
26 Federal Plaza
New York, NY 10278-0068
(212) 264-8068
(FTS) 264-8068

**Buffalo, New York
Office—(Category A)**
Joseph Lynch
Manager
HUD—Buffalo Office
Lafayette Court
5th Floor
465 Main Street
Buffalo, NY 14203-1780
(716) 846-5755
(FTS) 437-5733

**Camden, New Jersey
Office—(Category C)**
Elmer Roy
Manager
HUD—Camden Office
519 Federal Street
Camden, NJ 08103-9998
(609) 757-5081
(FTS) 488-5081

Newark, New Jersey
Office—(Category A)
Theodore Britton, Jr.
Manager
HUD—Newark Office
Military Park Building
60 Park Place
Newark, NJ 07102-5504
(201) 877-1662
(FTS) 349-1814

Albany, New York
Office—(Category C)
John Petricco
Manager
HUD—Albany Office
Leo W. O'Brien
Federal Building
North Pearl Street and
    Clinton Avenue
Albany, NY 12207-2395
(518) 472-3567
(FTS) 562-3567

Region III

Jurisdiction: Pennsylvania,
Washington, DC, Maryland,
Delaware, Virginia, West Virginia

Philadelphia, Pennsylvania
Regional Office
Harry Staller
Deputy Regional Administrator
HUD—Philadelphia
    Regional Office
Liberty Square Building

105 South 7th Street
Philadelphia, PA 19106-3392
(215) 597-2560
(FTS) 597-2560

Washington, DC
Office—(Category A)
I. Toni Thomas
Manager
HUD—Washington, DC Office
451 7th Street, S.W.
Room 3158
Washington, DC 20410-5500
(202) 453-4534
(FTS) 453-4534

Baltimore, Maryland
Office—(Category A)
Dean Reger
Acting Manager
HUD—Baltimore Office
10 North Calvert Street
3rd Floor
Baltimore, MD 21202-1865
(301) 962-2121
(FTS) 922-3047

Pittsburgh, Pennsylvania
Office—(Category A)
Manager
HUD—Pittsburgh Office
412 Old Post Office
Courthouse Building
7th Aveenue & Grant Street
Pittsburgh, PA 15219-1906
(412) 644-6428
(FTS) 722-6388

**Richmond, Virginia
Office—(Category A)**
Mary Ann Wilson
Manager
HUD—Richmond Office
400 North 8th Street
Richmond, VA 23240
(804) 771-2721
(FTS) 925-2721

**Charleston, West Virginia
Office—(Category B)**
Michael Kulick
Manager
HUD—Charleston Office
405 Capitol Street
Suite 708
Charleston, WV 25301-1795
(304) 347-7000
(FTS) 930-7036

**Wilmington, Delaware
Office—(Category D)**
A. David Sharbaugh
Chief
HUD—Wilmington Office
844 King Street
Wilmington, DE 19801
(302) 573-6300
(FTS) 487-6300

Region IV

Jurisdiction: Alabama, Florida,
Georgia, Kentucky, Mississippi,
North Carolina, South Carolina,
Tennessee

**Atlanta, Georgia Regional
Office**
Raymond A. Harris
Regional Administrator—
Regional Housing Commissioner
HUD—Atlanta Regional Office
Richard B. Russell
Federal Building
75 Spring Street, S.W.
Atlanta, GA 30303-3388
(404) 331-5136
(FTS) 841-5136

**Birmingham, Alabama
Office—(Category A)**
Robert E. Lunsford
Manager
HUD—Birmingham Office
600 Beacon Parkway West
Suite 300
Birmingham, AL 35209-3144
(205) 731-1617
(FTS) 229-1617

Caribbean Office—(Category A)
Rosa Villalonga
Acting Manager
HUD—Caribbean Office
San Juan Center
159 Carlos E. Chardon Avenue
San Juan, PR 00918-1804
(809) 766-5201
(FTS) 498-5201

**Louisville, Kentucky
Office—(Category A)**
Verna V. Van Ness
Acting Manager

HUD—Louisville Office
601 West Broadway
Post Office Box 1044
Louisville, KY 40201-1044
(502) 582-5251
(FTS) 352-5251

**Jackson, Mississippi—
(Category A)**
Sandra Freeman
Manager
HUD—Jackson Office
Dr. A.H. McCoy
Federal Building
100 W. Capitol Street
Room 910
Jackson, MS 39269-1096
(601) 965-4702
(FTS) 490-4702

**Greensboro, North
Carolina—(Category A)**
Larry J. Parker
Manager
HUD—Greensboro Office
415 North Edgeworth Street
Greensboro, NC 27401-2107
(919) 333-5363
(FTS) 699-5361

**Columbia, South Carolina
Office—(Category A)**
Ted B. Freeman
Manager
HUD—Columbia Office
Strom Thurmond
Federal Building
1835-45 Assembly Street

Columbia, SC 29201-2480
(803) 765-5592
(FTS) 677-5592

**Knoxville, Tennessee
Office—(Category A)**
Richard B. Barnwell
Manager
HUD—Knoxville Office
John J. Duncan
Federal Building
710 Locust Street, S.W.
Knoxville, TN 37902-2526
(615) 549-9384
(FTS) 854-9384

**Memphis, Tennessee
Office—(Category C)**
Bob Atkins
Manager
HUD—Memphis Office
200 Jefferson Avenue
Suite 1200
Memphis, TN 38103-2335
(901) 521-3367
(FTS) 222-3367

**Nashville, Tennessee
Office—(Category B)**
John H. Fisher
Manager
HUD—Nashville Office
251 Cumberland Bend Drive
Suite 200
Nashville, TN 37228-1803
(615) 736-5213
(FTS) 852-5213

**Jacksonville, Florida
Office—(Category A)**
James T. Chaplin
Manager
HUD—Jacksonville Office
325 West Adams Street
Jacksonville, FL 32202-4303
(904) 791-2626
(FTS) 946-2626

**Coral Gables, Florida
Office—(Category C)**
Orlando L. Lorie
Manager
HUD—Coral Gables Office
Gables One Tower
1320 South Dixie Highway
Coral Gables, FL 33146-2911
(305) 662-4510
(FTS) 350-6010

**Orlando, Florida
Office—(Category C)**
M. Jeannette Porter
Manager
HUD—Orlando Office
Langley Building
3751 Maguire Boulevard
Suite 270
Orlando, FL 32803-3032
(302) 648-6441
(FTS) 820-6441

**Tampa, Florida
Office—(Category C)**
George A. Milburn Jr.
Manager

HUD—Tampa Office
Suite 700
Timberlake Federal
  Building Annex
501 East Polk Street
Tampa, FL 33602-3945
(813) 228-2501
(FTS) 826-2501

Region V

Jurisdiction: Illinois, Indiana,
Michigan, Minnesota, Ohio,
Wisconsin

Chicago, Illinois Regional Office
Gertrude Jordan
Regional Administrator—
Regional Housing Commissioner
HUD—Chicago Regional Office
626 West Jackson Boulevard
Chicago, IL 60606
(312) 353-5680
(FTS) 353-5680

**Detroit, Michigan
Office—(Category A)**
Harry I. Sharrott
Manager
HUD—Detroit Office
Patrick V. McNamara
Federal Building
477 Michigan Avenue
Detroit, MI 48226-2592
(313) 226-6280
(FTS) 226-7900

Indianapolis, Indiana Office— (Category A)
J. Nicholas Shelley
Manager
HUD—Indianapolis Office
151 North Delaware Street
Indianapolis, IN 46204-2526
(317) 226-6303
(FTS) 331-6303

Grand Rapids, Michigan Office—(Category B)
Bill Harris
Acting Manager
HUD—Grand Rapids Office
2922 Fuller Avenue, N.E.
Grand Rapids, MI 49505-3409
(616) 456-2100
(FTS) 372-2182

Minneapolis–St.Paul, Minnesota—(Category A)
Thomas Feeney
Manager
HUD—Minneapolis–
  St. Paul Office
220 Second Street, South
Bridge Place Building
Minneapolis, MN 55401-2195
(612) 333-3002
(FTS) 782-3002

Cincinnati, Ohio Office—(Category B)
Norman L. Deas
Manager
HUD—Cincinnati Office

Federal Office Building
Room 9002
550 Main Street
Cincinnati, OH 45202-3253
(513) 684-2884
(FTS) 684-2884

Cleveland, Ohio Office—(Category B)
George L. Engel
Manager
HUD—Cleveland Office
One Playhouse Square
1375 Euclid Avenue
Room 420
Cleveland, OH 44115-1832
(216) 522-4065
(FTS) 942-4065

Columbus, Ohio Office—(Category A)
Robert W. Dolin
Manager
HUD—Columbus Office
200 North High Street
Columbus, OH 43215-2499
(614) 469-5737
(FTS) 943-7345

Milwaukee, Wisconsin Office—(Category A)
Delbert F. Reynolds
Manager
HUD—Milwaukee Office
Henry S. Reuss
Federal Plaza
310 West Wisconsin Avenue

Suite 1380
Milwaukee, WI 53203-2289
(414) 291-3214
(FTS) 362-1493

**Flint, Michigan
Office—(Category C)**
Gary T. LeVine
Manager
HUD—Flint Office
Gil Sabuco Building
352 South Saginaw Street
Room 200
Flint, MI 48502-1953
(313) 766-5107
(FTS) 378-5107

**Springfield, Illinois
Office—(Category D)**
Lawrence Morgan
Supervisory Appraiser
HUD—Springfield Office
524 South 2nd Street
Suite 672
Springfield, IL 62701-1774
(217) 492-4085
(FTS) 955-4085

Region VI

Jurisdiction: Arkansas,
Louisiana, New Mexico,
Oklahoma, Texas

**Fort Worth, Texas Regional
Office**
Sam R. Moseley
Regional Administrator—

Regional Housing
 Commmissioner
HUD—Fort Worth
 Regional Office
1600 Throckmorton
Post Office Box 2905
Fort Worth, TX 76113-2905
(817) 885-5401
(FTS) 728-5401

**Dallas, Texas Office—
(Category C)**
Clarence D. Babers
Manager
HUD—Dallas Office
555 Griffin Square Building
525 Griffin Street
Room 106
Dallas, TX 75202-5007
(214) 767-8308
(FTS) 729-8308

**Albuquerque, New
Mexico—(Category C)**
Michael R. Griego
Manager
HUD—Albuquerque Office
625 Truman Street, N.E.
Albuquerque, NM 87110-6443
(505) 262-6463
(FTS) 474-6463

**Houston, Texas
Office—(Category B)**
James M. Wilson
Manager
HUD—Houston Office
National Bank of Texas Building

2211 Norfolk
Suite 300
Houston, TX 77098-4096
(713) 229-3589
(FTS) 526-7586

**Lubbock, Texas
Office—(Category C)**
Henry E. Whitney
Manager
HUD—Lubbock Office
Federal Building
1205 Texas Avenue
Lubbock, TX 79401-4093
(806) 743-7265
(FTS) 738-7265

**San Antonio, Texas
Office—(Category A)**
Cynthia Leon
Manager
HUD—San Antonio Office
Washington Square Building
800 Dolorosa Street
San Antonio, TX 78207-4563
(512) 229-6781
(FTS) 730-6806

**Little Rock, Arkansas
Office—(Category A)**
John T. Suskie
Manager
HUD—Little Rock Office
Lafayette Building
523 Louisiana
Suite 200
Little Rock, AK 72201-3523

(501) 378-5931
(FTS) 740-5401

**New Orleans, Louisiana
Office—(Category A)**
Joe Brinkley
Acting Manager
HUD—New Orleans Office
Fisk Federal Building
1661 Canal Street
Post Office Box 70288
New Orleans, LA 70172-2887
(504) 589-7200
(FTS) 682-7200

**Shreveport, Louisiana
Office—(Category C)**
David E. Gleason
Manager
HUD—Shreveport Office
New Federal Building
500 Fannin Street
Shreveport, Louisiana
71101-3077
(318) 226-5385
(FTS) 493-5385

**Oklahoma City, Oklahoma
Office—(Category A)**
Troy Grigsby
Acting Manager
HUD—Oklahoma City Office
Murrah Federal Building
200 N.W. 5th Street
Oklahoma City, OK 73102-3202
(405) 231-4181
(FTS) 736-4891

Tulsa, Oklahoma
Office—(Category C)
Robert H. Gardner
Manager
HUD—Tulsa Office
Robert S. Kerr Building
440 South Houston Avenue
Room 200
Tulsa, OK 74127-8923
(918) 581-7435
(FTS) 745-7435

Region VII

Jurisdiction: Iowa, Kansas,
Missouri, Nebraska

Kansas City, Missouri
Regional Office
William H. Brown
Regional Administrator—
Regional Housing Commissioner
HUD—Kansas City Regional
Office
Gateway Tower II
400 State Avenue
Kansas City, KS 66101-2406
(913) 236-2162
(FTS) 757-2162

Omaha, Nebraska
Office—(Category A)
Roger M. Massey
Manager
HUD—Omaha Office
Braiker/Brandeis Building
210 South 16th Street
Omaha, NB 68102-1622

(402) 221-3703
(FTS) 864-3703

St. Louis, Missouri
Office—(Category A)
Kenneth G. Lange
Manager
HUD—St. Louis Office
210 North Tucker Boulevard
St. Louis, MO 63101-1997
(314) 425-4761
(FTS) 279-4761

Des Moines, Iowa
Office—(Category B)
William McNarney
Manager
HUD—Des Moines Office
Federal Building
210 Walnut Street
Room 259
Des Moines, IA 50309-2155
(515) 284-4512
(FTS) 862-4512

Topeka, Kansas
Office—(Category D)
Burl Baker, Chief
HUD—Topeka Office
Frank Carlson
Federal Building
444 S.E. Quincy
Room 370
Topeka, KS 66683-0001
(913) 295-2652
(FTS) 752-2652

Region VIII

Jurisdiction: Colorado, Montana, North Dakota, South Dakota, Utah, Wyoming

Denver, Colorado Regional Office
Michael Chitwood
Regional Administrator—
Regional Housing Commissioner
HUD—Denver Regional Office
Executive Tower Building
1405 Curtis Street
Denver, CO 80202-2349
(303) 844-4513
(FTS) 564-4513

Salt Lake City, Utah Office—(Category C)
Richard Bell
Manager
HUD—Salt Lake City Office
324 South State Street
Suite 220
Salt Lake City, UT 84111-2321
(801) 524-5237
(FTS) 588-5237

Helena, Montana Office—(Category C)
Christian Kafentzis
Manager
HUD—Helena Office
Federal Building
Drawer 10095
301 S. Park
Room 340

Helena, MT 59626-0095
(406) 449-5205
(FTS) 585-5205

Sioux Falls, South Dakota Office—(Category D)
Don Olson
Chief
HUD—Sioux Falls Office
300 North Dakota Avenue
Suite 116
Courthouse Plaza
Sioux Falls, SD 57102-0311
(605) 330-4223
(FTS) 782-4223

Fargo, North Dakota Office—(Category D)
Keith Elliott
Chief
HUD—Fargo Office
Federal Building
Post Office Box 2483
653 2nd Avenue, North
Room 300
Fargo, ND 58108-2483
(701) 239-5136
(FTS) 783-5136

Casper, Wyoming Office—(Category D)
Lawrence Gosnell
Chief
HUD—Casper Office
4225 Federal Office Building
100 East B Street
Post Office Box 580
Casper, WY 82602-1918

(307) 261-5252
(FTS) 328-5252

Region IX

Jurisdiction: Arizona, California, Hawaii, Nevada, Guam, American Samoa

San Francisco, California Regional Office
Robert De Monte
Regional Administrator—
Regional Housing Commissioner
HUD—San Francisco
  Regional Office
Philip Burton Federal Building
  & U.S. Courthouse
450 Golden Gate Avenue
Post Office Box 36003
San Francisco, CA 94102-3448
(415) 556-4752
(FTS) 556-4752

Indian Programs Office
C. Raphael Mecham
Director
HUD—Indian Programs Office
One North First Street
Suite 400
Phoenix, AZ 85004-2360
(602) 261-4156
(FTS) 261-4156

**Honolulu, Hawaii
Office—(Category A)**
Gordon Y. Furutani

Manager
HUD—Honolulu Office
300 Ala Moana Boulevard
Room 3318
Honolulu, HI 96850-4991
(808) 546-2136
(FTS) 546-2136

**Los Angeles, California
Office—(Category A)**
Charles Ming
Manager
HUD—Los Angeles Office
1615 W. Olympic Boulevard
Los Angeles, CA 90015-3801
(213) 251-7122
(FTS) 983-7122

**Sacramento, California
Office—(Category B)**
Anthony A. Randolph
Manager
HUD—Sacramento Office
777 12th Street
Suite 200
Post Office Box 1978
Sacramento, CA 95814-1977
(916) 551-1351
(FTS) 460-1351

**Reno, Nevada
Office—(Category C)**
Andrew D. Whitten, Jr.
Manager
HUD—Reno Office
1050 Bible Way
Box 4700

Reno, NV 89505-4700
(702) 784-5356
(FTS) 470-5356

San Diego, California
Office—(Category C)
Charles J. Wilson
Manager
HUD—San Diego Office
Federal Office Building
880 Front Street
Room 563
San Diego, CA 92188-0100
(619) 557-5310
(FTS) 895-5310

Las Vegas, Nevada
Office—(Category C)
Thomas C. Webster
Manager
HUD—Las Vegas Office
1500 East Tropicana Avenue
2nd Floor
Las Vegas, NV 89119-6516
(702) 388-6500
(FTS) 598-6500

Phoenix Office—(Category B)
Dwight A. Peterson
Manager
HUD—Phoenix Office
One North First Street
Suite 300
Post Office Box 13468
Phoenix, AZ 85002-3468
(602) 261-4434
(FTS) 261-3985

Santa Ana, California
Office—(Category C)
Earl G. Fields
Manager
HUD—Santa Ana Office
34 Civic Center Plaza
Post Office Box 12850
Santa Ana, CA 92712-2850
(714) 836-2451
(FTS) 799-2451

Tucson Office—(Category C)
Jean Staley
Manager
HUD—Tucson Office
100 North Stone Avenue
Suite 410
Post Office Box 2648
Tucson, AZ 86701-1467
(602) 629-6237
(FTS) 762-5220

Fresno, California
Office—(Category C)
Lily Lee
Manager
HUD—Fresno Office
1630 East Shaw Avenue
Suite 138
Fresno, CA 93710-8193
(209) 487-5033
(FTS) 467-5036

Region X

Jurisdiction: Alaska, Idaho,
Oregon, Washington

Seattle Washington Office
Richard Bauer
Regional Administrator—
Regional Housing Commissioner
HUD—Seattle Regional Office
Arcade Plaza Building
1321 Second Avenue
Seattle, WA 98101-2058
(206) 442-5414
(FTS) 399-5414

**Portland, Oregon
Office—(Category A)**
Richard C. Brinck
Manager
HUD—Portland Office
Cascade Building
520 SW Sixth Avenue
Portland, OR 97204-1596
(503) 221-2561
(FTS) 423-2561

**Boise, Idaho Office—
(Category C)**
Gary Gillespie
Manager
HUD—Boise Office
Federal Building/USCH

550 West Fort Street
Post Office Box 042
Boise, ID 83724-0420
(208) 334-1990
(FTS) 554-1990

**Spokane, Washington
Office—(Category C)**
Keith R. Green
Manager
HUD—Spokane Office
Farm Credit Bank Building
8th Floor East
West 601 1st Avenue
Spokane, WA 99204-0317
(509) 456-2624
(FTS) 439-2624

**Anchorage, Alaska
Office—(Category A)**
Arlene Patton
Acting Manager
HUD—Anchorage Office
222 West 8th Avenue, #64
Anchorage, AK 99513-7537
(907) 271-4170
(FTS) 271-4170

APPENDIX 2

U.S. GOVERNMENT PRINTING OFFICE BOOKSTORES

ATLANTA

Room 100, FB
275 Peachtree Street, NE
Atlanta, GA 30303
(404) 331-6947

BIRMINGHAM

2021 3rd Avenue North
Birmingham, AL 35206
(205) 731-1056

BOSTON

Room 179
10 Causeway Street
Boston, MA 02203
(617) 565-6680

CHICAGO

Room 1365
Everett McKinley Dirksen
    Building
219 South Dearborn Street
Chicago, IL 60604
(312) 353-5133

CLEVELAND

Room 1653
1240 East Ninth Street
Cleveland, OH 44199
(216) 522-4922

COLUMBUS

Room 207, FB
200 North High Street

Columbus, OH 43215
(412) 469-6956

DALLAS

Room 1050, FB
1100 Commerce Street
Dallas, TX 75242
(214) 767-0076

DENVER

Room 117, FB
1961 Stout Street
Denver, CO 80294
(303) 844-3964

DETROIT

Patrick V. McNamara FB
Suite 160
477 Michigan Avenue
Detroit, MI 48226
(313) 226-7816

HOUSTON

45 College Center
9319 Gulf Freeway
Houston, TX 77017
(713) 226-5453

JACKSONVILLE

Rm. 158, FB
400 W. Bay Street
Post Office Box 35089

Jacksonville, FL 32202
(904) 791-3801

KANSAS CITY

120 Bannister Mall
5600 East Bannister Road
Kansas City, MO 64106
(816) 765-2256

LOS ANGELES

ARCO Plaza, C-Level
505 South Flower Street
Los Angeles, CA 90071
(213) 894-5841

MILWAUKEE

Room 190, FB
517 East Wisconsin Avenue
Milwaukee, WI 53202
(414) 291-1304

NEW YORK

Room 110
26 Federal Plaza
New York, NY 10278
(212) 264-3825

PHILADELPHIA

100 North 17th Street
Philadelphia, PA 19106
(215) 597-0677

PITTSBURGH

Room 118, FOB
1000 Liberty Avenue
Pittsburgh, PA 15222
(412) 644-2721

PORTLAND

1305 SW 1st Avenue
Portland, OR 97201
(503) 221-6217

PUEBLO

Majestic Building
720 North Main Street
Pueblo, CO 81003
(719) 544-3142

SAN FRANCISCO

Room 1023, FOB
450 Golden Gate Avenue
San Francisco, CA 94102
(415) 556-0643

SEATTLE

Room 194, FOB
915 Second Avenue
Seattle, WA 98174
(206) 442-4270

WASHINGTON, DC AND VICINITY

Government Printing Office
710 North Capitol Street
Washington, DC 20402
(202) 275-2091

Farragut West
1717 H Street NW
Washington, DC 20006
(202) 653-5075

Retail Sales Outlet
8660 Cherry Lane
Laurel, MD 20707
(301) 953-7974

FB = Federal Building
FOB = Federal Office Building

INDEX